Nordic National Cinemas

Nordic National Cinemas explores the film histories and cultures of Denmark, Finland, Iceland, Norway and Sweden and examines each country's film production, social and political context and domestic audience.

Nordic National Cinemas traces the development of the cinema in the Nordic countries, from its origins in the early years of this century, through the golden years of film-making in the 1920s and 1930s, to film production and censorship during the war years, the new-realism in the 1950s and 1960s, the influence of American cinema and the international commercial and critical success of films in recent years. The authors not only explore the work of internationally-renowned film-makers such as Mauritz Stiller and Victor Sjöström, Carl Dreyer and Ingmar Bergman, but also nationally important film-makers such as August Blom, Gustaf Molander, Lau Lauritzen and Nils Malmros. They also discuss the films of contemporary film-makers such as Gabriel Axel, director of *Babette's Feast*, the Kaurismäki brothers, directors of *The Match Factory Girl* and *The Leningrad Cowboys* and Lars von Trier, director of *Breaking the Waves*.

The authors examine the phenomenon of Nordic cinema and, despite the similarities and collaborations between the countries, stress that Nordic cinema is the cinema of five particular traditions. Each chapter discusses the history and film culture of the individual country and considers three specific questions: state control and support of film production; the cultural characteristics of Nordic film which both unify and define peculiarities of each country; film production, content and form. In a final chapter, the authors assess the direction and future of the Nordic cinemas.

Tytti Soila and **Astrid Söderbergh Widding** are both Associate Professors in Cinema Studies at Stockholm University.
Gunnar Iversen is Associate Professor of Film Studies at the Norwegian University of Science and Technology, Trondheim.

National Cinemas series
General Editor: Susan Hayward

Reflecting growing interest in cinema as a national cultural institution, the new Routledge *National Cinemas* series brings together the most recent developments in cultural studies and film history. Its purpose is to deepen our understanding of film directors and movements by placing them within the context of national cinematic production and global culture and exploring the traditions and cultural values expressed within each. Each book provides students with a thorough and accessible introduction to a different national cinema.

French National Cinema
Susan Hayward

Italian National Cinema 1896–1996
Pierre Sorlin

Australian National Cinema
Tom O'Regan

British National Cinema
Sarah Street

Nordic National Cinemas

Tytti Soila, Astrid Söderbergh Widding
and Gunnar Iversen

Routledge
Taylor & Francis Group

LONDON AND NEW YORK

•

AG 19 '09

First published 1998
by Routledge
2 Park Square, Milton Park, Abingdon, Oxon, OX14 4RN

Transferred to Digital Printing 2005

Simultaneously published in the USA and Canada
by Routledge
270 Madison Ave, New York NY 10016

Typeset in Times by Florencetype Ltd, Stoodleigh, Devon

British Library Cataloguing in Publication Data
A catalogue record for this book is available from the British Library

Library of Congress Cataloging in Publication Data
Soila, Tytti
    Nordic national cinemas/Tytti Soila, Astrid Söderbergh Widding, Gunnar
    Iversen.
       p.   cm.—(National cinemas series)
       Includes bibliographical references and index.
       1. Motion pictures—Scandinavia—History. I. Söderbergh-Widding,
    Astrid. II. Iversen, Gunnar III. Title. IV. Series.
    PN1993.5.S2S65   1998
    791.43'0948—dc21   97–8287

ISBN   0-415-08194-7 (hbk)
ISBN   0-415-08195-5 (pbk)

Printed and bound by Antony Rowe Ltd, Eastbourne

Contents

Plates

Acknowledgements

.

Writing this book has been interesting and challenging. It would not have been possible without the invaluable help of friends, colleagues and institutions. We would like to thank Professors Richard Dyer and Jan Olsson for inspiration and encouragement. We also wish to thank Kari Uusitalo, the editor of *Finnish National Filmography*, for checking the facts in the chapter on Finnish film history, and our colleague Per Olov Quist who checked the facts in the chapter on Sweden. We would also like to thank Charlotte Jacobsson for help with the translation of the chapters on Sweden, Denmark and Iceland. Mary Jane Fox has kindly checked the English translation of the chapter on Finland.

The Department of Film Studies at Stockholm University has kindly supported us with travel stipends and the Finnish Film Archive, the Swedish Film Institute and the Danish Film Institute have helped with the picture research for this book. We would like to express our appreciation of their support, too.

Chapter 1

Introduction

Film production as a national project

Tytti Soila, Astrid Söderbergh Widding and Gunnar Iversen

The concept of national cinema has been central in several film historical texts and debates in recent years. As a departure point for the discussion of film in national terms, we find the assumption that a country's film history can be considered from certain stylistic or thematic parameters, related to the country's culture and the general background of the films which unite the country's production, to be a more or less homogeneous phenomenon. As a typical example one could mention France, where among other features poetic realism is often mentioned as a specifically national tendency in French production, or Germany, where expressionism or the new German cinema play a similar part. These national film cultures have often functioned as a counterbalance to the hegemony of Hollywood. During some periods, as, for example, in the new German cinema, the ambition to create a domestic film has been the expressed intention of the film-makers. In films by a Fassbinder or a Wenders there is clearly inscribed a critique of the Hollywood cinema, yet at the same time these films relate to Hollywood on several levels. They constitute an antithesis, a formulation of an individual alternative, and they have been interpreted as such by the audience. At other times it seems more reasonable to regard the national element largely as a reflection of the audience, as something that arises in the film's reception.

The concept of national cinemas has at the same time been questioned from many quarters. For example, Andrew Higson and Stephen Heath both claim that the device is a theoretical construction. The criticism of the concept originates among other things in the fact that, at the level of production only, it is difficult or impossible to isolate the films of individual nations from other countries' production. However, the device's characteristic of construction does not necessarily mean that it needs to be dismissed: it can after all be justified as an analytical tool. Furthermore, the degree of construction attributed to the term is dependent on whether, for example, one places the stress on production or reception. On revising sources like the companies' material, reviews and the like, it has become apparent in Nordic contexts that there was an early and distinct awareness of national distinction, which has remained permanent through the decades regardless of whether the films of that particular country have been fostered or rejected by the critics and the audience, and regardless of the national distinction simultaneously being subordinate to various changes as far as thematic and stylistic design is concerned.

The purpose of this study is twofold. The first is to offer a detailed description of the marginal film culture which the Nordic countries constitute in an international language, and thereby give them a place on the map of film history. The thought behind this is also to contribute with a corrective to the international film canon where Bergman and Dreyer, as virtually the only major names, have been made to represent Nordic presence. As we have observed, film and nationality today constitute one of the most vital fields of discussion within cinema studies – the existence of the National Cinema series, of which this book is a part, is but one example. This clarifies the second purpose behind this study, namely to allow this book to make a contribution to the debate on national film. The starting point of this contribution is to be found in the unique situation that exists in Nordic film contexts where there is a high degree of integration and exchange between the countries but it is also apparent that popular themes and genres specific to each country respectively can be traced through history.

PERSPECTIVES OF THE NATIONAL ELEMENT

In discussing Nordic cinema from a national perspective we have proceeded from three different ways of approaching the national element.

1 As opposed to several other countries' film cultures, Nordic cinema has been national in the specific sense that it has not, or to only a limited extent, been exportable to other countries. This means that it is national in a basic sort of way: a culture that stays within itself, something which exists only for that country.

   Even within the Nordic countries the different nations' domestic films are only exported to a limited extent. As an example, we will look at cinema in Norway during the 1980s. During this period, an average of ten Norwegian films were produced each year out of which only one was exported to Sweden, whereas some ten Swedish films were imported into Norway in the same period.

   An important exception to this trend was the large Swedish export of films following the so-called breakdown of the sex barrier. The reason for this is that Swedish films are not only exotic but also sensational. In the latter concept there is the preconception of news value. Thus a rough borderline is established where the aberration in Swedish film production in comparison with other countries (and in particular with the normative American production) suddenly appears to have acquired such news value. This also gives rise to a number of questions. How and when does the difference become sensation? The whole problem of the dichotomy of the difference–similarity, which is at the heart of every discussion on national cinema, is topicalized in this context.

The divergence of Nordic film versus, for example, American film is interesting: this is both national and international, and its national specificity at the same time constitutes the very basis for its distribution outside the borders of the own nation.

If one speaks of Nordic national cinema in this specific sense, however, it means that the very concept of 'the national' must be redefined. This is because earlier definitions of national Nordic film have been based on the exceptions – on the films of a Bergman or a Dreyer, which are paradoxically at the same time the most international films in the Nordic countries. We have instead proceeded from the basis of popular film, which has been seen by a majority audience in the country where it was made and which has been perceived by this audience to be specifically national.

2 This brings us to a second aspect of nationality in cinematic contexts, namely the question of the audience and its expectations in relation to national film.

National quality is enhanced in an interesting way if one considers the example of France. With the complete setback in production caused by the First World War, the French film industry, which at the time was the international leader, entered a prolonged period of crisis. It was only the breakthrough of sound film that brought about a revitalization of the French film, and then it had clear national overtones. This obviously goes to show the importance of language to national identity, but above all it is also an indicator as to what extent the film as a national phenomenon is a *project*. National cinema came into existence to the extent that a nation actively attempted to construct it, in a situation where external conditions allowed it. The state's influence on Nordic cinema is something which to a particularly high degree accentuates this fact, but the awareness of what is specific for the nation and its marketability is also an important factor which plays a part in the concrete production decisions for the private producers.

The creation of a national cinema is thus a decision which originates in a need that is presumed to exist, and which is thereby also presumed to arouse sympathy in the audience. These presumptions are confirmed if one looks at the audience ratings. Within the different national cultures in the Nordic countries the audience favours domestic films in a most singular way, something that is clearly apparent from the history of Nordic cinema. This is true independently of cultural value patterns:

during some periods the films of the home nation have been held up as models by the critics, yet during other periods they have been looked down upon.

It is thus with the audience in mind that one should seek the awareness of nationality in the first place. The knowledge that the rapids in the Finnish film version of the popular Finnish novel *The Song of the Scarlet Red Flower (Laulu tulipunaisesta Kukasta)* are in fact Finnish, for example – as opposed to the similar rapids in the Swedish version of the same film – created considerable differences with regard to the popularity of the respective films in Finland. However, it can also be said that the audience is deceived, so that the national authenticity of the images is something that only occurs in the film's reception. An interesting example is the Norwegian film *The Magic Moose (Trollelgen)* (1927). This film has been defined by audience and critics alike as being prototypically Norwegian in its images. In reality it contains footage which the film-maker has retrieved from a Swedish documentary and then cut into his story. That the images deceive, however, does not alter anything as regards the film as a national symbol, which clearly indicates that national quality is a construction which should primarily be defined from the point of view of the spectators.

Nationality in the area of film thereby implies a relation to the topical and to the specific for the culture. A certain country's national film is determined by the separate life values, in relation to other countries, which have been worked at in the form of fictions, rather than from any singularly demonstrable difference in stylistic measures between different countries' productions. The concept of national cinema in other words both presupposes and relates to a context. To speak of a national cinema in a given country is a construction which thus becomes specific to the country only in relation to other countries, to 'abroad'. At the same time it is of interest to analyse how the relationship between nationality and internationality changes. Particularly interesting in Nordic contexts are the complex relations which arise in the field between, first, each country's individuality as it is conveyed in the films; second, the Nordic affinity and collaboration which unite the separate national projects, and third, the influence of other countries, especially the USA.

3 The third way in which we have sought to approach the national quality in Nordic cinema is via the search for specific elements in the actual film texts which constitute national markers. Common to film in all the Nordic countries is that one can view it as a distinct alternative to the dominant American film. In this way, Nordic film constitutes a corrective of sorts, a way of asserting not only each country's national individuality, but the joint Nordic unity as an alternative, however

peripheral, in relation to Hollywood's style and mode of production. Here again, state influence enters the picture. The fact that these small nations also have numerically insignificant film production has made state regulation necessary to maintain production at a sufficiently high level both quantitatively and qualitatively, in order to resist the strong American influence.

THE RESEARCH SITUATION

In all the Nordic countries there exists a paradoxical situation in the area of film research. The state's influence over the cinema institution is, as mentioned above, common to all Nordic countries. Despite this interest of the state, however, the film still has a low status in all these countries. It is from this perspective that one must realize the fact that film as such, and more specifically film history in particular as regards national production, is a neglected area. It would also seem that the fact that Nordic cinema has had so few international hits has contributed to this. If Sweden to a certain extent is an exception to the situation outlined above, it is doubtless due to the fact that it was Sweden where Sjöström and Stiller, and later Bergman, were active. This inferiority complex seems to have been the most effective research obstacle. Only international success has been sufficient to legitimize research into the film history of each nation in its own right.

It has been only during latter years that a research proper into film has developed at the universities, and that a study of national film has become legitimate. This has also resulted in a situation which is in many ways problematic for the film scholar. Because of this, the literature on film has largely been made up of separate surveys, while the basic research proper has not been carried out until quite recently. Essential areas are still lacking basic research. The map of Nordic film history still has its blank areas.

When one exposes the Nordic countries to closer scrutiny one will find that there are simultaneously vast differences in the research situation between the countries. In Sweden and Finland the literature is thus far more extensive than in Denmark or Norway. In Sweden as well as Finland there are also detailed filmographies which map the countries' production. In Denmark and Norway, however, there have been as yet only filmographic attempts. It is interesting to compare Swedish and Danish literature in the field of cinema studies. If the Swedish body of texts would appear to be far superior in volume compared to the Danish literature, this is partly misleading. In Denmark, for example, there is a thorough and detailed mapping of the history of film production which lacks a Swedish counterpart, but virtually no aesthetic film history. It is also the case in both countries that extensive areas of film history fall outside of the writing of history. In both Denmark and Sweden the interest has been exclusively tied to certain periods and certain great auteurs.

At the same time the historical research into Nordic film is at present at a stage of dynamic development. Film history has appeared on the agenda at a number of Nordic universities. In Norway, for instance, this has resulted in a vast project covering the history of moving images. The research ranges over a wide field, from analysis of aesthetics and production-related aspects to the study of the films' reception.

Yet another problem concerning research from an international perspective is that what is published in the international languages on Nordic cinema is written in the main by people who have not mastered the language in question or who have no knowledge of the national culture. It has also been difficult for such people to make a selection from each country's national cinema, and they have thus been forced to trust in the official picture traded by way of the survey literature: starting from which films the film institutes have chosen to subtitle, and so on. The emphasis on secondary sources is thus extreme. The selection of films studied in these texts is also based on a consensus of sorts: it is exclusively the study of aesthetical masterpieces. In this book we are striving to place the exceptions in a particular context. International critics have not had access to the popular films and we think popularity is an important criterion in discussing national cinema. Which films have people actually seen? There is also a need for a comprehensive perspective on the complete production. The purpose of this work is specifically to fill this void by presenting a more complete picture of the film culture in each country respectively.

Chapter 2

Denmark

Astrid Söderbergh Widding

THE SILENT YEARS IN DENMARK: A PERIOD OF GREATNESS AND DECLINE

The history of Danish film begins in a grand way despite Denmark's small-ness, as the story of one of the world's leading film nations. During the first half of the 1910s the so-called golden age of Danish film occurred, when Denmark, alongside France, had the status of being Europe's most influential country in the realm of film production. But this period of greatness was to be short, and Denmark has since remained a marginal film country, with the exception of a few directors who have become inter-nationally known. Surveys of film history, with their focus on auteurs and great or artistic productions, give few or no clues to the consistent produc-tion of films in Denmark, apart from its relatively few international successes – films that have seldom been exported but on the other hand have had a solid native audience through the decades.

Denmark occupies a unique position among the Nordic countries through its dense population in relation to its geographic size. The natural scenery that in film history has often been pointed out to be the most characteristic feature in Nordic film also plays an important part in the history of Danish film. There is no wilderness however, only the cultivated agrarian landscape one meets in the films. Urbanization came earlier in Denmark and is more prominent than in the neighbouring Scandinavian countries. This is also evident in film production where urban types of film like melodrama, drawing-room comedy and street realism were already common from the earliest years.

The film came to Denmark only one year after its birth. In 1896 the first public screening took place, arranged by Vilhelm Pacht, the owner of a place of entertainment in Copenhagen. He had seen Lumière's show-ings in Paris and had brought home film and equipment. In that same year the first Danish film was produced by Peter Elfelt, who for ten years was virtually the sole film-maker in the country. From the beginning the film had an important, albeit limited, market in Denmark: films were shown

regularly at the music-halls in Copenhagen, and there were some travelling cinemas as well. In 1904 the first permanent cinema opened in
Copenhagen. It was followed by others in various parts of the country,
and from 1906 the growth was almost explosive. In the same year a cinema
owner in Copenhagen, Ole Olsen, set up his own film production company,
Nordisk Films Kompagni (Nordisk Film Company). It was almost coinci-
dental that he as well as his equals – businessmen in the entertainment
industry – came to invest in film as a possible new source of income, which
would turn out to exceed their wildest expectations.

By 1910 the Danish film industry was established and a stable production of considerable size had begun. Nordisk Films had within a few years
become the second largest film company in Europe, next to Pathé, with
a staff of 1700 people. Production was soon standardized in the company,
both on narrative and stylistic levels. A few genres were developed
in accordance with patterns similar to the American ones: mainly melodrama, farce and thriller. Besides Nordisk there were also a number of
small companies, twenty-five in all, most of which produced only a handful
of films before disappearing for good.

The film historian Ron Mottram describes the typical film style
characterizing Nordisk's productions. As a rule they comprise thrillers,
tragedies and love stories with an intense acting style and marked lighting
effects. Both interiors and exteriors are very realistic and natural scenery
as well as urban settings are exploited in an ingenious way. A few stock
characters appear and reappear in the Danish films of the period. Among
these we find the circus performer, the prodigal son, the officer, the
landowner and the earl. The film diva also makes her entrance in Nordisk's
films, such as Clara Wieth Pontoppidan and Asta Nielsen. Nielsen made
her name as a star in *The Abyss* (*Afgrunden*) in 1910, directed by Urban
Gad. It contained some innovative devices, for example, the lack of intertitles, but it achieved its reputation mainly as an erotic film with a touch
of dark fatalism. Nielsen appeared in two other similar films, both directed
by Gad, before leaving Denmark for Germany: *The Black Dream* (*Den
sorte drøm*) and *The Dancer (Balettdanserinden)*, both made in 1911.

The director August Blom, a former actor, was among the first to work
to produce longer films – Ole Olsen had an aversion to productions lasting
longer than one reel, that is, 15 minutes. In 1910 Blom staged *Hamlet* as
a play in three acts, but the film company cut it down to a one-reel play.
In the same year, however, the success of the 35-minute film *White Slavery*
(*Den hvide slavehandel*) – produced initially by a smaller company, and
immediately plagiarized by Ole Olsen – prompted the producers to begin
to make longer films with up to an hour's running time. In this way more
theatrical actors came to be tied to the cinema. In 1911 Blom took over
from Viggo Larsen as the leading director of the company. His *The
Temptations of a Great City* (*Ved Fængslets Port*) from the same year, an

erotic melodrama which made Valdemar Psilander a star, was 45 minutes long. It was a box-office sucess even internationally, and was sold in 246 copies. *Atlantis* (1913), an adaptation for the screen of the Nobel prize winner Hauptmann, comprised eight reels – the longest Danish film to date. It also enjoyed an immense success both in Denmark and abroad. Among its many spectacular scenes the sinking of an ocean liner is especially noteworthy, inspired by the Titanic catastrophe one year earlier.

The Danish melodrama of the same period was not exclusively popular, and was also criticized. The melodramatic subjects, the spectacular plots, the bold erotics and the descriptions of crime provoked a debate in wide circles, not only in Denmark. In Sweden many of these films were totally banned, and 'Danishness' became an abusive word referring to all films that were considered offensive to good taste.

As in the other Nordic countries, the Danish state also strived to establish a close relationship with the film industry. In 1913 state censorship was introduced as a consequence of the criticism from several sources that film-goers were inspired to commit crimes as a result of what they saw on the screen. As early as 1907 there had been local censorship, administered by the local police authorities. This foundered, however, on the inconsistencies of the system, with varying censor assessments in different countries. In the area of cinemas there is a state regulation in the law of 1922 which introduces restrictions on licensing, connected with an expressed purpose that the film should work in a manner 'ennobling and educating for the audience' ('forædlende og belærende på publikum'). There was also an entertainment tax levied on the proceeds. The law was preceded by a debate, where some advocated a municipal cinema system as in Norway, and others spoke for free competition. The Danish state took a clear stand, however, towards counteracting the formation of cinema chains in accordance with the Swedish model. Thereafter, the debate recurred regularly in Denmark: the next time it arose was in the early 1930s in connection with new legislation in the area of film.

The two directors of the period who have been integrated into the international canon of film history, namely Benjamin Christensen and Carl Theodor Dreyer, are, strikingly enough, marginal phenomena compared to the production giant. This is the more remarkable as – in contrast to their celebrated Swedish colleagues Sjöström, Stiller and Bergman – they remain relatively marginal in Danish film as a whole. Not even Dreyer occupies a position like Bergman, as an unchallenged central figure. Christensen made only two films in Denmark during the silent period, *The Mysterious X* (*Det hemmelighedsfulde X*) in 1914 and *Night of Revenge* (*Hævnens nat*) in 1916, both of which are stylistically innovative – and both outside the boundaries of Nordisk Films. His next film, the experimental semi-documentary *Witchcraft Through the Ages* (*Häxan*) (1922) was made in Sweden and landed Christensen in some trouble with the censors. Dreyer for his part made only two films for Nordisk, and this after the decline of the film company had begun: *The President* (*Præsidenten*) in 1918 and *Leaves from Satan's Book* (*Blade af Satans bog*) in 1921, inspired by Griffith's *Intolerance*.

Independently of Nordisk, *Mikael* – from a novel by Herman Bang – was brought to the screen by Dreyer in 1924, a version inspired by Stiller's Swedish adaptation of the same novel in 1916. This is a typical example of the circulation that has prevailed within Nordic film through the decades, where a filmic idea from one country is taken over and realized as an independent project in one of the neighbouring countries, sometimes as an immediate consequence of the fact that the import of the film in question has turned out to be unprofitable. Dreyer also directed two films in other Nordic countries: in Sweden – *The Parson's Widow* (*Prästänkan*) (1920), and in Norway – *The Bride of Glomdal* (*Glomdalsbruden*) (1926). In 1925, the naturalistic drama *Master of the House* (*Du skal ære din hustru*) was shot by Dreyer in the Palladium studios. The film was a box-office success and brought its director international fame. This provided the opportunity for Dreyer to make films in France, where in 1926 he directed *The Passion of Joan of Arc* (*La Passion de Jeanne d'Arc*), generally considered to be one of the most innovative achievements of the silent era. There are features in Dreyer's earlier film style that are here carried to their extreme: the predilection for closed interiors, the focusing on faces, his framings that either mask the lens or allow objects and people to be cut by the frame, leaving only a limited part of the image visible. The same stylistic features remain through the whole of Dreyer's very sparse production history.

The period of greatness for Ole Olsen's company was waning. With the outbreak of the First World War the situation deteriorated, but it was only after 1916 that the disaster became a reality. Still, in 1915, 143 films were released. Danish film historians cite artistic as well as structural reasons for the decline. Ole Olsen exploited successful concepts to the extent that they became stereotyped. The market potential was simultaneously shrinking, among other things as a result of the foundation of the state-owned UFA in Germany. In 1917 film production was discontinued, and when it resumed after the peace of 1918 it began from nothing. Denmark was never to regain her position on the international market.

The development of film in Denmark thus goes in the opposite direction from that in Sweden, where the 'golden age' took as its starting point Sjöström's *Terje Vigen* in 1917, and continued during the 1920s with an investment in quality and cultural hallmarks, secured through filmings of, above all, domestic literature. In Denmark, however, only a handful of films were made from literary originals during the period 1915 to 1930. The venture into quality film-making made by the resurrected Nordisk Films never achieved any real success. The only consistently renowned director from this period is Forest Holger-Madsen, August Blom's challenger as first director with Nordisk. He made an outstanding early production, *The Evangelist* (*Evangeliemandens liv*) (1914), with Valdemar Psilander in the leading role. The film has been provided with a narrative frame, introducing a flashback that occupies the greater part of the narrative, where a preacher tells a young man how he spent some time in prison, wrongfully accused of murder, thus saving the young man from a path of crime. The obligatory *femmes fatales* are there, as they were earlier during the decade. The cameraman Marius Clausen, however, gives an original touch to the film as well as to Holger-Madsen's other productions, with a marked feeling for setting, avant-garde lighting and inventive camera angles. Holger-Madsen also directed two films, *Down with Weapons!* (*Ned med vaabnene*) (1915) from a novel by Bertha Suttner, scripted by Dreyer, and *The Skyship* (*Himmelskibet*) (1918), the former dealing directly with the subject of war and the latter indirectly, within the frame of a science fiction story. These contemporary commentaries on the First World War occupy a unique position in Nordic film. Furthermore, their social commitment is exceptional for this period. Among the genres light comedy occupied an increasingly dominant position, followed by a handful of dramas. Lau Lauritzen was the singularly most active film-maker among the directors of light comedy. He was the force behind the international success of *Long and Short* (*Fyrtornet og Bivognen,* literally 'The Lighthouse and The Trailer') – forerunners of Laurel and Hardy. Lauritzen had left Nordisk in 1920 to be a party in founding Palladium, which, thanks to the success of '*Fy og Bi*', temporarily held a stronger position on the market than the former giant. Forty-six Long and Short films were produced in all, of which Lauritzen directed thirty. The films are set in a poor working-class environment and the two heroes who are the opposites of one another – as is indicated by their names: Long is lanky and Short is square – bear a resemblance to, among others, Charlie Chaplin.

SOUND FILM AND STATE REGULATION

The transition to sound film in Denmark was gradual and did not differ significantly from other countries. The system using gramophone records was the first to reach the cinemas, in 1926–27, followed by optical sound in 1929 after various experiments in the intermediary years. Among others *The Jazz Singer* was shown in the cinema with live music. The first Danish sound films premièred a few months before the American sensations arrived in Denmark. They were modest and small productions, but technically acceptable. The company Nordisk Tonefilm (Nordic Sound Film) was founded in 1928, and merged the following year with Nordisk Films, which had gone bankrupt but was subsequently revived. This created a new dominant film company in the Danish market which had ready access to an experienced production team, up-to-date equipment, as well as capital and patents.

In May 1931, the first domestic feature film with sound had its première in Denmark: *The Clergyman of Vejlby* (*Præsten i Vejlby*), directed by George Schnéevoight and produced by Nordisk Tonefilm. The film was an immediate success, and made three times its production cost. This promoted optimism for the future. It was apparently profitable, despite the diminutive domestic market, to make Danish films. Furthermore, the continued progress during the 1930s was to fulfil expectations, in spite of the pressure from American imports. Around 1930 many more American films were shown in Denmark, with German films in second place; the third place was held by Danish films.

In 1933 a new cinema law was introduced in Denmark. This law is a clear example of the social democratic politics of this period, which headed in the direction of increased state regulation with the purpose of creating protection against the unrestrained influence of foreign capital. The idea of the education of the nation was also a strong feature of the social democracy of the time. This is notable in the legislation which promoted the notion that better use be made of the film's cultural and social value and that it be made accessible to the Danish population.

With this in mind it was decided, among other things, that every cinema company was to be headed by a film expert with real control over the company, and who could not simultaneously head other cinemas. Moreover, prohibitions were introduced against the distributors investing in cinemas, which meant in practice that there was state regulation of film distribution. The law also strengthened the position of the cinemas in relation to the distributors for many years. In 1938 it was replaced by a new cinema law where several new state institutions were added, including a central purchase and letting body.

During the 1930s, sharp criticism was directed at the high entertainment tax (40 per cent of the price of a ticket in 1933), and there were demands for a state subsidy for film. It was some time, however, before these demands were realized. The pressure of taxation resulted in the situation that a Danish-produced film at this time had to be seen by half a million viewers in order to break even, a large percentage in a country with approximately four million inhabitants. This led to a certain conservatism in the industry, where staking safe bets came to the fore. Investors were especially sensitive to savings on the market: for example, when the audience polls of 1937 showed that three-quarters of the audience lived in the countryside, this was immediately followed by a venture into rural films. Towards the end of the 1930s there were three production companies in Denmark: besides Nordisk and Palladium there was also the recently started ASA. The rhythm of production became fairly steady: about nine Danish films were made each year.

The 1930s was in many ways a paradoxical decade for Danish cinema. Simultaneously with the educative ambitions of the film law, a gulf had in reality to be bridged between the broad audience of film and the quality demands of the critics, something which has endured through the decades. As during the 1920s when light comedy was singularly the most dominant genre, this now expanded into various musical features. Popular favourites, stars like Marguerite Viby or the comedian Chr. Arhoff, played a significant role during this period.

A typical example of Danish film of the 1930s is *Nyhavn 17* (1933), one of the films staged by George Schnéevoigt, which was denigrated all the more as he had previously enjoyed a certain goodwill from the critics after *Præsten i Vejlby*. In *Nyhavn 17* we meet the café owner's daughter Primula, who lives in the docklands area and who, while cycling to her work selling furniture at a department store gets hit by the store director's car driven by his future son-in-law. The director fires Primula for being late for work. The future son-in-law, however, who is there to buy furniture, falls in love the same day with Primula. Their meeting introduces the first of a series of musical acts in the film. Primula also turns out to be the director's illegitimate daughter, whose true populist heart is revealed when he goes to the café for a reunion with her mother, and eventually the young lovers can, after a few more complications, be united.

A comparison with Sweden in the 1930s shows striking parallels. In both countries film was a denigrated phenomenon. Explicit treatment of contemporary problems cannot be found. The economic crisis was largely presented as financial jams, which are consistently solved. The tension in the films was almost always based on some form of class difference or conflict which had to be resolved, usually through social climbing. The collision between two contrasting environments offered abundant opportunities for comic scenes. At the same time there was a fundamental mistrust of the upper class, whose stiffness and conventions are contrasted with the true joviality of the Danish. The stable idyll presented in the films was to be overturned, however, with the outbreak of the Second World War.

WAR AND OCCUPATION

Denmark, like Norway, was occupied by Germany in 1940, and thereafter the situation there was to be radically different from that in Sweden. Film production and the demand for film certainly increased throughout Scandinavia. But the German Occupation forces at the same time endeavoured to control all three levels of the film industry: production, distribution including import, and cinema screenings.

Already in 1940 all import of films from England had been banned, and American film was also subject to restrictions. There was also a severe and increasing pressure during the years of the Occupation to show more German films in the cinemas. Various state regulations were introduced to secure this. The Danish resistance to German films was striking for political as well as economic reasons. The German productions, made in a steady stream and often with low standards of quality, did not break even. Swedish films became very popular however; they could be imported thanks to Sweden's neutral status but were none the less completely free of German influence. The example of *The Inn of Kalle on the Footbridge* (*Kalle på Spången*) (1939) deserves a mention. This Edvard Persson film ran for a year and a half in the same cinema in Copenhagen, and the citizens of the capital went to see it time and again to keep it on the repertoire as an act of resistance. In the years from 1941 to 1943 the Swedish film made up no less than 10 per cent of the total turnover. In Denmark too, ninety-two domestic films were produced during the years of occupation: here, as in Sweden, the import restrictions came to be important for film production.

The entertainment film – light comedy, comedy and farce – dominated to a large extent. Some were blatantly copied from American and English concepts to fill a gap in the market. But at the same time another genre was beginning to make itself known, which was given the term 'problem drama'. This has been called a Danish variation of the film noir: black film distinguished by psychological realism, not all that different from its contemporary Swedish counterpart. Examples are Bodil Ipsen and Lau Lauritzen's *Astray* (*Afsporet*) (1942), a violent and realistic portrayal of the life-story of a woman in the underworld of Copenhagen, or Ipsen's *Occupation* (*Besættelse*) (1944) (the Danish 'besættelse' means both occupation and possession). Carl Th. Dreyer's historical drama of the seventeenth-century witch burnings, *Day of Wrath* (*Vredens dag*) (1943), which can in its stinging depiction of intolerance be effortlessly interpreted as an allegory of the contemporary, is also a milestone in the Danish film history of the war years.

PEACE AND PROBLEM DRAMA

In Denmark, everyone looked forward with anticipation to peace, in the cinema business as in society in general. The demand for feature films from the allied nations was great, and many films were awaiting distribution. However, it turned out that once the first flush of victory had subsided the situation was to be far from straightforward.

First and foremost, audience ratings did not increase to the extent expected by the cinema owners. Certainly the lack of consumer goods in the wake of the war, which went hand-in-hand with the country having become financially strong, contributed to there being money to spend on film-going, but state regulation led simultaneously to severe restrictions on film import. At the heart of this policy was the belief that more urgent financial problems had to be resolved before the country could be allowed luxury items. Concurrent with these restrictions the entertainment tax for the cinemas was raised, and the film prices were fixed at a level that was unacceptably low to the American studios. Hollywood on its part began to exert pressure, and several film boycotts during 1947, of Sweden as well as Denmark, resulted. This rid the Danish cinema of its most dangerous competitors, and in this relatively undisturbed period producers were able to secure the domestic market. A newly set up company still bought and distributed a number of American films in the intermediary period, mainly B and C productions. Denmark thus handled the film boycott without any major difficulties, and it was the Americans who had to ask for renegotiations to once more get a share of the Danish market.

A new agreement was struck which came into effect in 1948, where free import on a licence basis was secured by the American studios, but where, in the event of any surplus on the films, this would be fixed and taxed in Denmark. The agreement was undoubtedly a victory for Danish interests. Its immediate effect was that the supply of American films grew, which, although advantageous for the cinema business, treated producers and distributors unfairly. Parallel to this development, however, there was the onset of a decline in cinema ratings. This had to do with changes in the market: the financial surplus from the end of the war had been spent at a time when the supply of goods had reached a normal level. The decreasing audience ratings were yet another blow to Danish film production, which had to adjust to drastic cut-backs. This struck all the more hard since the different parts of the industry had been kept separate as a result of Danish politics. Now the producers strove to find underhand ways of simultaneously being able to distribute film, and thereby secure some profitability.

Between 1945 and 1949, the average production rate was ten films a year for Danish cinema (Dinnesen and Kau 1983: 264). Four major production companies were responsible: ASA, Nordisk, Palladium and Saga, which were now all integrated companies, apart from ASA. However, in 1950 ASA also opened a large cinema in Copenhagen and thus became equal to the other companies.

Technically, the end of the war meant a modest revival for Danish film. A cycle of films from the second half of the 1940s dealt with the years of occupation. At the same time and parallel to these films there continued some productions of light comedies as well as detective stories. The films about the Occupation were of various kinds: for example, there were documentaries like the one produced by Frihetsrådet ('The Freedom Council') in 1946, *Your Freedom Is at Stake* (*Det gælder din frihet*) (Theodor Christensen), which settled the score with the spirit of collaboration during the war years. Most famous, however, was a feature film, *The Red Fields*

(*De røde Enge*) (1945), directed by Lau Lauritzen and Bodil Ipsen, which became something of a filmic monument to the struggle of the resistance movement.

A special genre that appeared during the 1940s was the travel film. It ceased to exist when the Danes began to travel abroad to a larger extent – only one or two stray films were produced in the 1950s. This was a very varied group of films, from lavish 35 mm colour films to cheap 16 mm productions. They were shown, not only in cinemas but also at clubs, church halls and the like. They had the advantage of being free to be shown on church holidays when there was otherwise a ban on film screenings. Furthermore, from the point of view of production the films had the unique characteristic of combining exoticism and escape from reality with a cultural hallmark and the prospect of a quality subsidy, since they were counted as documentaries.

Denmark has produced a number of distinguished documentarists, perhaps most notably Jørgen Roos, who worked in the Flaherty tradition, for example, portraying life in the Danish dominion of Greenland. Furthermore, the new generation of film-makers who stepped in after the war had often worked as makers of documentaries during the war years – for example, Bjarne and Astrid Henning-Jensen or Ole Palsbo. This becomes apparent in the unvarnished realism which began to appear in the narrative. The striving towards authenticity is noticeable in a predilection for location shoots, or in the changes in dialogue, for example, when a novel like *Ditte Menneskebarn* was filmed by Bjarne and Astrid Henning-Jensen as *Ditte, Child of Man* (1946), changes which have the purpose of increasing the degree of realism in the narration. Another expression of realism was when documentary features were included in the fiction film. This occurred for instance in a crime drama from 1950, *Smedestræde 4*, where the film poster advertised: 'Filmed with the assistance of the Copenhagen police department.' This refers specifically to one sequence in the film which shows in great detail the work of the police at the scene of a murder, how to secure evidence and if possible establish the events that took place.

Among the realistic films of the 1940s we can also mention *While the Front Door Was Closed* (*Mens porten var lukket*) (1948), directed by Asbjørn Andersen from a Swedish script by Hasse Ekman, who filmed a Swedish version of it. The film is about the different tenants occupying flats in the same house, and the events which take place in their flats during the nocturnal hours. It constitutes an interesting example of the exchange between the Nordic countries at this time: instead of importing each other's films they imported the scripts, which were given a suitably Danish 'touch' when filmed. The two versions are in effect strikingly similar. They work with *Kammerspiel* aesthetics, and tell the story of the individual dramas that are conducted behind anonymous front doors in the city's interiors.

In Denmark, the dominating group of films during these years was the social problem films – a continuation of the genre that was introduced during the war years. There were films made about the difficult conditions of young people growing up, both in the city and in the countryside, about alcoholism, crime and social outcasts. One of the more spectacular films was *We Want a Child* (*Vi vil ha'et barn*) (1949) by Lau Lauritzen and Alice O'Fredericks, which caused something of an outcry because it showed an authentic childbirth. Thus, it was considered to be breaking the sexual taboo. Towards the end of the 1940s there was a new censorship debate, which had its origin in the social problem film. The demands for tightening state censorship were largely motivated by the critics of the too realistic portrayal of a bank robbery in the film *Kristinus Bergman* (1948). Denmark had at this time a censorship law dating back to 1933. After a new inquiry this was largely retained – it was only twenty years later that Denmark was to abolish its adult censorship.

A specific set of circumstances was associated with the upswing in the fortunes of the social problem films. In 1949 a change in the legislation brought about the possibility of the Danish state partially or completely granting exemption from entertainment taxation for films with an educative content. Here the aforementioned sequence with the police seen at work is an excellent example. The productions were thus not without underlying financial motives. This caused many of the films to lack the dark and sharp qualities which made their Swedish counterparts so well worth seeing. Here the uncompromising social criticism ran the risk of being replaced by sermons. In 1950 a state film subsidy was introduced in Denmark – as in Sweden – to help promote domestic productions. Part of the subsidy was determined by their possible effects on the common good, but a 25 per cent repayment of the entertainment tax was granted to all films, regardless of content and quality. Helped by this law of film subsidizing, the Danish cinema was ensured some good years in the 1950s – and it was during the first half of this decade that the Danish film industry reached its absolute peak. The year 1955 marks the turning point when audience ratings began to decrease (Dinnesen and Kau 1983: 256).

THE 1950s AND THE GENIAL FILM

At the beginning of the 1950s, the notion of quality film appeared as one of the central concepts of the Danish film debate. The call for state subsidies was motivated by a need to guarantee a qualitatively superior production and to avoid a staking of safe bets, namely popular film. The film critics posed demands for a film production with serious overtones. As for Swedish film, several Danish films received international recognition during this period: *The Invisible Army* (*Den usynlige hær*) (Johan Jacobsen 1945), *The Red Fields* and *Ditte Menneskebarn*. There arises in this situation a clear dichotomy between the official and the unofficial film culture: the recognized quality films on the one hand and the popular culture on the other. The first group is in Danish contexts distinguished by its very issues of moral problems which are eventually resolved by some plan of action. The latter films, often represented by the so-called genial film ('hyggefilmen') with the Danish national virtue congeniality in focus, often treat similar problems, but solve them according to the patterns of the melodrama, which was condemned as simplifying when decisions were made about the quality subsidies.

Within the renowned quality film, nothing very much happened during the 1950s. Only one film followed up the international successes of the 1940s. This was made by Carl Th. Dreyer, who at the time ran the cinema Dagmar in Copenhagen, and who returned to film-making after twelve years of silence since making *Day of Wrath*. In 1955 his film *The Word* (*Ordet*) opened, a film of a play by the clergyman and resistance fighter Kaj Munk who was murdered by the Nazis. The play had incidentally already been filmed in Sweden during the war by Gustaf Molander. It is a strong drama of faith, and depicts a young woman in a farm on Jutland, her death and subsequent resurrection to life by a 'holy fool' (as in the great Russian tradition) in Danish shape. While Molander's film is a well-made melodrama, Dreyer's film becomes an incredibly naked drama, with slow, insistent camera movements that follow characters and objects. Dreyer's film won the Grand Prix in Venice that year and became a financial success, as well as one of the greatest artistic successes in the history of Danish film.

Paradoxically, however, the film subsidy law of 1949 was to bring about a decline in the general quality of films. Film production was secured, as was the audience turnout – but the fact remained: serial productions which were disdainfully termed 'trivia film' by the critics largely replaced the artistic ventures from the first years of peace.

A hit concept which was pioneered in this area was the film *The Red Horses* (*De røde heste*) (1950), directed by Jon Iversen and Alice O'Fredericks, the very prototype of a genial film ('hyggefilm'). It was based on a novel by Morten Korch and contained – in the words of the producer – 'Danish humour and Danish scenery'. Its success ensured a number of sequels and the Korch films became legion: eighteen such films were made up to 1976. All of them take place in an indeterminate modern age, prior to the existence of war and misery. The family is at the centre, they often live in a country house, and the object of the films is to solve financial or practical difficulties which threaten to cloud such domestic bliss. The rural romanticism flourishes as never before. The iconography is familiar: a blonde-haired girl standing in billowing fields of corn, but also detailed and almost educational close-ups of various types of corn. The critics were horrified at the stereotyping of the narrative and the aesthetics. Imagewise, the films were often cliché-like copies of American models.

But the audience flocked to the cinemas. In a short period of time 2.3 million tickets were sold to see *The Red Horses* – Denmark had a population of 4.2 million in 1950. In terms of production, the 1950s were a golden decade thanks to these films. Investments in previously known, popular originals predominated – out of 138 films made during the 1950s no less than fifty-seven were based on other media products. Besides the Korch novels there were also plays, other films, and cartoons, such as the inestimably popular series *Father of Four* (*Far til fire*), in which eight films were made between 1953 and 1961, with one straggler in 1971.

The overall dominance of popular film also stands out clearly when examining the genres on offer. Of the 138 films, forty-eight were counted as belonging to the genre of folk comedies and thirty-eight as being light comedies. To this we can add twelve farces, six crime films, thirty-three 'serious' films and one travel film. Even Nordisk Films, for a long time the stronghold of artistic film, threw in the towel and prioritized financial concerns, following in the wake of ASA, Palladium and Saga. Thus the entire Danish film industry adopted a similar approach, even if there were differences in nuance. The reorientation meant among other things that Erik Balling became head of production at Nordisk in 1954. He backed light comedies, which had a somewhat higher status than the Korch films. The Danish film of the 1950s can in several respects be compared with the 1930s film in Sweden, a decade which heralded major popular successes for Swedish folk comedy, a remarkable mainstreaming of production and a unanimous critique from the cultural establishment. The Danish criticism was, however, somewhat milder of tone than the Swedish one, perhaps because the gap between the critics and the audience had not generally been as wide in Denmark as in Sweden.

The turning point in 1955 was the onset of a deepening crisis for film. Criticism of the charges on cinema tickets was sharpened. It was especially the charge to the State Film Fund (Filmfonden) which was attacked from time to time. Such criticism is hardly surprising. Towards the end of the 1950s only 60 per cent of the Fund's means were being used for film purposes: the film censor, the state film central, the Film Council, and so on (Dinnesen and Kau 1983: 366). The remainder of the funds were transferred to the Ministry of Education or were used for public utility purposes like the theatre or sports – in business terms the very competitors of the film industry.

The breakthrough of television in the same year (1955) did not initially affect the Danish cinema as much as elsewhere, as a new American boycott between 1955 and 1958 created a shortage which could be filled by domestic productions. In 1958 however, an invasion of American films flooded the Danish cinemas – hits like *Gone With the Wind* (1939), for example, only now had their Danish premières. A few years into the 1950s the

Plate 2.1 The Nordic touch *The Abyss* (*Afgrunden*) (Gad, 1910)

Plate 2.2 Stylistic innovations *Night of Revenge* (*Haevnens nat*)
(Christensen, 1916)

Plate 2.3 Sound comes to Denmark *The Clergyman of Vejlby* (*Praesten I Vejlby*) (Schnéevoight, 1931)

Plate 2.4 Danish film noir *Astray* (*Afsporet*) (Ipsen and Lauritzen, 1942)

Plate 2.5 Striving for realism *Ditte, Child of Man* (*Ditte Menneskebarn*) (Henning-Jensen, 1946)

Plate 2.6 A Danish auteur film *The Word* (*Ordet*) (Dreyer, 1955)

Plate 2.7 Modern Danish art film *Element of Crime* (*Forbrydelsens element*) (von Trier, 1985)

Plate 2.8 Feminism and comedy *Hearts Flambé* (*Flamberede hjerter*) (Ryslinge, 1987)

development also tended increasingly in the direction of large première cinemas, while the small local cinemas had a more difficult time. This was primarily a result of technical innovations which had the audience preferring better conditions for showings, not least the popularity of the different wide-screen formats. During the 1950s the cinemas and the showing rights were also under debate in Denmark. The rights of several cinemas had been transferred to collectives – either to counties or to various associations. People began to talk of underhand socialization. At the same time, in 1952, Carl Th. Dreyer was made head of the renowned cinema Dagmar in Copenhagen, home of the artistic film. It was a symbolic victory for individual cinema ownership interests – but it still remained Danish policy to transfer cinemas to institutions rather than private citizens.

As in the neighbouring country of Sweden – or in the USA – there was during the 1950s a significant change in the composition of the cinema audience in Denmark, which had to do with a fundamental structural change in the society as a whole. A substantial part of the audience disappeared with the advent of television. But the change must above all be viewed in relation to the generally increasing prosperity and the thereby altered living standards of much of the population: car ownership, more money for luxuries, and so on. The original audience was to some extent replaced by a smaller but new group: teenagers. The development of youth culture into a completely independent culture form was a phenomenon which saw the light of day in this decade. As far as Danish film was concerned, this came to be a decisive factor, since it created a breeding-ground for the genre which was to renew the Danish film of latter years and was to become a characteristic of it both domestically and internationally, namely the youth film.

THE BREAKTHROUGH OF THE MODERN FILM

The crisis experienced by the film industry at the shift of decades to the 1960s, before the breakthrough of the French new wave, was closely connected with a surfeit phenomena of sorts in a number of countries. The grand film spectacles could not get any grander. The sensations and masterpieces had ceased to be sensations. The stereotypes of film advertising could not conceal the fact that film in its previous form had had to concede defeat to television. So it was in Denmark. Despite the fact that the films of the new wave were marketed in the same fashion as earlier productions, they found an audience. The audience of the artistic film together with the youth audience was for the first time in a long while a factor, however small, for the film producers. The transition was slow and hesitant in Denmark – in Sweden, the process was considerably swifter. The general tendency during the first years of the 1960s was a comparatively substantial and widespread decline.

An attempt to halt this development resulted in a new film law in 1964. Already, in 1963, it was decided that the means of the Film Fund were no longer to be used to support the theatre. People looked to the developments in Sweden, where a film institute had been set up, and the discussion of film as art began to seriously appear in the debate – previously arguments had primarily focused on film as culture. The law of 1964 therefore abolished the entertainment tax, and instead introduced a charge of 15 per cent of the price of a cinema ticket going to the Film Fund. The quality subsidy was at the centre of the new law, and it was stipulated that this subsidy was to be completely independent of the films' popular success. It was also at this time that the Danish Museum of Film (Det danske filmmuseum), founded as early as 1941, became a state institution under the Ministry of Culture. The museum aimed to promote film-cultural work through, for example, archives, magazine publishing and film showings. The revival was modest in practice however, at least to begin with. The art film ventures, with Dreyer's *Gertrud* (1964) leading the way, all ended up, not unexpectedly, with a deficit. *Gertrud* had a scandalous première in Paris and the critics tore the director to pieces. Even Denmark's Paris ambassador Eyvind Bartels chose publicly to denounce the film in a leading Danish newspaper. The film was to be revived by and by, after various leading personalities in French film – such as Jean-Luc Godard and the founder of the French Cinemathèque, Henri Langlois – had leapt to its defence. The whole debate concerning *Gertrud* clearly illustrates how such values as – to borrow a term from Bourdieu – the cultural capital of the debaters play an important part in the critical judgement of a film.

Two years earlier, a film had opened that is usually regarded as the starting point of the Danish new wave: *Weekend* (1962), directed by Palle Kjærulff-Schmidt in collaboration with the writer Klaus Rifbjerg. It also belongs to a genre which was to become a characteristic of the new Danish film, namely the youth picture. It is a quiet film, naturalistically told. But there are also scenes involving alcohol and sex, corresponding well to the common international view of Nordic film. Thus it was doomed as regards export; in many countries it was totally banned. In 1966, Kjærulff-Schmidt and Rifbjerg returned to youth film with *Once there was a War (Det var engang en krig)*, a description of the years of Occupation seen from the point of view of a 15 year old boy. This was to become a classic among Danish films describing the Occupation.

A renowned director like Henning Carlsen was forced to step in as producer of his own films, even for the Swedish-Norwegian-Danish co-production of his film of Knut Hamsun's *Starvation (Sult)* (1966), and he had problems finding a distributor for it. The film offers a personal vision of the Hamsun story, with the starving writer and the city of Kristiania (Oslo) as the two main protagonists. Carlsen here tries a subjective narrative style, completely breaking down the boundaries between reality and fiction, in his portrayal of the writer's confinement in a stuffy and suffocating urban environment. Later, Carlsen also made several satirical films, among them *Oh, To Be on the Bandwagon* (*Man sku'være noget ved musikken*) (1972), criticizing the modern consumer society in his portrait of a group of Copenhageners who meet in the bars to talk about life.

The structure of the Danish film companies also changed dramatically during this time: apart from the ten or so larger companies which produced between five and twenty-four films from 1965 to 1972, no less than thirty small companies made between one and three films in the same period. The debate was occasionally fierce between the Film Fund, which awarded the grants, and the State Film Council, which was ultimately responsible for the films' distribution. In spite of everything, a peak was reached in 1967, when twenty films were produced.

A crucial movement towards something new had also begun. In 1966 the first Danish film school was set up, and in 1968 the first generation of directors were examined from it, among them such names as Dirk Brüel and Christian Braad Thomsen. The latter has played a considerable role in importing art films to Denmark, and has also directed several films of his own. More directors than previously became qualified – at least two in 1969 – and consequently a larger number of directors came to be active in Danish film: during the period 1968 to 1991 an average of sixteen films a year were made. The emphasis is on the first half of the period, however: in 1971 no less than twenty-eight Danish feature films were released. At the same time the cinemas began to merge into chains in order to achieve greater stability.

An important change was also constituted by the establishment of the state-run Danish Film Institute in 1972, modelled on the Swedish one. In a new film law of the same year the state became a co-producer of film and the charges levied on tickets were abolished. A system of advisory officers was introduced, each of whom assumed responsibility for their feature film projects before the Film Institute, which mediated the state subsidy. This law replaced the loan guarantees, script subsidy and quality premiums of the Film Fund, which constituted the production subsidy in the law of 1964. In practice, this meant that the Danish cinema went from being a mainly private mode of financing to a public one. The advisory model was retained in the film law of 1989 which in its turn replaced the regulation of 1972. The purpose of retaining the advisory officers was to continue to guarantee artistic quality. However, the so-called fifty-fifty order was also introduced which meant that a producer who could finance half of a film project received the remaining half (up to 3.5 million DKR) from the state without the project needing to be subjected to artistic evaluation from the advisory officers. Besides, in the early 1990s when Sweden was about to draw up a new state film agreement it copied the advisory model from the Danish.

Independently of swings on the market and the quality subsidy, a constant production of commercial film continued during the 1960s and 1970s. With the abolition of the adult censor in 1969 a new wave of sex comedies saw the light of day, produced by Palladium. The most famous example is probably the *Sengekant* series (the *Bedside* series (begun in 1970)) which comprises eight films and became a box-office success not only in Denmark, but also in other Nordic countries. The venture into the erotic realm, but also the venture into series such as this proved financially viable. There was moreover already a tradition of series based on the films of the 1950s. Besides the sex comedies, several family series were also made, such as, for example, *The Goldencabbage Family* (*Familien Gyldenkål*) (1975–77). There were also attempts at genre parodies around this time, above all of crime films and westerns.

Yet another hit concept of the same period which was related to the genre parody, but which was to exceed all expectations, was *The Olsen Gang* (*Olsenbanden*), when the first film opened in 1968. The films depict a gang of three petty criminals who plan the perfect crime, but who always go astray on the way to realizing their big *coup*. It is a study of Danish *petty-bourgeoisie* and the dream of an unexpected windfall, which is doomed to fail in a world where capital and major crime rule. During the period up to the early 1980s no less than thirteen films were made, all directed by Erik Balling. The films were to provide a stable income for their producer Nordisk Films Kompagni. They are also interesting as variations on the earlier genial film ('hyggefilm'). Here, Danish joviality also rates highly and is presented as a national virtue of sorts. The recurrent scenes with beer and sandwiches are legendary. *The Olsen Gang* has through its incredible popularity with audience and critics alike obviously played an important role in the national self-affirmation process. The scripts of the films were sold to Norway after a failed attempt to export them, and revised to suit Norwegian needs. It is interesting to see what kinds of revisions were made in the transition. For instance, there is a sequence with a guard whom the Olsen Gang want to temporarily neutralize. In Denmark he is distracted with a pornographic magazine, which in Norway is replaced by a bag of sweets – a typical example of the attitude towards the representation of eroticism in each country respectively. Sweden also took over the concept under the title *Jönsson-ligan*.

Towards the end of the 1970s a genre that had dominated Danish film for decades disappeared, namely the privately financed folk comedy Korch & company. This was connected with the changes in the composition of the audience as well as with the fact that television had now taken over as the forum for this kind of entertainment.

The new model for financing from the Film Institute became the subject of much criticism. A number of films were rejected by the audience as well as by the critics. There were exceptions however. Ole Roos's *Destruction* (*Hærværk*) (1977), the filming of a classic Danish novel, was the most expensive production thus far in Danish film at a cost of 3 million DKR. It was received fairly well by the audience however. Yet other audience hits in the 1970s were taken as justification for defending the subsidies by the Institute. Anders Refn's psychological detective story *Cops* (*Strømer*) (1976) was an example. Astrid Henning-Jensen's film of the novel *Winter Children* (*Vinterbørn*) (1978) written by Dea Trier Mørch, about the pregnancies and deliveries of a group of women, was an unexpected success. The film recouped the money owed for the advanced subsidy granted to it with plenty of margins and on top of that it received a Silver Bear award at Berlin. That same year Bille August came out with *Moon of Honey* (*Honningmåne*), which was also greeted with appreciation by both audience and critics. It also distinguished itself by being co-funded with Danish Television, a model that turned out to be here to stay.

The biggest scandal of the decade was brought about through the advisory officer Stig Björkman's subsidy to Jens Jørgen Thorsen's controversial film project *The Many Faces of Jesus Christ* in 1975. The subsidy was revoked, and the film project caused a debate which resounded far beyond film circles. As a consequence, much more caution was exercised in which projects one dared to back. The censorship of the self became – as so often in the history of film – far more efficient than any outer censorship.

During the 1980s the number of film companies in Denmark rose still further, even though the dominance of a few greats, both Danish and local American companies, was strong. During the 1980s there was an American expansion of previously unheard of extent. The major film successes were accompanied by a number of other products in the mass culture industry which consumers were enjoying, such as hamburgers, My Little Pony, etc.

The youth films of the 1970s and 1980s are part of the most important of Danish productions. If the genre has a long tradition in Denmark it is with the aforementioned youth film trend of the 1950s that one can say that it was established as a specific genre, and it was then that it began to primarily address itself to a young audience; and it is only from the 1970s that one can begin to speak of a youth film in the modern sense. The prosperity of the genre had also received support from state measures aimed at benefiting it. In the revision of the film law that was approved in 1982 a special section was addressed to both children's film and youth film, where it was established that a quarter of the total resources was to be spent on this section of the industry. Already at the introduction of the advisory system a specific advisory officer had been appointed to be responsible for children's film.

In 1975 the film *Let Us Be* (*La' os være*) was released which formed the basis of a new wave of youth films addressed primarily to a teenage audience. It was directed by Lasse Nielsen, originally a youth educationist. The film was based largely on improvisation and had the expressed purpose of wanting to show the reality and actual conditions of young people. Like its successors in the genre it draws a dark picture of youth with all kinds of social problems: insecurity, violence, group dependency, etc. At the same time the Danish youth film is often balanced by a disarming humour and a lightness of tone which modulates the bleakness of the societal depiction. One of the more renowned youth film directors is Nils Malmros, with films like *The Tree of Knowledge* (*Kundskabens træ*) (1981) and *Beauty and the Beast* (*Skønheden og udyret*) (1983), which depict with feeling and without embellishment the time of unrest and upheaval of youth and the relationship between young people and the adult world. Bille August's *Zappa* (1983) is also one of the youth film classics, featuring three boys who each represent a different social group.

The 1980s were also a decade when several art film-oriented directors became seriously established, achieving international status as well. Bille August belongs with them too, with a success like *Pelle the Conqueror* (*Pelle Erobreren*) (1988), which guaranteed his international breakthrough and won several awards, both in Scandinavia and abroad (the Golden Palm at Cannes as well as an Oscar). *Pelle the Conqueror* is an episodic film fresco, set in Denmark in the 1890s and based on a series of novels by Martin Andersen Nexø. It opened the way to an international career for August, who also collaborated with Ingmar Bergman on a series for television, also released for the cinema, *Best Intentions* (*Den goda viljan*) (1991). Gabriel Axel, who had been an eccentric in Danish films for decades, had a hit with *Babette's Feast* (*Babettes gæstebud*) (1988), which was exported to several countries and became immensely popular in Scandinavia. It also received an Oscar in 1989. Lars von Trier deserves mentioning as well, with *Element of Crime* (*Forbrydelsens element*) (1985) and *Europa* (1991). Von Trier's films are extremely stylized, often working with light and black-and-white imagery, and evoking a hopelessness and a timeless mood of anxiety.

Helle Ryslinge's comedy *Hearts Flambé* (*Flamberede Hjerter*) (1987) deals with stereotypes with an absurd humour. It became a broad audience success and was followed by another, more satirical comedy, *Syrup* (1990). Ryslinge also deserves special mention, as female directors have been remarkably sparse in Danish film in comparison with, for example, Norwegian film. Besides Ryslinge, Jytte Rex has to be mentioned: she made her first critically acclaimed feature film *Isolde* in 1989.

During this decade there were comparatively few productions of the classical Danish series type, apart from, for example, the series about Walter and Carlo, two video amateurs, three films of which were axed by the critics in spite of an audience of over a million. In 1988 a new detective parody was released, *The Jutland Company* (*Jydekompagniet*), which was followed by a sequel in 1989.

That the shift of generations in Danish cinema during the period between 1960 and 1990 has been nearly complete is hardly surprising; neither is the fact that several of the new directors work in other media such as television and video. What is striking during the latter decades ever since the film crisis first became noticeable is the strong position of the Danish film in Denmark. In comparison with the other Nordic countries the Danes see considerably more domestic films per year. National identity would appear to be significantly less ambivalent in Denmark than, for example, in Sweden. But – as the Danish fairy tale author Hans Christian Andersen would have put it – that is another story.

SELECT BIBLIOGRAPHY

Bordwell, David, *The Films of Carl Theodor Dreyer*, Berkeley/Los Angeles/ London: University of California Press, 1981.

Jeppesen, Peter *et al.* (eds), *Danske spillefilm 1968–1991*, Esbjerg: SDF, 1993.

Dinnesen, Niels Jørgen and Kau, Edvin, *Filmen i Danmark*, København: Akademisk Forlag, 1983.

Engberg, Marguerite, *Dansk Stumfilm I–II*, København: Rhodos forlag, 1977.

Le cinéma danois, Paris: Editions du Centre Pompidou, 1979.

Mottram, Ron, *The Danish Cinema Before Dreyer*, New Jersey: The Scarecrow Press, 1988.

Troelsen, Anders (ed.), *Levende billeder af Danmark*, København: Medusa, 1980.

Chapter 3

Finland

Tytti Soila

When the sensation of moving images was first introduced in Finland, the country was still a Grand Duchy under the Imperial Tsar of Russia (from 1809), and as it was experiencing efforts from the central power to obliterate ideas of autonomy, strong nationalist aspirations filled the minds of the Finnish people. National Romanticism was powerfully expressed through the fine arts and within the quite new and burgeoning Finnish literature. In spite of the fact that the Bible had been translated into Finnish by 1550 and thus established the basis for the written language, the first novel written in Finnish was not published until 1870. Until then the language of the educated public had been Swedish, a state of affairs that was to continue for at least two more decades. This had a particular meaning for the development of the film medium in Finland: Swedish as the mutual language made the mode of exchange easy between the Scandinavian countries and it was, for instance, practical to employ competent Swedish photographers to educate Finns interested in the profession. It also demonstrated that the current was not only running in one direction: many Finnish craftsmen moved to Sweden, among them Mauritz Stiller who was one of the directors responsible for the global prominence of Swedish film.

Those interested in exploiting the new medium in the first place were not only businessmen, but also patriots. Their expressed idea was to distribute images of their native country among fellow citizens in order to awaken and maintain national sentiments. It is important to note that the country was suffering from a period of severe oppression and Russification. Censorship was harsh and patriotic sentiments could only be expressed through music and images. The first short newsreels and documentaries reproduced – not surprisingly – the nature of the different provinces of the fatherland, especially its watercourses, with descriptive titles such as 'Images from the beautiful spots of the surroundings of Tampere and the factories of Nokia'. Other popular motifs were sports events, celebrities – especially their funerals – and city scenes with crowds on the streets.

Atelier Apollo, situated in Helsinki, was the first company to produce and distribute film. It also owned the first permanent cinema in the country: Världen Rundt-Maailman ympäri (Round the World). The owner, an engineer called K. E. Ståhlberg, was a cousin of the first future president of Finland and an active Fennophile. He declared that his intention was to promote the beauty of the fatherland among Finnish people and perhaps even abroad. In order to realize this he employed two photographers: the Swedish-born Frans Engström and a Finn, I. K. Inha. The pair travelled around the country and captured on camera its landscapes, meadows and woods, and especially its lakes and rivers: during the first ten years (beginning with 1904 when Atelier Apollo entered into business) different rapids and waterfalls were reproduced in no less than sixteen separate films. The impressive rapids would later rank among the most significant symbols in the national iconography, where they represented contradictory mythical elements and characteristics.

Nature is of course a common source for myths and beliefs all over the world but it is important to keep in mind that for Scandinavian people and for life in Scandinavia nature has a special meaning. The wilderness and its woods and lakes are in particular regarded as a utopia of abundance and power. Its anomalies, such as mountains and waterfalls, were – and perhaps still are – believed to carry secret forces. In fiction these anomalies have developed into signs that combine mythical and contradictory meanings.It should be noted that, within Scandinavian fantasy, nature is almost always a positive element. Occasionally it may show itself to be dangerous, even in fiction, but that is because it must guard itself against intruders.

The first feature film in Finland was made by Atelier Apollo in 1907 and was a result of a script competition announced in several newspapers in which the participants should 'make suggestions for such domestic themes that would be suitable for a show as living images'. The Finnish historian Hannu Salmi concludes that the initial phase of the film industry in Finland was not a temporary experiment. The creation of the country's film culture was instead a conscious national enterprise aimed at heightening the identity and self-esteem of the Finnish people. In a similar manner the National Theatre and the National Opera had been initiated two decades earlier in order to provide a basis and setting for the Finnish language.

The Moonshiners (*Salaviinanpolttajat/Lönnbrännarna*) (Sparre and Puro, 1907) was the name of the winning script, the author of which was to remain a secret forever. The film contained a mixture of comic scenes and fights between bootleggers and the police. The theme was remarkably up to date: during the early spring when the film was made, the Social Democrats won the election and the majority supported the legislation behind a proposal for the prohibition of alcohol; Finland would be the first country in the world to do so. The law was passed in October of that same year. The Tsar, however, refused to confirm it, and this controversial law was not passed until 1919, when the country had already been independent for two years.

The film itself, *Salaviinanpolttajat*, like all the feature films from this early period (with the exception of a few scenes from Teuvo Puros's film *Sylvi* (1913)) has disappeared. Studies have shown that it contained the embryos of several repeated themes: the action takes place in deep woods; the comic figure who escapes from the police resembles the lumberjack, the archetypal hero of Finnish fiction; and alcohol abuse, which in future was to become a permanent fixture in films, giving domestic censorship reason to interfere repeatedly.

During this early period before the declaration of the country's independence, twenty-seven feature films were made, most of which were short comedies based on original scripts. There were also other films in this collection which indicated a trend that was to remain permanent in the country's film production: the producers went in for adapting popular domestic plays and literature for the screen. For example, two larger investments that Teuvo Puro, a well-known actor of the national stage and second director of *Salaviinanpolttajat*, took on with his colleagues Frans Engström and Teppo Raikas, were two plays by Minna Canth: *Anna-Liisa* and *Sylvi*. Minna Canth (1844–97) was the widow of a schoolmaster and one of the most controversial authors of her time, an author of societal 'indignationrealistic' (i.e. realistic to a degree that aroused audiences' indignation) and often clearly feminist dramas where the conflicts of the plot were expressed through the fate of a female character.

The production of both Canth films was fraught with difficulties and *Anna-Liisa* was never finished: most of the negatives of the film were ruined, since the film-makers had to postpone the development of the film due to financial difficulties. *Anna-Liisa* was remade in 1922 (Teuvo Puro) and this time with much greater success: it was the first film to be exported abroad, including to Sweden.

Along with these ambitious projects with literary origins, several short farces were produced, among others by an industrious family called Pohjanheimo who established· the Lyyra cinema to compete with Atelier Apollo. The company soon engaged in the distribution of film in addition to a photographic studio and a laboratory for photo developing. Film production was initiated in 1911, and the first newsreels in the country were produced by Lyyra Filmi. In the spring of 1913 the company bought the rights to *Sylvi* and during the summer the first fiction films were shot. Kari Uusitalo, a film scholar, offers a lively description of how the director-father, Hjalmar, worked as an attendant in the cinema, the mother sold tickets, one of the four sons played the violin, another was the usher and the two remaining sons worked as projectionists. Film production worked according to similar principles: the boys wrote filmscripts and shot a series of slapstick, action-filled detective stories and comedies of about 8–15 minutes in length. According to hearsay the mother used to appear on location and exhort her sons: 'Wind slowly, boys, so you won't waste the film stock!'

Apart from 'lighter entertainment', the Pohjanheimo clan produced serious melodramas, many of which were based on the plays written by the well-known theatre manager and playwright Kaarle Halme. Halme even directed his plays, among them a film called *The Young Pilot* (*Nuori luotsi*) written by a certain Yrjö Veijola. The film was released in 1913; the author of the play is now forgotten, but the film was remade in 1927. In spite of its unparalleled success the Pohjanheimo company suffered financial difficulties: the business was mismanaged by the sons in the uncertain market conditions of the First World War, and Hjalmar Pohjanheimo was forced to sell his last cinema in 1922.

The leading company of the industry, Atelier Apollo, however, faced competition from other quarters as early as 1907, for example, Pohjoismaiden Biografi Komppania. Furthermore, a former employee of Atelier Apollo, Hjalmar Hårdh, founded a smaller cinema company: Premier Biografi. The first production company outside Helsinki, OY Maat ja Kansat, was founded in Tampere in 1907 and it completed about forty short documentaries between 1907 and 1912. There were no less than forty-four production companies in total in the country during the early period. The numbers, however, reflect curiosity as to new means to earn money rather than the actual amount of produced film. During the Russian period Atelier Apollo produced 110 films which accounted for one-third of all domestic film production. The production of film was, with few exceptions, concentrated in the capital, a state of affairs that was to continue well into the future.

Yet another company should be mentioned in this context; namely Finlandia Filmi, the owner of which, an engineer called Estlander, had great plans to bring domestic film production to the same level as in Sweden and Denmark. In 1915 he built the first Finnish film studio with glass walls. The studio was used for only two productions before high-level international politics put an end to all film production in Finland: in the autumn of 1916 all filming activities were forbidden by the Russian authorities.

Earlier, censorship authorities had considered it necessary to interfere on only a few occasions. One of the films produced by the company OY Maat ja Kansat in Tampere, *Judge Blom's Return from St Petersburg to Turku* (*Raatimies Blomin paluu Pietarista Turkuun*), was banned in 1912, probably for political reasons – as was *Images from the Funeral of Ida Ahlberg* (*Kuvia Ida Ahbergin hautajaisista*). It is difficult to understand the reason for banning the latter film; Ida Ahlberg was however a celebrated actress at the National Theatre and it is possible that some undue patriotic sentiments had overcome the participants at her funeral. In 1916 still another feature film was banned, namely *The Tragedy of One Life* (*Eräs elämän murhenäytelmä*) which contained a scene where a Russian officer was shot. The authorities obviously considered it far too risky to show in the prevailing political climate.

After this film was confiscated Finnish film production ceased for almost three years. Even documentary film production was limited to a handful of short works about the Civil War and the military parades following it. A lengthy documentary film produced by Pathé Frères was registered and approved by the censorship authorities in the spring of 1918: *Finland's Present Fight for Freedom* (*Suomen parhaillaan käytävästä vapaustaistelusta*). The title testifies to the mood of contemporary history writing: the ongoing war was to be seen as the liberation from the Russian regime, not as the communist revolt and civil war which it purported to be.

THE FIRST TWO DECADES OF INDEPENDENCE

When feature film production resumed after the war, Finland had become an independent republic. Many critics believe that the Civil War caused irreparable damage to the development of Finnish film, particularly its modes of narration and other characteristics. They maintain that since the film industry was not able to develop in a similarly expansive way as was the case in Sweden and Denmark, the means of expression through domestic cinema remained undeveloped. It is true that the innovative use of camera angles and editing remained rather marginal and the producers were satisfied with theatrical shots (picture stills and actors portrayed in full figure). It is nevertheless important to note that such opinions are ruled by normative values of retrospective criticism and its wish to understand cinema as an art form. Already during the 1920s the controversial writer Olavi Paavolainen criticized films that were 'too bad to be praised and too good to be put down' – and thus, according to him, drove the critics to despair. However, the domestic audiences did not care. Finnish film was to keep its unique position as the public favourite into the 1950s, and even beyond. The film producers themselves seemed only too anxious to angle their products in such a manner that they would appeal to the largest possible audiences. If they had any other ambitions apart from this, it would be those of professionally conscious craftsmen.

The film industry that was created in the new Republic of Finland kept to the old patriotism, indeed reinforcing it with more extended views and new energy and pride: 'Finland should be made familiar to Finns and to the whole wide world!'

With the establishment of Suomi-Filmi in 1919, initially called Suomen Filmikuvaamo, Finnish film production entered a new era with long-term strategy planning and a clearly formulated policy. One of the founders of the company and soon-to-be chief manager and chief director, Erkki Karu (a former prop painter and theatre director) proved to have far-sighted visions and, in the long run, the ability to feel the pulse of the audiences. From the beginning the company invested in a grandiose manner. The first film was based on a story written by Anni Swan, a popular and well-known author of juvenile novels, and the President of Finland and members of the Cabinet attended the première. This ambitious enterprise was not, however, very successful; the losses amounted to around 50,000 marks, about half of the company's investing capital.

Other investments also led to losses, and the future of the company seemed very precarious. Thus the company directors decided to trust their intuition as experienced theatre men and invested the last of their capital in the old, well-known popular rural melodramas they had played during their tours around the country. This proved to be the turning point. The remake of the Minna Canth play *Anna-Liisa* in 1922 sealed the pact between the producers of Suomi-Filmi and the Finnish audiences; this was Finnish popular cinema. Another similar film was released the same year: *The Logger's Wife* (*Koskenlaskijan morsian*), shown for an entire seven weeks in Helsinki.

These two films changed the luck of Suomi-Filmi. *Koskenlaskijan morsian* was sold to the other Scandinavian countries and even to continental Europe. According to Kari Uusitalo's estimation it was this film that signified Erkki Karu's breakthrough as a professional film director. *Koskenlaskijan morsian* tells the story of a family feud, revenge and reconciliation on the brink of wild and dangerous rapids. The rapids provide a dramatic background to the story and featured the most long-lived male stereotype of the Finnish film fiction: the lumberjack.

Lumberjacks (log-rollers) were itinerant labourers who cut timber in the northern wilderness during the winter and drove it down the great rivers to the sawmills by the sea during the summer. The work was poorly paid, difficult and dangerous. The great rivers both in northern Finland and Sweden have many rapids and waterfalls, and getting the timber past them often involved danger for the men. The adventurous and relatively free life in the wilderness was a hotbed for all kinds of myths and stories, and from the beginning of this century the lumberjack has been an archetypal character in Finnish popular fiction where he stands for freedom, virility and individuality as well as for mastery of nature's forces.

Interestingly enough, in *Koskenlaskijan morsian* it is the bride, Hanna, who is the driving force behind the story and who with her blonde hair dancing in the wind finally steers the raft herself in order to save the life of her fiancé, caught in the middle of the rapids. Perhaps one might say that the fortune of Suomi-Filmi, and thus the future of Finnish cinema, was established by portraying the lives of two strong female figures: Anna-Liisa and Hanna. Subsequently, many Finnish films were to have a strong female character at the centre of the action. It would be easy to describe the history of Finnish film as an enterprise of only a handful of men. The fact remains that the most popular Finnish-made films told the tales of women and were written by women.

In the same year as *Koskenlaskijan morsian*, Teuvo Puro directed Aleksis Kivi's comedy *The Betrothal* (*Kihlaus*) and immediately afterwards Erkki Karu produced *The Village Shoemakers* (*Nummisuutarit*), another Kivi play. Aleksis Kivi (1834–72) was the son of a poor country tailor and lived his short life more or less in poverty. He wrote his fourteen novels and plays during a period of seven years, lacking any real predecessors as a Finnish-speaking prose writer. In his works Kivi described the rural culture of the deep Finnish woods, and he has created the most original and memorable characters ever in Finnish fiction. In his characters Kivi managed to combine the sublime with comic banality in a manner that has invited repeated interpretations: his classic plays are still those most performed and enjoyed in Finland.

Kivi's innately Finnish play about Esko, the stupid, uncompromising son of the village shoemaker, whose tragicomic character always has its place in the hearts of Finnish people, was a guaranteed investment for Suomi-Filmi. The role of Esko was played by a well-known actor called Axel Slagus, who had received excellent reviews when the play was staged at the Swedish Theatre of Helsinki. The film had its première at the National Theatre and became an outstanding success. The appreciative critics especially noted that the director of the film had managed to conserve the 'spirit of Kivi'. Technically, the film demonstrates innovative camera use in depicting the drunkenness of Esko. The deeper Esko sinks into intoxication, the wilder are the movements of the camera, which finally ends up rotating around Esko's head. This effect astonished the audiences, and was accomplished by hoisting the photographer Kurt Jäger and his camera up a tree in a box that rotated while suspended from a rope.

The production of these films illustrated a policy that was to be characteristic of Finnish film for several decades. During the first ten years of independence (before the introduction of sound film) eleven rural melodramas were made, all of which proved to be popular. Of these, three were set by the sea among fishermen instead of the traditional farming society, but the plot was similar to the others. Considering that the entire production of this period did not consist of more than approximately forty feature films, it is possible to understand their persistence in Finnish imagery throughout decades. However, other films, for instance those staged in upper-class mansions (*Love Almighty/Amor Omnia* (*Rakkauden kaikkivalta/ Amor Omnia*)) (1922) or in a contemporary city setting (comedies such as *Summery Fairytale* (*Suvinen satu*) (Karu, 1925)) were not at all successful.

Continental melodramas usually had a happy ending, whereas the Finnish rural melodramas tended towards tragedy. Central to the plot is a loving couple, where one belongs to a land-owning peasant family and the other is one of the servants. The archetypal story, then, takes place on a prosperous farm with generation or class conflicts as its central themes, themes which in the melodramatic manner are embodied in the destinies of individual characters. The contemporary political situation is outlined only briefly. In many of the films the action takes place in a utopian, but not very distant past, and only a few of them, such as *The Bothnians* (*Pohjalaisia*) (1925) describe the conflicts between the free peasants in the Finnish Ostrobothnia and the Russian rulers, and then only on the periphery of the plot. In this context it is important to note that wounds inflicted by the Civil War were still quite fresh and the healing and unifying of the country's population was making very slow progress. It is thus not surprising that the political conflicts were not openly expressed in the fiction films until the 1950s, and a feature film about the Civil War was not released until during the 1960s. If the Finnish film industry had wished to describe deep national traumas such as the Civil War and its consequences (among other things the fascist Lapua movement), it obviously had to be done in a circuitous way.

One exception, a clear political demonstration, was the film *Fugitives from Murmansk* (*Muurmanin pakolaiset*), in which Erkki Karu wished to mark the tenth anniversary of his fatherland in 1927. The film was based on a novel written by Kaarlo Hänninen and tells the story of a group of German war prisoners who were deported to build the railway to Murmansk. In the film, the men manage to escape, but one of them drowns and the others are helped by the Finnish people to continue their journey to Sweden and then on to Germany. The story offers many exciting opportunities for chase and fighting scenes, and indeed it was also possible to weave in a minor love story. The film ends with the hero, the German lieutenant Braun, returning to the family who has protected him against the Russians. The point is that he returns to an independent Finland, and the last image in the film shows the Finnish flag fluttering in the wind.

The film' was photographed by Frans Ekebom, who together with the German Kurt Jäger was the most qualified photographer in the country. At this time the film-makers were already using cinematic devices such as panning, fade-in and fade-out, flashbacks, close-ups and subjective camera in a competent manner. One example of this is the emotional climax of the film, where Lieutenant Braun finds the place where his drowned comrade is buried; the sunlight is filtering between the trees, glittering on the waves behind him, when he respectfully bows his head in a last salute. The text on the headstone reads: 'It was not allowed that you should rest in the earth of your fatherland, but you died for your country in the wilderness. We honour and thank you, comrade!'

Muurmanin pakolaiset was one of the few films whose thematics deviated from the usual fare of the period and which was, in spite of this, well received. Two years earlier Karu had directed a contemporary mundane comedy, *Suvinen satu*, which clearly showed that the Finnish audiences were not entertained by the amusements of the upper classes. As a consequence, Suomi-Filmi abandoned all experimentation of thematic character and kept to the rural melodramas and a narrow range of other popular genres. It is worth mentioning *Noidan kirot* (Puro, 1927), a dramatic story about a curse which a persecuted Sami shaman had cast over a farm and its people. The film utilizes beautiful wintery landscapes and natural scenery and gainfully exploits, as does *Muurmanin pakolaiset*, every opportunity to let the camera wander through the wilderness of northern Finland. Thus the beautiful landscape which the first documentary photographers had used to perpetuate political goals also found its way into fiction.

Documentaries about the nature of the country remained popular. The production company Aho & Soldan, which was to develop a special style in visual nature lyricism, was founded at the end of 1920s and finished its first full feature, the lengthy documentary *Among Wild Birds* (*Villilintujen parissa*) in 1927. The greatest documentary producer during the silent era however was Suomi-Filmi, with its 106 short and documentary films. Among these was a feature-length documentary which was commissioned by the Finnish Ministry of Foreign Affairs. The film, which 'described the Finnish life and landscape as foreigners should see it', was called *Finlandia* and the titles of its six instalments closely reflected its contents: *The Fairy Tale of the Woods* (*Metsän satu*), *Helsinki Arising from the Sea* (*Merestä kohoava Helsinki*), *Finnish Sports Life* (*Suomen urheiluelämää*), *The Song of the Green Meadows and Yellow Butter* (*Laulu viheriäisistä niityistä ja keltaisesta voista*), *The Descendants of the Hackapelitas*[1] (*Hakkapeliittojen jälkeläiset*) and *Finnish Water Falls* (*Suomen kosket*) [*sic*]. The films were shown at the Diplomatic Conference in Genoa in 1922 and were received enthusiastically even by domestic audiences. They were shown for four weeks in all in the Helsinki cinemas. The films were later distributed throughout the Finnish embassies and legations in forty countries.

In 1927 another 'great film' was released: *On the Highway of Life* (*Elämän maantiellä*). This tells the story of a wandering barrel organ player's daily, tragic life in the back streets of the cities. The film, which in an international context had a rather ordinary melodramatic pattern and actually is an impassioned and psychologically plausible character study, was not accepted by native audiences, or, as Kari Uusitalo puts it: 'the adventures of the barrel organ player didn't put fire in the Finnish hearts that exclusively seemed to beat for the descriptions of rural life furnished with the signum of Erkki Karu'.

Elämän maantiellä was produced by Komedia-Filmi, one of Suomi-Filmi's few competitors. It was established by Kurt Jäger, the photographer whom Karu had invited to join him from Germany in 1921 (and who became a Finnish citizen in the early 1930s). Jäger left Suomi-Filmi at the beginning of 1925 and established a company called Jäger Filmi OY.[2] His company produced newsreels and provided laboratory facilities for the development of film. When it did not seem to flourish, Jäger founded, together with Teuvo Puro and Karl Fager, who had by now both left Suomi-Filmi, the new company OY Komedia-Filmi. The first production of Komedia-filmi was called *Meren kasvojen edessä* (Puro, 1926). After the première however Puro returned to Suomi-Filmi, complaining that several days could pass without his hearing a Finnish word in Komedia-Filmi.

Jäger then joined Gustaf Molin, who was born in St Petersburg but had managed to escape to Finland during the Revolution. Jäger and Molin, as the two 'miscellaneous foreigners', met shortly after Komedia-Filmi was set up. The company produced only two feature films, one of them *Elämän maantiellä*. Molin also owned a few cinemas and in two years he managed to create the largest distribution company in the country: OY Ufanamet AB, a company that held film rights from Paramount, Metro and the German UFA. By the end of the 1920s Molin was expanding in a manner that probably worried Karu and Suomi-Filmi. Karu managed to secure Suomi-Filmi's position in 1926 by buying the Suomen Biografi OY's chain of twelve nationwide cinemas.

THE SOUND FILM

As in many other countries the breakthrough of sound cinema brought with it great consequences, especially economically due to the massive investments it would require. At the same time the modestly flourishing domestic film industry seemed threatened from other directions too; the market showed signs of satiation towards the end of the 1920s, and when the international crisis reached the country, the future suddenly looked grim for the film-producing business. Certain erroneous investments in sound equipment exhausted Suomi-Filmi's finances, and the film *The Supreme Victory* (*Korkein voitto*) (Carl von Haartman, 1929), a sophisticated spy film, made only a modest profit. On top of all that the company faced other financial problems, since expenses had become much higher than expected.

As a consequence, only three films premièred in 1930, all of them silent. The only film produced by Suomi-Filmi during the summer of 1930 was the comedy *Dressed like Adam and a Little Like Eve, Too* (*Aatamin puvussa ja vähän Eevankin*) (1931) based on a novel by a popular writer known as Agapetus (really Yrjö Soini). This showed itself to be a kind of a lucky strike since the audiences seemed to have matured enough for another genre, the contemporary comedy, and Agapetus's plays and novels were to be among the most popular in the Finnish cinema. The film was a harmless comedy, but just to be sure, the censorship authorities prohibited children from seeing the film, perhaps because of the gentlemen's scanty clothing during certain scenes!

In addition to the arrival of the sound film in Finland, a company was established in Turku, Lahyn-Filmi[3] that had started experimenting with sound film in 1926. *Aatamin puvussa* was filmed silent, and the sound track added later in the Lahyn studios because Suomi-Filmi still lacked sound equipment at this point. The film sound consisted of background music and a few other effects, such as animal noises, which the impressed critics discussed in detail. Suomi-Filmi's own programme flyer read: 'The sound cinema has invaded the world! Finnish enterprising spirit and the power of initiative triumph in this film (*Aatamin puvussa*) – the first domestic sound film is even recorded in our home country. Such an honour has endowed but few countries!'

Lahyn-Filmi even produced a full-length feature film of its own, which premièred in 1931 and became the first feature film with 'real' synchronized sound: *Say It in Finnish* (*Sano se suomeksi*) (Nyberg, 1931).The film may be described as a show comprising different kinds of sketches, musical and song items, interviews and so on. It was not until the end of 1931 that the first narrative film with real dialogue had its première, a film called *The Lumberjack's Bride* (*Tukkipojan morsian*) (Karu, 1931). The title referred to the ever popular *Koskenlaskijan morsian*, and the film was a king-in-disguise story that was subsequently to be repeated many times in Finnish fiction: thanks to his personal charisma and courage, a certain lumberjack or vagabond wins the heart of a rich farmer's daughter. Later the vagabond shows himself to be, if not a rich farmer, then at least a college student with a promising future. The producer himself proudly presented the film: '*Tukkipojan morsian* is a cinematic "Our land" ',[4] which can be understood by everyone and which is meant to be seen by everyone!' Even the censorship authorities gave their consent and allowed the film to be shown to children.

At the same time Suomi-Filmi was completely insolvent, as the investments made by the company had been substantial and some of them unwise. Erkki Karu, who was both the executive director and film director-in-chief, had had grandiose ideas about building a skyscraper in the middle of Helsinki to indicate the power and status of the company. His plans unexpectedly consumed a great deal of company funds without any return. Certain erroneous investments in unprofitable films and economic setbacks caused by the subsidiary company Suomen Biografi OY, which owned the cinema chain, failed, and the accountants finally suggested filing a bankruptcy petition. This and other circumstances, such as the fact that

Karu had allowed himself generous privileges and director's honoraries, caused the company board to gradually lose confidence in him. Karu managed to save the company temporarily with two well-chosen productions, both comedies, and especially the film *Our Boys at Sea* (*Meidän poikamme merellä*) (Karu, 1933) which exploited the success of the 1929 film *Our Boys* (*Meidän poikamme*) – a patriotic and partly humoristic story about recruits in the Finnish army. This new film focused on the navy, and as Karu managed to hire the popular singer Georg Malmstén to sing a couple of his greatest hits in the film, its success was assured.

However, the success with *Meidän poikamme merellä* was not enough to mend the relationship between Karu and the company Board. The breach became final when Karu, in the summer of 1933, found that the Board had gone behind his back by increasing the share capital stock of Suomi-Filmi and selling it, an act which caused him to resign. It is possible that he did not quite believe the Board would accept his resignation; in many ways he was still the guarantor for ongoing production success, and it was apparent that there was no obvious successor as film director. However, his resignation was accepted in August 1933, and even if he was surprised, he was not paralysed; by October he had set up a new production company called Suomen Filmiteollisuus (after the Swedish example) with an official abbreviation SF. The new company was not registered until January 1934, which thus became the official 'launch year' of SF – the year that gave Suomi-Filmi its first serious competitor.

After some initial difficulties in the early 1930s the film industry in Finland came to be seen as a flourishing enterprise, and practically every film produced seemed at least to cover its production costs. The reason for this success was simple: 'the possibility of hearing their mother tongue spoken on the silver screen literally infatuated the Finnish spectators', writes Kari Uusitalo.

It was not only feature films for which people had a craze; the film producers also made a point of making short films. The production of short films had decreased markedly at the beginning of the 1930s. Since 1922 the Finnish state had collected between 20 and 30 per cent stamp duty on all films shown. The domestic feature film had been somewhat favoured since 1927, when stamp duty was reduced to 15 per cent, and further since 1929 when most Finnish films were released from liability to pay taxes (the first tax-free film was *Meidän poikamme*). After a suggestion from the film branch organizations, support measures were undertaken in order to safeguard the future of the short film. In January 1933 a new tax regulation took effect, according to which all films liable to tax (meaning foreign) were allowed 5 per cent reduction of the duty if a short[5] film made in Finland was shown together with it. A requirement was that the content and purpose of the short film had to deal with science, fine arts or education.

Needless to say, the interest in short films immediately increased and even induced some cheating: since the regulation did not say anything about the content of the film material, some inventive profiteers retrieved old films made in the silent period, re-edited them and sold them at a profit. As a consequence, short film production increased tenfold between 1932 and 1933 (from twenty-four to twenty-five films). The following year production stabilized to about 150 films per year, a number that would remain so to the end of the decade. The two largest short film producers were Suomi-Filmi and Aho & Soldan.

The production of feature films was gradually established as an industry, and towards the mid-1930s a handful of companies consolidated, among them of course SF and Suomi-Filmi and, in addition, Jäger-Filmi – Kurt Jäger's own company after Komedia-Filmi and Adams-Filmi.[6] The origins of Adams-Filmi seem to be characteristic of this period: the Finn Aapeli Korhonen had emigrated to North America and made himself a fortune there as Abel Adams. He had come to Finland for a visit and was already on his way back to the USA when he happened to see an advertisement for a cinema for sale. Following an impulse, he bought the cinema, and in no time at all he was an important man within the film industry. He was, for instance, a founding member and the first Chair of Suomen Biografiliitto (The Movie Theatre Owner's Union) in 1923 – which later changed its name to Suomen Filmikamari (Finland's Film Chamber).

From the mid-1930s, Kurt Jäger produced several nationalist and national romantic documentaries, for example, the film *From the Land of Kalevala* (*Kalevalan mailta*) (Kaarna, 1935). This film was not a success and, in spite of the fact that it seems to have contained valuable ethnologic material, it was edited down to two short films. Jäger was more fortunate with another production, a remake of *The Log Drivers* (*Tukkijoella*) (Kaarna, 1937): national romanticism in fictive guise seems to have been more appealing to audiences than documentaries. Jäger, who was German by birth, seems to have been fascinated by Finnish rural romanticism and produced quite a few films based on lumberjack stories.

During this decade Jäger-Filmi produced a total of seven films and thus ranked number three in size. Of eighty-six feature films produced in Finland during the 1930s, SF and Suomi-Filmi were responsible for fifty-four in all. Adams-Filmi, which started as a cinema chain and distributor, contributed with three feature films during the 1930s. Abel Adams died in 1938 and it was not until ten years later that the company produced another feature film. During the war only a handful of short films were produced.

In the mid-1930s there were only two companies seriously competing for cinema audiences. The future of the newcomer, Suomen Filmiteollisuus (SF) seemed just as bright as it had for Suomi-Filmi some ten years earlier. In order to establish himself on the market Karu, who was aching for revenge, decided to exploit the success of the two *Meidän poikamme* films. He lacked proper funding, but was still able to rely on the benevolent support of the Finnish Army when staging his next film, *Our Boys in the Air – We on the Ground* (*Meidän poikamme ilmassa – me maassa*) (Karu, 1934). Not surprisingly, the film was about the Air Force and starred the newly appointed Finnish Miss Europe, Esteri Toivonen. Nevertheless, the film was a failure and severely jeopardized the future of the new company.

One of the reasons for *Meidän poikamme ilmassa*'s failure may have been that Suomi-Filmi had presented its latest feature, *The Foreman at Siltala* (*Siltalan pehtoori*) (Orko, 1934) only three weeks earlier. *Siltalan pehtoori* was to be one of the greatest film successes ever in Finland and the first film to be seen by over a million people. The director of the film, Risto Orko (originally Nylund), had been employed in 1933 as an assistant director to Karu to make a film with an ideological goal, *Those 45,000* (*Ne 45,000*) (Karu, 1933), a film based on a novel written by a celebrated author, Maila Talvio, involving propaganda against tuberculosis.

Siltalan pehtoori, which secured Orko's position in Suomi-Film (the company Board had offered him a position as production manager in 1933), was not his first film. Between *Ne 45,000* and *Siltalan pehtoori* the new film director had managed to direct two light comedies, and had started shooting a film with a Sami motif, when the company decided to make a film of the novel written by Harald Selmer-Geeth. The writer is completely unknown, but the film is archetypal in its way of combining private enterprise and nature-worship with primitive patriotism. It tells the story of the proud and beautiful ruler of the manor Siltala, Lilli Lind (Hanna Taini) and the bailiff Kurt Alarik (Jalmari Rinne). The handsome stranger (who finally shows himself to be socially one of Lilli's peers) is hired to reorganize the neglected estate. Apart from doing his job he even wins the heart of the proud owner of the house. The comic figure of the story is Alarik's rival, an effeminized Finnish-Swedish lieutenant called Mandelcrona, a stereotypical character who always managed to amuse Finnish audiences.

After the disappointment with *Meidän poikamme*, SF managed to secure its position with the help of two films that followed a well-tested pattern: one was another rural melodrama and the other a comedy set in a contemporary middle-class milieu. The latter was written by Agapetus, who also wrote *Aatamin puvussa*. The first film to be made was *Scapegoat* (*Syntipukki*) (Karu, 1935), then *All Kinds of Visitors* (*Kaikenlaisia vieraita*) (Särkkä-Norta, 1936) and *The Assessor's Woman Troubles* (*Asessorin naishuolet*) (Särkkä-Norta, 1937). A series of films based on rural melodramas opened with *On the Roinila Farm* (*Roinilan talossa*) (Karu, 1935), yet another film based on a play written by Minna Canth – and the following year SF repeated the success that Suomi-Filmi had attained eleven years earlier with *The Bothnians* (*Pohjalaisia*) (Särkkä and Norta, 1936), SF's greatest success to date. Another melodrama that further contributed to the dichotomizing of genres presented a motif from the farms of the purest part of Finland, Ostrobothnia, and was called *As Dream and Shadow* (*Kuin uni ja varjo*) (Särkkä and Norta, 1937).

Erkki Karu died suddenly from the complications of a common ear inflammation in December 1935, and his successors T. J. Särkkä and Yrjö Norta followed the policy laid down by him. Norta returned to Finland after two years in Sweden where he had been employed as a sound technician, attaining a solid background as a film worker. Särkkä in his turn was an uninitiated but keen newcomer to the industry. Karus's patriotic disposition was a fact generally vouched for and it was possible that he had been looking for a like-minded person when he contacted T(oivo) J(almari) Särkkä when setting up SF and suggested that he join the company Board. Särkkä was the president of a federation called Kotimainen Työ[7] – later Kotimaisen Työn Liitto (The Union of Domestic Work) – and in the federation's newsletter had shown active interest in promoting the Finnish film industry.

Särkkä very soon became the company's leading personality, due above all to his organizing ability. He utilized the company resources in a purposeful manner and saw to it that when one of the two film teams was shooting exteriors during the summer, it was done for not only one but several films at once. Using such a routine, a record number of four films was produced during the summer of 1937. The following year SF surpassed Suomi-Filmi as leading film company in Finland, a position that it was to keep for the next twenty-five years, producing five or six feature film premières per year. In fact, during the late 1930s both companies expanded by establishing new facilities and employing new staff; for instance, the first professional film editors were employed in 1939; furthermore, Suomi-Filmi built a new studio in Munkkisaari (in 1938) and SF came to own three studios in the city.

An important ideological project the young nation had to struggle with during the first decades of its independence was to unite its people after the Civil War of 1917–18, the aftermath of which had claimed many victims and split the small population into two factions.[8] The film industry was owned by the patriotic middle class, and the conscious or unconscious consequence was that this popular mass medium became a mediator of its values and goals, promoting the healing and homogenizing of the country.

In its effort to address as many people as possible, the domestic film contributed to creating a common, imaginary past that could be accepted by everyone regardless of his or her social background. The films of the 1920s had frequently taken place in a nostalgic past, marked, for instance, by the vaguely old-fashioned costumes of the characters, and in a country setting that was familiar to the majority of the audiences. The stories were set on prosperous farms, people worked in the fields and in the grounds, surrounded by the traditional wooden houses built on one level with a porch in the middle. The birches would cast shadows over their surroundings and at the rear one could see the woods, not dark and threatening, but as secure domains where cattle could graze and the timber was cut in winter. This was the imagery that consolidated and confirmed the familiar and common, the surroundings that most of the audiences recognized in a country where the urbanization process would not get started until towards the end of the 1940s.

The rural melodramas that took place in this milieu initially focused on a class and generation conflict, where parents opposed young love across class boundaries. According to the melodramatic model the fiercely controversial question of class was reduced to a private problem that could be overcome with the help of personal understanding, and the transgression from one class to another was done with the help of all-embracing love.

Characteristic of the productions of the 1930s was how producers utilized contemporary popular literature to a greater degree than before. It is apparent that the film industry kept its eye on the bestseller fiction lists, and popular novels were filmed as often as folk comedies. In fact the popular literary genres accounted for almost a half of the films of the decade. Interestingly, the original manuscripts were written exclusively as slapsticks and comedies, resulting in a number of harmless and relatively popular products that were soon to irritate the film critics.

An important 'innovation' among the few new film genres introduced towards the end of the 1930s was the military farce that had several popular predecessors in Sweden. As with many other Swedish films, military farces had been imported to Finland; these were obviously quite successful, since the domestic companies ventured to produce a few. The first, *The Black Sheep of the Regiment* (*Rykmentin murheenkryyni*) (Särkkä/Norta, 1938), was received enthusiastically, and became one of the greatest box-office successes ever in the history of SF. It was followed by several similar productions sufficiently interesting despite the fact that during the war audiences were tired of the subject, and *Murheenkryyni* itself was remade in the 1950s.

The film companies also showed high cultural ambition through several investments during this stabilizing period. Quite a few plays written by such celebrated authors as Kivi and Canth were filmed, among them remakes such as *Nummisuutarit*. Juhani Aho's *Juha*, a classic novel which the Swedes had filmed during the 1920s, was made into a film as a domestic enterprise. Svensk Filmindustri, Sweden's largest film company, had investigated the possibility of remaking this successsful film, but Heikki Aho, the son of the famous author and a joint owner of Aho & Soldan, considered that the story would be best made in Finland.

Juha (Tapiovaara, 1937) was to be Aho & Soldan's only feature film during the twenty-five years of the company's existence and was directed by the young and gifted Nyrki Tapiovaara. This attractive young man, whom Kari Uusitalo has characterized as the 'very angry young man' of Finnish film criticism, was to become one of the most cherished legends of Finnish film history. Tapiovaara, originally a law student, admired expressionism and French films, voicing his opinion about contemporary domestic film in such an indignant manner that he was banned from the Finnish Broadcasting Corporation, where he began his career as a film critic. He maintained that the Finnish film was provincial and lacked artistic ambition. As a result, there were quite a few people in the film industry who wanted him to fail when he made his debut with *Juha*. However, Tapiovaara showed himself capable of realizing his ideas successfully: 'The beginning and the end of the theatre are the words, the means of cinema are instead image and sound, a cinematically utilized sound.' *Juha* was unanimously well- received, and Tapiovaara went on to make another four films before – as were so many other gifted young people – he was killed in the Winter War. The fact that he disappeared as a leader of a reconnaissance group far behind enemy lines contributed further to the legend.

The first professional film script writers were also introduced during the 1930s, the most outstanding of whom was Mika Waltari, author of, among other things, the world-famous novel *Sinuhe the Egyptian*. During the 1920s he had belonged to the modernist artist group Tulenkantajat, and his debut work was characterized by expressionistic preferences for strong emotions and the exotic. During his long career Waltari showed himself to be a prolific writer and wrote thrillers as well as political dramas. He wrote his first manuscript based on his novel *The Unruly Generation* (*Kuriton sukupolvi*) in 1937 and his first original manuscript for the film two years later: *February Manifesto* (*Helmikuun manifesti*) (Särkkä/ Norta, 1939).

Helmikuun manifesti was a melodrama and as such was one of the few films not based on a novel or a play that had first proved to be popular in another media. It is possible that the producers believed in the subject itself, since it corresponded to the serious political situation into which Finland was drifting. As with the films *Activists* (*Aktivistit*) (Orko, 1939) and *The Great Wrath* (*Isoviha*) (Kaarna, 1939), it was a retrospective view of the relations between Finland and its powerful eastern neighbour. *Helmikuun manifesti* proved to be the most expensive film ever made in the history of SF, and was presented as a 'historic cavalcade over the fatal occurrences of our fatherland'. The box-offices sold out all over the country, and the film's audiences were larger than those for the military farce *Rykmentin murheenkryyni*.

SF's rival Suomi-Filmi hung on, and *Aktivistit*, their answer to *Helmikuun manifesti*, had its première two months later. *Aktivistit* also had an original script, written by its director Risto Orko together with Ilmari Unho. The film was 'dedicated to the memory of the men who offered their lives for the freedom of Finland 1917–1918' and formed part of the patriotic tissue of images to which Orko had devoted himself even in his earlier work. Hannu Leminen, the set designer who had made his name with the highly praised *A Yager's Bride*[9] (*Jääkärin morsian*) (Orko, 1938), and who was to become one of the most skilled directors of melodrama, planned the extraordinarily well-made and expensive set decor for this 'domestic film of top class' which even the Swedish film critics considered to be grand cinema.

Together with some other popular films (for example, *Jääkärin morsian*), *Aktivistit* and *Isoviha* had both been banned by the end of the Second World War because their contents were considered to be a threat to the relationship with the Soviet Union. Already in the autumn of 1939, before the outbreak of war, Jyrki Mikkonen's story *Isoviha* had had several clashes with the censors, mirroring the insecure state of foreign affairs. At the end of September about a hundred metres of film stock were removed because they contained some insulting lines about the Russians, for instance, expressions such as 'Bull-eyed Muscovites'. Even things that would disgrace the Finns themselves were cut: in the censor's notes it is possible to read laconic commentaries such as 'Cut out the carcasses of the Muscovites – they were accomplished by ourselves, weren't they?' (in other words, the deaths of the Muscovites were caused by the Finns, so why show the bodies to the people?). The film was initially shown for adults only, but four days after making this decision the authorities concluded that, when cut, the film might also be shown to children. Uncertain of the status of the film, the authorities had decided to stage another viewing, to which representatives from the Ministries of Defence and Foreign Affairs were also invited. Yet, a few days later the Ministry of Education recommended the prohibition of the entire film. To the already existing list of forbidden film subjects had thus been added even those which might endanger the neutrality of the country. However, in December, after the outbreak of the Winter War, the film was passed by the special censorship board established during the war, and could now be shown to children in its entirety.

THE WAR YEARS

Towards the end of the 1930s Finland's strained relations with her eastern neighbour contributed to the general hardening of world politics. From the autumn of 1938 the Soviet Union made repeated demands on Finland, suggesting, first, that it should yield strategically important land to the

Plate 3.1 Patriotic iconography *The Logger's Wife* (*Koskenlaskijan morsian*) (Karu, 1922)

Plate 3.2 Love across class barriers *The Foreman at Siltala* (*Siltalan pehtoori*) (Orko, 1934)

Plate 3.3 Abducting the bride *The Vagabond's Wife* (*Kulkurin valssi*) (Särkkä, 1941)

Plate 3.4 Finland and the Soviet Union at war *Yes and Right Away!* (*Jees ja just*) (Orko, 1943)

Plate 3.5 The sins of the cities *The Cross of Love* (*Rakkauden risti*) (Tulio, 1946)

Plate 3.6 The new realism *Children of the Wilderness* (*Putkinotko*) (af Hällström, 1954)

Plate 3.7 The most popular film ever in Finland *The Unknown Soldier* (*Tuntematon sotilas*) (Laine, 1955)

Plate 3.8 Revising history *Flame Top* (*Tulipää*) (Honkasalo, 1980)

Plate 3.9 Deconstructing the military Uuno Goes Military (Uuno Turhapuro armeijan leivissa) (Pasanen, 1984)

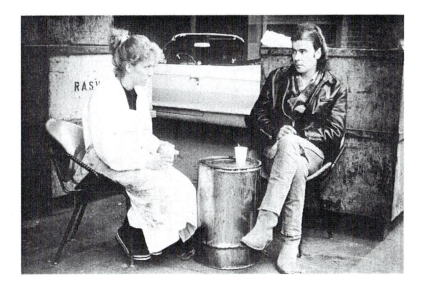

Plate 3.10 International success Ariel (Kaurismäki, 1988)

USSR. Second, it was suggested that Finland endorse a treaty ensuring that no attacks on the Soviet Union would be allowed from Finnish territory and that Finland would accept help from the Soviet Union if it was attacked.

The Soviet Union did manage to force the Baltic countries to accept similar agreements, which led to the occupation of Estonia, Latvia and Lithuania in August 1940. During the negotiations the Finns, who had their suspicions about such consequences, endorsed the politically neutral status of their country and assured the Soviet Union that no further treaties would be necessary. In October and November 1939 additional Finnish delegations were summoned to Moscow for negotiations. Those concessions the Finns considered themselves to be capable of were not, however, enough for Stalin. On 30 November 1939 the Soviet Union declared war against Finland, commencing an instant military offensive along the entire border (1,000 kilometres in length), together with extensive bombing of civilian targets. The Russian strategy was to break down the defensive spirit of the country and to occupy it within two weeks.

The war was total, and there was barely any means of relief since all public amusements such as dance halls became forbidden. The cinemas were still allowed to operate and this led to the paradoxical situation where film production was more difficult than ever, but the demand for films of all kinds was quite substantial. Feature film production ceased entirely during the first weeks of the war and thereafter became difficult. The National Defence started film production for obvious reasons and completed 102 short films as well as five feature-length documentaries during the war years. It is worth observing that the executive director of Suomi-Filmi, Risto Orko, himself conducted the shooting of documentaries on the front line. The Olympic Games of 1940 were planned to take place in Helsinki, and Suomi-Filmi had, among others, provided brand new equipment for rapid production of reportage films. It already trained staff and worked out a distribution net abroad; now these skills and resources were to become useful in another context.

Finland had mobilized her small army of 330,000 men by October 1939 and managed, in spite of the severe lack of war equipment and poor odds, to resist the superior enemy for 105 days while the rest of the world, well informed by more than three hundred foreign reporters, held its breath. On 13 March 1940 the country was forced to accept a peace where large territories were surrendered to the Soviet Union. The peace treaty was received as mournful tidings and all over the country flags were hung at half mast, in many places with mourning crapes.

Yet the fate of the Baltic countries demonstrated that the sacrifices the Finns had made were worthwhile. However, it also proved that the threat from the Soviet Union had by no means diminished, especially when the situation in the rest of Europe developed according to Hitler's plans. Finland alone was facing this threat, and when Germany offered cooperation, it was accepted gratefully. When Germany launched Operation Barbarossa in June 1941, Finland responded immediately to the Soviet declaration of war announced three days later. During the months of peace the Finns had, with the help of Germany and others, managed to modernize and equip its army, which now comprised half a million soldiers. During the following five months the Finns managed not only to reoccupy the lost territories but also to occcupy large areas of Soviet Carelia and to hold on to them until the summer of 1944.

The fresh outbreak of war in 1941 indicated another pause of several months in film production that had been resumed during the short period of peace. There was a general lack of personnel and material, and when production resumed, the companies had to switch cameramen and other workers depending on who was on leave. Even the state contributed to the difficulties; for obvious reasons its need of funds was constant and the domestic feature films, which had been exempt from taxes during the past fifteen years, became liable to taxation in 1941.

Against all odds some new production companies were actually established during this period, of which Fenno-Filmi, with the well-known veteran Yrjö Norta, became one of the most long-lived, finally merging with Adams-Filmi in the 1950s. The cinemas became a lucrative business during the war; there was little competition from other entertainment forms because of the prohibition and every new domestic film was seen by about 10 per cent of the entire population. As the war continued, Finland emphasized that even though it was allied with Germany, the war it was involved in was a separate one and against the Soviet Union only. Thus a great many American films were shown in the cinemas even though their market share decreased from 60 per cent to 20 per cent of the total amount (the domestic films occupied 11.6 per cent of the market). The largest US companies had their own representatives in the country for the duration of the war, whereas German films were imported by Adams-Filmi and Suomi-Filmi. Naturally all Russian film disappeared from the cinemas whereas the share of German films represented 30 per cent of the entire market.

POPULAR THEMES IN HARD TIMES

During the 1920s the audiences seemed to have overlooked films with contemporary themes and especially those where the action took place in a class that was relatively unknown and nonexistent in Finland: the gentry, which in the past had either been foreign or Swedish-speaking. A significant shift occurred in the mid-1930s when the comedies which had been adapted into films became staged not only in contemporary settings but also in the cities. The audiences now seemed to be ready to accept larger variations and it is worth noting that the number of contemporary comedies increased steadily during the war.

Towards the end of the 1930s the market had shown certain signs of satiation, and for the first time the producers began to look for new subjects outside the borders of the country. Several scripts of successful Swedish films were bought and translated into Finnish. The contents were sometimes changed in order to better correspond to domestic circumstances but, for instance when remaking Gustaf Molander's popular comedy *Vi som går köksvägen* from 1932, the producer made painstaking efforts to accomplish an exact copy of the film *In the Kitchen* (*Kyökin puolella*) (Orko, 1940), to the extent that the actress Helena Kara was persuaded to use similar kinds of mimics to Tutta Rolf, the star of the Swedish version.

Among the most characteristic products of this period are undoubtedly the many and enjoyable comedies of Suomi-Filmi accomplished by cooperation between the script writer Kersti Bergroth (pseudonyme Tet), the director Valentin Vaala, and the dazzling and intelligent actress Lea Joutseno. These films, where the female character brings (a well-needed) chaos into the masculine order, were similar to the screwball comedies produced in Hollywood. The military farce was also developed during the war years, surprisingly enough for some, and nine different comedies in a military milieu were produced between 1938 and the end of the war. According to Kimmo Laine this was the period of the first 'wave' of the military farce in Finland. He differentiates between real military farces and adventure films in the war setting. The latter are represented by Armas J. Pulla's novel series about a pair of comrades similar to Stan Laurel and Oliver Hardy. The fat sergeant Ryhmy and his companion, private Romppainen, made jokes about the hardships of war. The pranks were occasionally quite coarse and humiliating for the Russians and consequently the second film in the series *Yes and Right Away!* (*Jees ja just*) (Orko, 1943) received a total ban after the war. The producers made three films on the subject, the last one in the early 1950s.

Yet another film series, which apparently created a momentary illusion of security and order for the home audiences, was introduced during the war years and dealt with the Suominens (the Finn family). There were five Suominen films and they portrayed an average family comprising the father Väinö, a judge by occupation, the wordly-wise mother Aino, four children, and last but by no means least, the cook Hilda. This series broke with the standard family imaginary in Finnish film fiction in that, instead of the earlier model of a farmer family, it opened the doors to the home of a middle-class family living in the capital.

Interestingly, this type of family and setting had been quite common in the Swedish films of the 1930s. The scope of the series dealt with ordinary

problems in a household with several children instead of those of generation conflicts that had governed earlier fiction, even if problems between
the children and their parents came into focus while time passed and the
children grew up. One of the films, for instance, deals with the adjustment
problems the eldest son Olli experiences when he returns to school after
completing his war service. Thus the films did reflect quite directly the
reality faced by many families during and at the end of the war.

Another cycle in an unusual setting which was introduced was a number
of elaborate costume films which in a way were connected with the patriotic melodramas produced immediately before the outbreak of the war.
These melodramas took place in the nineteenth century and gave the
producers the opportunity to make films portraying uninhibited and
romantic fantasies about the upper class and the gentry that had never
really existed. These spectacular romantic stories were made in costly environments. The dramatic conflicts were plotted between the characters who,
in spite of the fact that they belonged to the gentry, gave expression to the
virtues of the bourgeoisie: diligence, honesty, orderliness and patriotism.

Suomen Filmiteollisuus produced its first costume film in the summer
of 1939: *The King of Poets and the Bird of Passage* (*Runon kuningas ja
muuttolintu*) (Särkkä, 1940) which related the love story between the
national poet, the 'Poet King', J. L. Runeberg and Miss Emilie Björkstén.
Many expected a scandal when it became clear that SF was making a film
about the relationship between the elderly married poet and the young
and beautiful middle-class girl. This was in vain, since the completed film
showed all possible consideration for the historical characters in question
and was even allowed to be shown to children, becoming one of the
greatest box-office successes in the history of SF.

Before the end of the war another five costume films were completed
by the same company: *Beautiful Regina of Kaivopuisto* (*Kaivopuiston
kaunis Regina*) (Särkkä, 1941), *The Vagabond's Waltz* (*Kulkurin valssi*)
(Särkkä, 1941), *Catherine and the Count of Munkkiniemi* (*Katariina ja
Munkkiniemen kreivi*) (Elstelä, 1943), *Ballad* (*Ballaadi*) (Särkkä, 1944)
and *Sylvi* (Särkkä, 1944). Other companies made similar investments;
based on the short story written by Stefan Zweig, *Briefen einer
Unbekannten*, was Hannu Leminen's well-made melodrama *White Roses*
(*Valkoiset ruusut*) (1943). This was made a few years before Max Ophuls's
famous film *Letter from the Unknown Woman*. *Valkoiset ruusut* starred
one of the most popular actresses of the time, Helena Kara, the wife of
Leminen, who had great influence in shaping the characters she played.

Mika Waltari was the script writer of the costume film which was to
become one of the most popular Finnish films ever and a grandiose spectacle: *The Vagabond's Waltz* (*Kulkurin valssi*). The film had its première
simultaneously in two cinemas in Helsinki in 1941; it was an expensive
accomplishment, built upon a popular melody, a kind of early hit before

hits were invented. The plot is really a loosely composed series of episodes about a Finnish nobleman, a certain baron Robert Arnold who, after having wounded a Russian rival during a duel, roams around the country disguised as a vagabond. While wandering around he ends up in a circus as well as in a gypsy camp, places where he meets love, rivalry and friendship. Finally he finds his way to a large manor where the beautiful daughter of the house, Helena, in order to save her family's estate, has agreed to marry Eric, the degenerate offspring of a Swedish-speaking [sic] noble family.

Helena takes charge of the apparently simple vagabond, teaching him some manners and how to read. They are naturally drawn to each other, but they are from different backgrounds. Helena is oppressed by her parents, and in a desperate moment she accepts Eric's proposal. Incensed, Robert Arnold leaves the estate, under the impression that Helena has betrayed love for money.

The climax of the story takes place when Arnold, now disguised as a gypsy prince, returns with his nomadic friends in order to abduct Helena. The wedding is already being celebrated at the manor and the flaming beacons stand in the garden, the tables are laid with silver, crystal and flowers and the distinquished guests have just taken their seats. But the bride, Helena, looks unhappy. There is a noise from outside and suddenly Arnold breaks in. Shuffling forward in his dragging vagabond gait he approaches Helena, then sweeps off his hat with an extravagant flourish and boldly poses a question: 'Sallitaan kai kuokkavieraan laulaa laulu morsiamen kunniaksi/Hopefully a singer too is allowed to sing a song to honour the bride!'

Helena is at first hesitant but is soon reassured when, still singing, he invites her to dance. She rushes into his open arms and waltzes with him out of the room while the fiancé and guests gape stupidly after her. When Arnold asks if she wishes to follow him she removes Eric's engagement present from her neck, throwing it into a corner, and rips off her bridal crown and veil which finally end up under the feet of the pursuing crowd. But by then Arnold and Helena are already out of reach.

Kulkurin valssi was the first of the Finnish films to be seen by over a million spectators (the second was to be *The Unknown Soldier* (*Tuntematon sotilas*)), and Kari Uusitalo reports that during the first three months when the film was shown in Helsinki, it was seen by every second inhabitant of the capital, in other words, about 160,000 people. It included the most well-known stars of the period and the main characters were played by the number one couple of Finnish cinema: Ansa Ikonen and Tauno Palo.

In this film, as in many others, Ansa Ikonen's light blonde hair and Madonna-like, oval face with its large, serious eyes contrasted with Tauno Palo's dark masculinity and his laughing, superior attitude in a manner that had fascinated the Finnish people for decades. In several aspects *Kulkurin valssi* is centred around its male star, the unforgettable, incomparable Tauno Palo, who was loved by three generations of film-goers. Anu Koivunen points out the centrality of his performance for contemporary audiences. The combination of these characteristics make him into an idealized image of the Finnish man who in reality lived in dirt, terror and pain in the trenches. To reinforce his perfection, the rival characters of Robert Arnold are portrayed according to the ideas of the imaginary 'other' of the Finnish people: the drunken, deceitful and false Russian officer; the Swedish-born cowardly Eric with his feminine gestures and, finally, the capricious, unreliable and therefore dangerous gypsy.

As an explanation for the appearance of the costume films it has been suggested that there was a need in wartime for escapist entertainment from the cruel circumstances of reality. Of course there is some truth behind such speculations, the wartime reality being depressing and frightening. For instance, Leif Wager, the sensitive and handsome young hero of Ossi Elsteläs's film *Catherine and the Count of Munkkiniemi* (*Katariina ja Munkkiniemen kreivi*) (1943) told the story, while having a break from the production of this romantic film with its park promenades by the lake, how he, as an 18-year-old schoolboy, drove an ambulance in the bombed Helsinki and helped dig out the wounded and dead from the ruins. At least for those directly involved in film production, the situation created strange paradoxes as both dream and reality actually existed side by side. In this context it is also important not to ignore an account of the film producers' desire to show off their professional skills and those resources which the different companies had acquired during the formative period of the 1930s. These grandiose films should thus also be seen as evidence of professional pride over able craftsmanship within the film industry. The melodramas from the war period were well made and carefully planned and it is not surprising to discover that it was the scenographers Hannu Leminen and Ossi Elstelä who directed some of them. As professionals they were able to see the possibilities of the *mise-en-scène* designed to express the ineffable, the energy of displaced and forbidden feelings, which melodrama is often about.

FEMALE–MALE

It may be difficult not to see the history of Finnish film as a result of a handful of men's willpower and dexterity. In addition, it is important to remember that Finland is a small country and it was – and still is – possible for a small group of people to gain a dominant position within one or another area and leave their stamp on it. Thus it is possible to describe the professional activities of some people's efforts to document major parts of Finnish film history from the 1920s to the 1950s and 1960s. First is Erkki Karu, the most energetic of the founders of Suomi-Filmi and also founder of the historically most dominant Finnish production company, Suomen Filmiteollisuus (SF). After his death the leaders of the two companies, Risto Orko for Suomi-Filmi and T. J. Särkkä for SF, commandeered extensive areas of the country's film production until they retired and a new generation began to make films in the early 1960s.

Both directors were emblematic of, if not identified with, Finnish film. They acted as chief directors as well as executive directors for the two companies respectively. Moreover, it was their decision whether or not a certain film was made. Large areas of production within the film industry were and still are dominated by a patriarchal system where the respective leader of the large companies was able to influence and control the smallest details in the production chain. It was not necessary for them to be present everywhere in a system where everybody knew each other and consequently the taste and sentiments of the top man.

Focusing on the beliefs and views of a handful of men is however the kind of auteuristic approach which cannot be justified. It is important to note that from the very beginning women, both in reality and as representations, have been important for the domestic film and its popularity in the domestic market. The industrious heroines in the films of the 1920s are worthy of everyone's interest and even in the 1930s and 1940s women and the female stars have been the hub or the driving force in both comedies and more poignant dramas.

There have not been many female film directors. The actress Glory Leppänen directed one film in 1936, *A Stroke of Luck* (*Onnenpotku*), based on a Swedish film *Kärlek och kassabrist*, and eight years later, in 1944, Ansa Ikonen directed *The Woman is the Trump* (*Nainen on valttia*), a comedy where she herself played the leading lady. In 1950 Brita Wrede directed *Tukkijoella tapahtuu* with Felix Forsman, but otherwise no female film directors were active until the 1960s.

It is worth mentioning that many novels written by female authors have continuously been the source of numerous successful feature films, especially during periods when original manuscripts for film were not as common as they are today. In spite of this it is difficult to find the names of such female authors in the literary history books, a sign, first, of their low status in popular literature, and second, an indication of the way women are made invisible in entire society, not only within the film industry.

The female authors of popular fiction seem to have been those who in the first place managed to express the sentiments which reflect the views of contemporary readers. Whether it is called the 'spirit of the time' or the 'expression of the ineffable', they had the ability to transfer these sentiments into easily manageable forms of fiction that were well received by their readers. The film industry seems to have followed sales rates of contemporary literature and has never been late in exploiting these forms. Yet, because of the male leadership of the production apparatus and male directors, the female background figures have disappeared, if not for the contemporary world, then certainly in historical accounts.

In this context Hilja Valtonen should be mentioned. She was a teacher by profession, and the author of the most well-known popular fiction; practically every book she wrote was adapted for the screen. The first Valtonen film was *Surrogate Wife* (*Vaimoke*) (Vaala, 1936) and her *The Stopgap* (*Hätavara*) (Saarikivi, 1939) became the jubilee film of Suomi-Filmi. During the war, two of these films were directed by Valentin Vaala, with Lea Joutseno as leading lady: *Safety Valve* (*Varaventtiili*) (Vaala, 1942) and *Miss Hothead* (*Neiti Tuittupää*) (Vaala, 1943). The standard story of Valtonen was centred around a brisk and independent young woman, quick at repartee and usually well educated according to the standards of her time or profession. Without quite understanding it herself, she falls in love with an inexperienced, taciturn bachelor whose feelings, after a few setbacks, she manages to arouse, and finally she marries him.

Another successful author of the period was Aino Räsänen, whose romance in twelve parts became extremely popular, and tells the story of a beautiful teacher and violin player, Helena. The first novel in the series, *Play for Me, Helena!* (*Soita minulle, Helena!*) (which thus far has been printed in at least twenty-five editions) was adapted for the screen in 1948 (Leminen, 1948) and was the third most popular film of the domestic productions made that year (NB: the placement was possible even though the film was only released in the autumn!). The film was produced by Adams-Filmi since the director Hannu Leminen had left SF in order to direct his social problem film *Ruined Youth* (*Tuhottu nuoruus*) (Leminen, 1947). Leminen made the scenography and wrote, as often, the script for this story of passion, guilt and duty.

It is worth mentioning that Adams-Filmi employed during this period a female film producer, Signe af Forselles, who was responsible for the *Helena* films, as well as another Tauno Palo spectacle *Rob the Robber* (*Rosvo Roopesta*) (Leminen, 1949), which imitated the successful *Kulkurin valssi*. The second film, *And Helena Plays on* (*Ja Helena soittaa*) (Pöysti, 1953) heralded Lasse Pöysti's debut as a film director and starred Irma Seikkula as Helena. Two more *Helena* films were released during the 1950s: *Farewell Helena* (*Näkemiin Helena*) (Pöysti, 1955) and *Chin up Helena!* (*Pää pystyyn Helena*) (Töyri, 1975); the title role in the former was played by Emma Väänänen and in the latter by Irma Seikkula. Even though these sequels were by no means financial failures, they never reached the kind of popularity achieved by the first Helena film, starring Helena Kara.

An interesting question in this context is the degree of influence exercised by these many great and outstandingly popular actresses in the films they contributed to: actresses such as Ansa Ikonen and Helena Kara were obviously able to shape the characters they played. As mentioned above, Ansa Ikonen even directed one of her films, whereas Helena Kara negotiated her characters in a detailed manner with her director and husband Hannu Leminen. The dazzling comedienne Lea Joutseno in her turn contributed to the scripts of her films.

One of the important personalities behind the most popular films was the Estonian-born author Hella Wuolijoki (1886–1954) who used the pseudonym Juhani Tervapää. Wuolijoki wrote among other things a play, *Mr Puntila and his Servant Matti* (*Herr Puntila und sein Knecht Matti*), in cooperation with Bertolt Brecht, who during a short period in 1940 lived in exile in Finland. Wuolijoki's important position in Finnish drama stems from the series of five plays about the Niskavuori estate and its passionate owners. The story of the women born out of the earth of Tavastlandia in the middle of Finland has its background partly in reality, in the history of the family at the Wuolijoki estate in Sahalahti, Finland. As drama, the Niskavuori epic represents the essence of the Finnish rural melodrama. The core of the story deals with a conflict between the fulfilment of duties and giving way for love. The story-line is built upon several generations of strong women who carry on their shoulders the responsibility of the estate, its people and its traditions while their men are absent.

This is a setup which goes against the grain of the mainstream melodrama in which the female character in the first place is seen and not heard. No matter whether the Niskavuori men are in the city escaping from their responsibilities or in public service, they always seem to be consumed by a craving for the unattainable. The women in their turn stay at home, immutably rooted in the earth, and lace up their corsets in order to face the day and control their emotions which can only be traced in the scant retorts and the skilful mimicry of the actresses.

One example of this theme is a piece of dialogue from the film *Loviisa, Niskavuoren nuori emäntä* (Vaala, 1946), an exchange between Loviisa – the married hostess of the estate – and Malviina, the penniless mistress of Loviisa's husband. Loviisa confronts Malviina and says that all three of them should now somehow pick up the pieces of their lives together and go on living. Malviina retorts bitterly: 'It is easy for you who owns the man, the house and the honour', to which Loviisa replies in a soft voice: 'And you've got love.'

WORLD POLITICS AND WAR WITHIN THE INDUSTRY

The Second World War not only affected the general conditions of film production in Finland but also relationships between the producers and distributors as well as cinema owners. The political animosity within the industry that persisted throughout the war did in fact reflect the ambivalent position of the Finnish people between the central fighting powers. The companies within the industry were concerned with different parts of the war-waging world depending on where each respective company found itself in the production chain. The large companies which produced the majority of films felt obliged to show solidarity with Germany. It was necessary for them to grant the supply of raw film which, like laboratory equipment and film carbon was exclusively provided by German industries.

Suomen Biorafiliitto (the Society of Finnish Cinema) had participated in the meetings of the European Cinema Society and became an official member of the society in 1935 in Berlin. The Society of Finnish Cinema was the central organization for several other interest organizations, among others one for distributors founded in 1937 and another for cinema owners established in 1938. The European Cinema Society in its turn belonged to the International Film Chambers (IFC), of which the Finns became a member in 1939 when the activities of the former European Society ceased. On this occasion the Finnish group changed its name to Suomen Filmikamari (Finnish Film Chambers), a central organization set up for members of the film industry.

In 1941 the representatives of the IFC's member organizations were summoned to a meeting in Berlin on the initiative of the German Film Chambers, which demanded that in the name of European solidarity its member societies should refrain from showing American films; such a decision had already been made in Germany and in the countries allied with it. The representatives of the independent countries considered themselves unable to make such a decision. The Finnish representatives were especially hesitant, since Finland did not wish to join the front hostile to the USA under any circumstances; Finland had, for instance, publicly regretted the breach that had occurred in its relations with Great Britain in December 1941. Naturally even sole economic factors were important here since the US films were the most lucrative in the market, apart from the domestic films.

On the other hand, the film-producing companies knew that if they resisted the plans Germany had put forward, the importation of all raw material would sooner or later be stopped. This predicament was discussed at the Society's meeting in Helsinki in February 1941. In spite of the fact that the board of the Film Chambers risked its entire authority in order to forbid the showing of American films, the proposal was put before the board, which voted at 103 against and 95 for the prohibition.

This vote initiated the 'film skirmish' that was to last for almost three years. Characteristic of this problem was that the censorship authorities forbade all discussion concerning it in the daily newspapers, whereas the debate continued in the industry magazines and newsletters. Suomen

Kinolehti was the supporter for the phalanx friendly to the Germans and the magazine *Elokuvateatteri* resisted the prohibition of American film. The Finnish government wished to remain outside the conflict. Industry members did contact the Foreign Ministry for advice but the question was dismissed as a purely economic one.

The Germans repeated their demands in April 1942 through a decision wherein all showings of American films would cease by the end of the year in all the member countries of the IFC. It was simultaneously concluded that all the benefits the society provided to its member organizations, such as exchange of films and raw materials, would only pertain to the member organizations. The underlying message was that those countries which refused to follow this decision could not be members.

The leaders of Suomi-Filmi, Orko and Schreck, campaigned intensively for the prohibition, but they lost significantly in another vote with only 60 votes out of 208. It is interesting to note that the amount of votes for the prohibition was considerably smaller now than in the first vote. When the result of the vote was clear, the German-minded members announced that they would leave the Film Chamber and found a society of their own. Thus *Suomen Filmiliitto* (Finland's Film Union) was established in July 1942 to compete with the Film Chamber. In accordance with the pro-German ideas of the new society the rhetorics used for recruiting members entertained fantasies of the powerful position that European film would hold after the war.

The Film Union ruled that films produced by its members would be exclusively sold to the distributors who were members of the Film Union. In September of that year the Film Union was accepted as a rightful member of IFC and at the same time that Finland's Film Chamber was excluded from the society. The IFC also declared its support for the measures taken by the Film Union and as a reward its members were granted a supply of raw film stock for the future. The Film Chamber in its turn received the whole-hearted support of the US companies, which was among other things expressed by the Finnish distributors of US films being allowed to pick up films they wished to show in their cinemas. Thus the joint sales policy, so well known for US marketing, did not apply in Finland.

When Finland pulled out of the war in September 1944, all contacts with Germany were broken. Finland's Film Union immediately decided to withdraw all its restrictions on US film and two months later it halted its activities altogether. The decisive reconciliation between all interfering parts in the 'film skirmish' did not fully take place until the new rules of the Film Chamber were approved in 1947.

THE PERIOD OF REBUILDING

When Finland pulled out of the war in September 1944 the Finnish Parliament was once again forced to ratify a rigid agreement of peace which, among other things, confirmed the 1940 borders with the Soviet Union. This meant that Finland was obliged to leave about 12 per cent of its territorial area to Russia, forcing almost half a million people to leave their homes and find new ones in the remaining Finland. Some forty-two cinemas (about 11 per cent) were lost to the Soviet Union. During the war 86,000 lives were lost and 57,000 people were wounded or hand-icapped for the rest of their lives. Considering that the entire Finnish population amounted to only 4.5 million before the outbreak of the war, the losses were heavy and affected almost everyone. On top of this the country had to settle a war debt of close to US$300 million within the next six-year period.

Peace heralded an immediate reorganization in the politics of the film industry as far as the programmes of the cinemas were concerned. Four domestic films that were considered as offensive to their Eastern neigh-bours were banned or voluntarily withdrawn from distribution. Apart from this, the production of two films was interrupted when the German situation became insecure: Suomi-Filmi Wilho Ilmari's film *Disappearing Borders* (*Katoavat rajat*) and in SF Topo Leistelä's *We Belong to Europe* (*Me kuulumme Eurooppaan*). All German films of a political nature were forbidden from the suspension of arms, and from December 1944 all German and Hungarian films were also banned, a prohibition that was maintained until October 1947. The vacuum created in the cinemas by the disappearance of the German films was soon filled by US films which reached 60 per cent of the market, the number one position it had occupied before the war. Even Russian films were shown frequently in Finnish cinemas: 10 per cent of the total market, whereas the domestic films held only 5.3 per cent.

As in the rest of Europe, there was a substantial lack of everything in Finland: from foreign currency to electricity and fuel, to food and clothing. The times were bad for the film industry; dance halls and other evening entertainments that had been forbidden during the war were now competing for the people's attention and the lack of raw materials drove up production costs. It was difficult to compensate for production expenses by the box-office income since ticket prices remained under the general price regulation. And in fact, even though the import regulation of technical apparatus was abolished in 1946, and the first import licence for raw film from the USA and Belgium was granted in the same year, the problems with the lack of raw film lasted to the beginning of the 1950s.

For a few years after the war, before the peace treaty was signed in Paris in 1947, a control commission of the Allies (which was almost all-Russian in practice) was placed in the capital. About ten years later, in 1956, the national regulation authorities and the surveillance of the Russian control commission became a target for a film comedy, *Our Wife in Common* (*Yhteinen vaimomme*) (Vaala, 1956). The film tells the story of a woman whose husband disappears during the war and is presumed dead, after which she remarries a zealous under-secretary in the Regulation Authority. All of a sudden the first husband returns home and the woman faces the delicate problem of bigamy in which the first husband represents love and the second one security. The question of missing soldiers and returning war prisoners was naturally a painful one, and it is interesting to note that it was possible to deal with such problems in the dichotomized world of comedy rather than melodrama.

The war debts were heavy and the Soviet control delegations spread insecurity and fear. The Russians made claims, especially in two areas: first, that the government would take measures against war criminals. For this purpose a humiliating and, in a Finnish sense of justice, adverse retroactive law was passed, a law which made it possible to persecute and punish people for deeds and decisions that during their execution were not considered crimes. Consequently, it became possible to press charges against the wartime president, Risto Ryti, his prime minister and other members of the council of the realm in February 1946. Ryti was convicted and sentenced to ten years in prison, but was pardoned three years later, as were the other councillors.

The Russians also made claims that the substantial war debt would be largely paid in metal goods instead of the ordinary export products of the country, that is, cellulose, paper and timber. The positive consequence of this was that the country was forced to modernize and expand its metal industry perhaps sooner than otherwise would have happened, increasing employment as a consequence. When the war debt was paid in 1952 it was possible, then, to use the industry for further export. The first trade agreement with Finland and the Soviet Union spanned the years 1951 to 1955. This was to contribute to the mood of mutual understanding and confidence between the two countries which was to characterize the coming years.

Finland Pays (*Suomi maksaa*) (Leistelä, 1951) was a one-hour long documentary about the industry that provided war compensations. The way the film was edited, describing among other things long series of freight trains being sent towards the East, provoked contradictory reactions; while the Communist newspapers held that the purpose of the film was to arouse the indignation of the spectators over the amounts of goods the country was forced to yield, the Conservatives saw the film as a homage to the workers, 'in praise of labour'. The representatives of the Communist party, SKDL, made an interpellation concerning the film. In fact *Suomi maksaa* was not seen by many people since it was only shown in six towns for just a few days.

In April 1948 the Agreement for Friendship, Cooperation and Mutual Assistance was signed between Finland and the Soviet Union. The contents of the agreement corresponded to Finnish ambitions since it deviated significantly from the other agreements the Soviet Union had made with the Eastern countries and explicitly confirmed the sovereignty of Finland. The West, which immediately after the war had indicated doubts concerning the possibility of total independence for Finland, changed its attitude. Finland had its supporters from the West even earlier and by 1945 was able to send political representatives to the USA and Great Britain. Another important step had been taken towards stabilization when Finland was granted substantial credit by the USA at the beginning of 1946. After pressure from the Soviet Union, Finland declined aid from the Marshall Plan, but the USA still continued to provide Finland with loans and material for rebuilding the country. The Olympic Games were held ten years behind schedule in Helsinki in 1952, the same year that Coca-Cola and chewing gum were introduced to the country. Finland was orienting itself culturally and economically towards the West.

The insecure period after the war was indirectly reflected in an unusually high amount of so-called problem films with motifs based on the lives of the poor and the unemployed. Edvin Laine, who was to become one of the most productive and well-known Finnish film directors ever through his film *Tuntematon sotilas* (1955), directed his second film *In the Shadow of the Prison Bars* (*Ristikon varjossa*) (1945), a story set against a prison background with realistic ambitions; for example, parts of the film were shot in an authentic setting. The film incurred heavy costs and received enthusiastic reviews, but the audiences did not show much interest in it.

Laine himself announced a policy for the problem films in a newsletter of the film company: 'In my opinion both the theatre and film should look for subjects that appear living and humane for the spectator.' In 1946 only twelve feature films were produced in the entire country, half of them dark and pessimistic in mood. A year later, fourteen features were completed, five of which belonged to the group of problem films. This trend ceased surprisingly quickly; of the sixteen feature films that were produced in 1948 only three may be regarded as problem films, the inclination in production policy obviously being directed instead towards light entertainment.

Most of the problem films were what was referred to in popular speech as 'syphilis films'. The standard syphilis film told the story of a young, innocent woman who comes from the country to the city. In the city she soon becomes corrupt and enters prostitution, eventually contaminating her lover with a venereal disease. A few of these films contain a moralistic viewpoint of the authorities (Väestöliitto), which promoted moderation in sexual relations and, if a misfortune takes place, the right kind of treatment. Occasionally, in films such as *Leeni of Haavisto* (*Haaviston Leeni*) (Salminen, 1948), based on the Swedish film *Anna Lans*, the young woman converts to a better life and begins a career as a Salvation Army soldier. It is easy to see in these female characters a metaphor for the raped country. What makes them more ambiguous and complex is the burden of guilt shouldered by the female character in these films. The director of many syphilis films *par excellence* was Teuvo Tulio who, after upsetting the widow of Abel Adams with his films, worked as an independent producer, director and editor.

Tulio, together with the then 17-year-old Valentin Vaala, had made his first films during the silent era when he was 14 years old. The few films they made deviated from mainstream nationalist film production and were clearly influenced by enthusiasm for the exoticism of *The Fire Carriers* and the more popular films by Rudolph Valentino. The two teenagers ventilated their romantic sentiments about the gypsy life (especially its erotic side), utilizing for the first time this motif which was to become the privileged sign of otherness in Finnish cinema. In *Dark Eyes* (*Mustat silmät*) (Vaala, 1929) and *The Gypsy Charmer* (*Mustalaishurmaaja*) (Vaala, 1929) Tulio plays the role of the mysterious hero with a bare chest and his head wrapped in a bandanna.

As already mentioned, Vaala was to direct some of the most charming comedies as well as to act as a supportive colleague of many female artists, whereas Tulio dedicated himself to portraying the mysteries of the female body. Most characteristic of Tulio's films, apart from the strong contrasts of light and shadow, is the face of the actress Regina Linnanheimo with her provocative smile and her open and bold gaze which returns and challenges the eye of the spectator.

THE STATE AND THE FILM INDUSTRY

The state controlled film production in Finland in four different ways: first, censorship, which regulated what was allowed to be shown; second, the censorship authorities decided on age limits – i.e. who would see what. The third and more subtle way of control was executed through the stamp duty that was generally based on certain quality criteria concerning how the images were constituted: domestic films considered to be edifying or artistic usually benefited from tax deductions. The fourth means of control employed from the 1950s onwards was to be the state subsidies and, before the subsidy system, the state prizes.

The censorship authority of the state was founded in 1919; a nationwide organ whose responsibility was to scrutinize all the films to be publicly shown in the country. In its execution of power the censorship authorities basically seem to have taken steps towards banning films which have exposed their audiences to too much sex and alcohol, as well as films which might have been offensive to its Eastern neighbour, the Soviet Union. During recent years, violence has increasingly been a reason for interference.

Either the Finnish film producers were especially restrained or, rather, their self-censorship was already alert in the script writing phase, since throughout the 1930s the authorities did not interfere more than fifteen times. One trailer was cut, and some images of naked people and whatever might be perceived as promoting alcohol were banned from one or two documentaries or short films. In a film about the life of the Sami people one scene, where a man castrated reindeers by biting their testicles off with his teeth, was shortened. Seven feature films were cut; the aim was usually to shorten or cut explicit love scenes, especially if the lovers found themselves in bed (or a haystack). Even the consequences of love could occasionally disturb the authorities: in the film *Song of the Scarlet Flower* (*Laulu tulipunaisesta kukasta*) (Tulio, 1938) a scene showing a pregnant woman during labour, and her cries, was cut out.

The film *The Women of Niskavuori Farm* (*Niskavuoren naiset*) led to a confrontation between the censors and the producer. The authorities disliked a love scene which the producer considered crucial to the plot. Removing it would make parts of the remaining film unintelligible. Consequently the producer refused to make the cut, whereupon the authorities threatened to ban the film altogether. Finally, an agreement was accomplished where twelve metres from the crucial scene were cut, including a close-up with the loving couple resting their heads on the same pillow.

During the 1940s the censors exercised their powers in the case of sixteen domestic feature films. It is possible to surmise the themes of the films by their names: for example, *The Way You Wanted Me* (*Sellaisena kuin sinä minut halusit*) (Tulio, 1944), *Love's Sacrifice* (*Rakkautensa uhri*) (Söderhjelm, 1945), *The Cross of Love* (*Rakkauden risti*) (Tulio, 1946), *Restless Blood* (*Levoton veri*) (Tulio, 1946). Three of the trailers were shortened and a group of thirty-five documentaries and short films were subject to intervention. As may be observed, Teuvo Tulio, the *enfant terrible* of Finnish film, was the director whom the authorities loved to persecute. Interestingly, the censors not only cut explicit sex scenes but quite often, in a fit of bigotry, any that might end in sexual contact. In the 1940s this was represented by shabby bars and private parties where large amounts of alcohol were consumed and there were risqué dance scenes.

It is possible to find such comments as 'abandon 10 metres of dead bodies' or 'Get rid of the cat's ass' in the censors' notes. The most usual reason for cuts in short films and documentaries was basically hidden commercial advertising, and every now and then the authorities intervened when they came across political propaganda. During the 1950s the censors intervened in ninety cases when it came to short and documentary films. Out of seventeen feature films a few sex scenes were abandoned. Drunk driving and violence were new topics considered extensive enough for the authorities to intervene, and obviously scenes containing police brutality were also banned.

In the 1960s a new era in the history of Finnish censorship was introduced in that the producers wished to protest to a greater degree, maintaining that the censors intervened in the artistic intentions and rights of the directors. It became possible to appeal to two different instances when wishing to file a complaint. In the 1950s the most frequent reason for complaints was due to the tax situation. The producers stressed the artistic values of their films in order to avoid the higher tax charge, and the argument for freedom of speech was also frequently used.

The censorship authorities decided upon tax rates when domestic film again became taxable in 1941. Those domestic films with artistic qualities were subject to 10 per cent stamp duty and all other films were liable to 15 per cent tax from their box-office income. 'The others' were non-artistic (entertainment) films, such as certain low-brow comedies. Two years later the tax was raised to 25 and 35 per cent respectively, and in 1946 the state secured 30 and 35 per cent of a film's net income. Of course the film industry considered itself to be in big trouble; box-office numbers had fallen steadily since 1944 and apart from this, rationing caused other kinds of difficulties. The film producers complained loudly and the taxes were lowered by 5 per cent in 1948. From this year even the length of a film was considered as a criterion for the tax percentage: in order to get some relief from the burden the film had to be at least 2,500 metres long. Certain films could now escape tax altogether and in 1950 three tax classes were created: tax-free, 15 per cent and 25 per cent.

It is interesting to note that the classification of the films was carried out on the basis of a division between artistic and non-artistic films, a classification system that was created early on and utilized by the censorhip authorities themselves. It is possible, then, to consider the allotted tax category, if not as a means of regulation, at least as a kind of indicator of taste in regard to the eventual status of certain films. Initially, as the authorities started to apply the system of three tax categories, it is obvious that almost every domestic film was considered artistic: the definition was thus quite generous. The films that were punished with a high percentage tax class seem to have been 'bush' comedies produced by temporarily constructed speculative companies, and only a handful of films found themselves in this class of pariahs during the war. Among them was, interestingly, a remake of a military farce that had been quite popular in Sweden: *65.66 och jag*, directed by a certain Weyler Hildebrand. The Finnish name was *Varuskunnan 'pikku' morsian* (*The 'Little' Bride of the Garrison*) (Levä, 1943). According to Kari Uusitalo, the film was considered to be humiliating to national defence during the grave times that reigned; the film contained a scene where an officer was put in gaol. The film was initially totally forbidden, but was allowed to be shown about six months later, now with 35 per cent tax as its punishment. The film '*I Live*' ('*Minä elän*') (Unho, 1946) which told the life story of the writer Aleksis Kivi, was the first film to escape tax altogether since the 1930s.

It is not easy to follow the criteria of the censorship authorities, but it would appear that those films which were considered educational in one way or another, as when dealing with an acknowledged artist's tragic life, were considered worth promoting, as were films such as *Ruined Youth* (*Tuhottu nuoruus*) (Leminen, 1947) which, in an educative fashion, told the story of the negative consequences of free love, and was awarded a tax deduction.

Even in the mid-1940s the authorities were suspicious of any comedies written by unknown writers, and the censors always kept a watchful eye on Teuvo Tulio's erotic productions. It is worth noting that the film *In the Grip of Passion* (*Intohimon vallassa*) (Tulio, 1947) was awarded the highest tax percentage (then 30 per cent) without any hesitation, whereas just two weeks later another film containing sexual violence and implicit incest was considered artistic and was thus liable to 5 per cent less tax. The film *The Destruction of Pimeänpirtti* (*Pimeänpirtin hävitys*) (Unho, 1947) was based on a novel by Maila Talvio, an acknowledged female writer, and it seems that the authorities allowed themselves to be impressed by the literary flavour of the film. How could it otherwise be possible for a film with the illustrious name *Love is Even Quicker than Piiroinens's Ram* (*Rakkaus on nopeampi Piiroisen Pässiäkin*) (Ilmari, 1950), to escape stamp duty altogether? Scrutiny of the censor's note on the latter film – 'Describes the country life strikingly' – implies that the quality criteria must have been quite arbitrary.

At least the producers shared this opinion; since the year 1950 more systematic debate was initiated in order to question the decisions made by the censors. It was possible to appeal to the State Film Board, which was an organization superior to the State Office of Film Censorship, and which seems to have made its decisions basically in favour of the plaintiff. In those cases where the Film Board was still not satisfied, it was possible to appeal to the Supreme Administrative Court, a right that was enforced now and again. The film *Behind the Mirror in the Window* (*Katupeilin takana*) for instance, the hundredth film produced by SF and the fifteenth anniversary jubilee film of the company, was awarded 20 per cent tax before its appeal to the Film Board. The Board reduced the tax by 5 per cent and three months later, when the film was again viewed by the censors, it was exempt from taxes altogether. It is, indeed, difficult not to gain the impression that many such decisions were made quite randomly.

A new law in 1966 concerning film censorship replaced the previous one of twenty years earlier. The well-known film critic Jerker A. Eriksson was appointed director and chair of the authority. On taking up the post, he announced that the decisions of the authority were to be liberal, following the general line practised by the other Scandinavian countries. Interestingly, it was Eriksson who was to fight the most contentious dispute in the history of the Finnish censorship authorities when the *enfant terrible* of the Finnish film industry at the time, Jörn Donner, directed certain films with such explicit love scenes that they were inevitably caught up in the wheels of the authorities. One of the most famous disputes was that concerning Donner's film *Portraits of Women* (*Naisenkuvia*) (1970) and which finally resulted in the incensed Donner publishing a book about the process and the press reactions surrounding the case.

THE MARKET POLICIES DURING THE 1950s

The 1950s started with an ascending economy curve for the film industry. The state made certain concessions as regards film taxes, and ticket prices could be increased since the regulations were abolished and the supply of material such as film stock improved. The film companies launched an offensive against the other, competing entertainment forms and SF especially increased its annual production from nine to fourteen films in 1954, a top achievement of the decade for a company that produced ninety-nine films in all. Suomi-Filmi made thirty-three films during the decade, but was surpassed by the newcomer Fennada-Filmi, with its forty-five films.

Characteristic of the expansive production policies of the 1950s were the remakes of old public favourites, new film genres and thematically restrained series of films. After a period of decline probably caused by war weariness, the military farce had a second heyday during which about a dozen films were made. The old comrades Ryhmy and Romppainen had already started their adventures during the war and a revival in 1952 resulted in a fantastic adventure with imaginary international gangster leagues operating in Helsinki in connection with the Olympic Games. In spite of its topical nature, the film was a failure.

Two other films were *The Dead Man* (alias Colonel Rainer Sarmo) played by Joel Rinne, and his supporter Captain Mikko Vehmer (Reino Valkama), who became involved in fantastic adventures in exotic parts of the world during the war. The film *The Dead Man Falls in Love* (*Kuollut mies rakastuu*) (Unho, 1942) was based on an idea by Simo Penttilä (real name Uuno Hirvonen): Penttilä had won a competition for comedy and adventure scripts arranged by Suomi-Filmi in 1940. The two first film adaptations were quite successful, but the third one, *The Dead Man Walks Again* (*Kuollut mies kummittelee*) (Nortimo, 1952), was a failure and the Dead Man was buried forever early in the 1950s.

Joel Rinne, who had played the part of the Dead Man, successfully played another character within the popular genre ten years later, namely the detective Chief Palmu in four detective stories. The cigar-smoking, moustached character created by Mika Waltari resembled Hercule Poirot and Maigret, but solved murder riddles according to a unique Finnish formula together with his companion Detective Kokki and a law student, Virta. The first film *Police Inspector Palmu's Mistake* (*Komisario Palmun erehdys*) in 1960 was a great success and led to a further three sequels, the last of which was made in 1969.

Another thematic cycle created during the early 1950s was the ballad film, a group of films that could be characterized as a national variant of Hollywood musicals, namely, based on popular folk melodies or hits. The story was developed around an uncomplicated moral standpoint in favour of good and law-abiding people in the countryside in a diffuse, ahistoric past. An entertainment artist and a barefoot poet by divine right known all over the country, Reino Helismaa, played a large part in the genesis of this popular genre. These films were known as 'cheerio-films' by those who looked down on them and Helismaa himself had a hand in many of these films, the first of which contributed to the nickname of the genre, 'Cheerio' (the Finnish term is *Rillumarei*). This was to become the refrain for the most popular song in *At the Rovaniemi Fair* (*Rovaniemen markki-noilla*) (Nortimo, 1951). Helismaa was to be the script writer of another twenty-eight films as well as the lyrics for many of the songs composed by Toivo Kärki.

The ballad films deviated from each other in content: *Rovaniemen markkinoilla* and its successors adopted a masculine style. They were connected to the lumberjack romanticism in that the films exploited the mythical character of the lumberjack, and they were set in the mountains of Lapland among gold prospectors. Some discoveries of gold in the rivers of Lapland gave the producers the idea of exploiting Western themes in this cycle of films with songs, lavish natural scenery, open air life and 'real' men. Interestingly this was a period when the mythical character of the lumberjack degenerated from a dramatic hero to a comic trickster. One of the most frequent characters in these films was Tapio Rautavaara, a guitar-playing bard who had won a gold medal in javelin-throwing at the Olympic Games in London in 1948. His healthy sportsman's body, broad white smile and deep voice with its alveolar r-sounds pronounced distinctly in a 'masculine' manner, stands as the ideal male character of the time.

Another variant of the ballad films was a group of romantic films which were perhaps culturally more ambitious than the others in that they combined an elaborated *mise-en-scène* with the well-cut costumes of the actors. The story takes place among the imaginary gentry in Helsinki at the turn of the century and relates the life of an artist, for instance, imitating the air of historical novels, as does the successful film *A Summer Night's Waltz* (*Kesäillan valssi*) (Leminen, 1951).

One of the first romantic ballad films was *Beautiful Veera* (*Kaunis Veera eli ballaadi Saimaalta*) (Salminen, 1950). The film was seen by 900,000 people and thus became one of the most popular films in the history of the Finnish film industry. *Veera* is a changeling story: a beautiful girl has been kidnapped by a wandering gypsy couple and now, being a gypsy girl of a marriageable age, gets a job as a cook on a wooden barge. The good-natured crew of the barge was played by four singers who later, as a result of the film, were to form the famous singing quartet, Kipparikvartetti. Apart from the popular hit songs in which the film invested was the picturesque gypsy motif and the beautiful lake landscapes in the middle of Finland. While sailing on Lake Saimaa towards the Baltic Sea Veera falls in love with a white man. On her travels she meets a mysterious man who in the end turns out to be her real father, a Finnish nobleman and a patriot fighting against the Russian oppressors. The appearance of Veera's father naturally annihilated the possible ethnic scruples concerning the marital fitness of the young couple in love. In spite of the fact that the Finnish film industry and in particular the popular music industry frequently exploited the exoticism of gypsy life, the Finnish gypsies have always been the most shunned ethnic group in the country.

All these new, popular forms of film were probably motivated by the singular purpose to bring the audiences back to the cinemas. And indeed, films such as *Rovaniemen markkinoilla* and *Kesäillan valssi* were the most popular in 1951, until which time the Finnish film producers and their audiences had a mutual understanding of each others' taste. Yet, the preferences of the average film-goer did not match those of the film critics in the newspapers and magazines. Domestic cinema had been a target for the critics throughout its history, but the reaction that *Rovaniemen markki-noilla* and its successors received resembled more a reaction to rabies than anything else!

Professional film critics were still rather rare in Finland, but during the 1950s the group increased. The reviews of the earlier period were usually written by freelancers with an interest in film rather than by professional journalists, especially in the newspapers published in the countryside. When the cinema and the nation were young, the expectations that the domestic films met had to do with a quest for realism; the reviewers appreciated films that were true to the letter and copied the novels and plays as best they could. Another implicit wish was that the professional design of the films would stand out in comparison to the foreign films. When this proved to be the case, the prize was considerable, as was the will to overlook eventual flaws.

Critics such as Paavola and Tapiovaara in the 1920s and 1930s belonged to those professional intellectuals who started to demand artistic performances from the domestic producers. In the first place this meant a quest for originality in the formal design and *mise-en-scène*. The expectations concerning the thematics of individual films were that they should express the originator's (i.e. the director's) individuality and eventual philosophy.

Yet the ambitions of the Finnish film industry were in the first place those of professional craftsmen wishing to produce an acceptable product, and in combination with the producer's actual knowledge of the preferences of the audiences, they seldom lived up to the (quite normative) expectations of the intellectuals. This discrepancy became more pronounced when the import of European films was made possible after the war, and comparison became easier on home grounds. When the critics were able to travel abroad again and participate in international film festivals, the breach between the expectations of the critics and the ability and ambition of the producers increased even further. The attitudes of the critics were to have a significant impact on the attitudes of the new generation of film directors in the 1960s.

Another sign of public interest in cinema as an art form was the establishment of film clubs at the beginning of the 1950s. The first ones were established in 1952, and a nationwide central organization, the Federation of Finnish Film Societies, was founded four years later. Film magazines had been published very early, in the 1920s and the 1930s; the longest survivor was called *Elokuva-Aitta*. From then on the film clubs and the more specialized film critics contributed to cultivating a normative attitude, according to which film as a means of expression should be understood as an art form, not as 'entertainment', and that domestic film should contribute to creating a favourable image of Finland abroad and even at home. The intention was still the same as it had been at the beginning of the century, but the norms had changed. As the reader may remember, the purpose at the beginning of the century had been to promote the knowledge of the beautiful nature of Finland and the customs of its people. Now the critics wished for original and individualistic works of art that hopefully would win prizes at the international festivals.

Interestingly, the critics were not always positive when their demands were met, for example, by Erik Blomberg's film *The White Reindeer* (*Valkoinen peura*) (Blomberg, 1952), a film that won international prizes in Cannes (1953), at Karlov Vary (1954) as well as in Hollywood (1956). The film tells the story of a witch who turns into a deer in the wilderness and kills anyone who tries to capture her. The main character, Pirita the Sami (indigenous tribe) woman, is played by Blomberg's wife Mirjami Kuosmanen. The auteur of the film seems to be in question: it was photographed, directed and edited by Blomberg himself, but the idea as well as large parts of the script belonged to Kuosmanen, as was her almost palpable presence on the screen.

Valkoinen peura was produced by Junior-Filmi, a new company with Blomberg among its founders. Matti Kassila and Aarne Tarkas were the two other members who were to be among the country's best-known film directors in the future. Another company called Fennada-Filmi, a newcomer quite able to compete with the older ones, was oriented towards making films of classic novels, a genre that was once a guarantee of success for the older companies. Fennada made successful adaptations of two of Joel Lehtonen's novels: *Children of the Wilderness* (*Putkinotko*) (1954) and *Joseph of Ryysyranta* (*Ryysyrannan Jooseppi*) (1955), both directed by the veteran Raoul af Hällström. *Ryysyrannan Jooseppi* was to be the last work of its director; Hällström died during the winter of 1956 and the following summer he was posthumously awarded a personal prize for his artistic achievements at the Karlov Vary Film Festival.

Two of Hällström's films deviated from the kind of politics that the film companies had exploited for decades, avoiding the description of the origins of the Finnish class society, and the moulding of the conflicts within its defined limitations. *Putkinotko* was to be the most popular film in 1954, thus proving that the audiences were mature enough to appreciate an unvarnished description of the Finnish lumpenproletariat at the turn of the century. It is possible to see a connection between these films and the film *The Unknown Soldier* (*Tuntematon sotilas*) (Laine, 1955) which in its capacity as a war film was a rather odd phenomenon in the national inventory: the particularly popular military farces did not describe war and the waging of war from its realistic side.

Väinö Linna's novel *The Unknown Soldier* was published in a rather modest edition during Christmas 1954. The author himself was a self-taught person and factory worker who had previously published one or two novels without arousing much interest. *The Unknown Soldier* immediately became one of the most read novels ever in the country: in the first four months an additional 100,000 copies were printed. With the help of its mixture of realism and biting humour the novel records vividly the everyday life of a war as it is experienced by a small group of uneducated and unsentimental men who, despite their smallmindedness, are somehow transformed into men of quality to the point that the novel ultimately stands as a homage to the Finnish soldier.

SF hurried to secure the rights to adapt Linna's novel into a film and the première took place the day before Christmas Eve in 1955. The company was desperately hoping that the film would recoup its production costs since it had ended up with a budget of an unbelievable 50 million marks (50,000 in current currency). By the end of 1956 all such anxiety proved to be unwarranted as the company was able to show a fourfold profit. The surplus was massive enough to cause problems. It is said that the profits made by *Tuntematon sotilas* steered the continued production of SF in a negative direction, contributing to the crisis that hit the Finnish film industry at the end of the 1950s. In order to avoid paying taxes for the income from *Tuntematon*, as it came to be called all over the country, SF invested immediately (and, many thought, unwisely) in a large number of productions which were later to be called 'shelf films'. These films were hastily made and literally placed on the shelves in order to wait for a sufficient time for release.

The way *Tuntematon sotilas* was received is unique in the history of Finnish cinema and in many ways difficult to describe. It is as if the film turned out to be too great for this small country. It made a record at the box-office (over two million people – more than one-third of the entire population – saw the film) and at the same time it seems to have had such a universal applicability that it had no comparable successors for at least two decades. It seems as if all the other war films became superfluous after *Tuntematon sotilas*.

In a similar manner it is difficult to estimate the impact of the novel itself on cultural life in Finland. Sentences from the novel soon found their way into the everyday vernacular. As an example, it is said that when Rauni Mollberg directed a new version of the film in 1985, the land was hit by a complete mass media hysteria. The weekly magazines, for instance, published long series of portraits of the actors with descriptions of the fictive characters' personal qualities and background stories as if they had been real people.

The production of the first version of the film did not go entirely smoothly. The novel had its antagonists, according to whom it lacked proper respect for professional officers, and its rough humour dragged patriotic values into the ground. The Finnish army, for instance, refused to put its equipment and personnel at the film team's disposal. Another film, a military farce called *The Major off the Highway* (*Majuri maantieltä*) had upset the leaders of the army by its obvious lack of respect for military life. For scenes requiring large crowds, the company was forced to hire students from the University of Helsinki; weapons as well as other war material were borrowed from the Frontier Patrol. It has also been said that T. J. Särkkä would never have dared to invest in this film had there not been the very steady income from the Pekka and Pätkä (Pete and Runt) films.

The Finnish variant of the *Fyrtornet* and *Bivognen* was based on a popular cartoon, published in two magazines *Elanto* and *Kuluttajain lehti*, designed by Ola Fogelberg. Altogether, thirteen films were produced during the years 1953 to 1960. In most of the films the director was Armand Lohikoski together with a well-known writer of easy pieces, Reino Helismaa. A characteristic feature of these swiftly produced and improvised films is a carelessly trusting note in the film script: 'Shoots 15–35: funny mishaps – the director will know.' The content of these films was built upon situation comedies that demanded much from the actors' ability to improvise. The main character of *Pekka Puupää* was played by Esa Pakarinen, already well known from the ballad films. Together with Masa Niemi they formed an unforgettable couple. The films were pronounced low budget productions; for example, *Pete and Runt in Suez* (*Pekka ja Pätkä Suez'illa*), set in the Sahara, was filmed at a sand-pit near Helsinki.

In the series featuring Pekka Puupää it is possible to see a predecessor of the extremely popular series of films with oddly individualistic figures that during the 1960s and 1970s were embodied by the comedian Pertti 'Spede' Pasanen, and in the 1980s were condensed into the anarchistic character of Uuno Turhapuro (Numbscull Emptybrook) played by Vesa-Matti Loiri. The latter character appealed to an adult audience, whereas Pekka Puupää's films addressed children.

The children's film was a comparatively unknown genre during the earlier decades. One of the tasks of the censorship authorities was to decide which films were suitable for younger audiences. The film scholar Jukka Sihvonen maintains that the few films made before the 1950s and characterized as children's films in fact seem to have been targeted at adult audiences. This is why the early children's films in Finland should rather be defined on account of their main characters than by a specific film's possible target group. On the other hand, one of the very first feature films ever in the country, *Olli's Apprenticeship* (*Ollin oppivuodet*) was based on a novel written by Anni Swan, an author of popular adolescent and children's books.

Long after *Ollin oppivuodet*, the majority of children's films had their origins in the stories of Anni Swan's imaginary world where the main theme, according to Sihvonen, seems to have been different variations of loss: someone has disappeared – a father, a mother, an inheritance, a home – that the child must somehow win back. The portraits of children that these films promote are idealistic and didactic, and replete with qualities such as honesty and obedience. After the war, more emphasis was placed on openness, cheerfulness and an ability to sing as being ideal characteristics for children.

It is interesting to note that the hero in the earliest films is always a boy (for example, *Tottisalmen Perillinen, Pikku Matti maailmalla, Onnen-Pekka*). In the 1950s however, some films featured a girl as the heroine instead. In the post-war stories the child finds herself in a lost or split world trying to find a new life with new parents and/or in new surroundings. These films even contain contradictory features, as Jukka Sihvonen shows, and the child may feel afraid or anxious. Several films of this kind were made during the 'shelf film' period and were the most successful, such as *Tirlittan* (Kurkvaara, 1958). The question remains unanswered whether the films with young heroines would ever have been made had there not been a cash surplus and a reason to invest as much as possible as soon as possible.

According to Sihvonen, *Little Iris Klewe* (*Pikku Suorasuu*) (Laine, 1962) ends the period of the 'older' Finnish children's films, focusing on edifying stories about a young country child who finds his or her way from the countryside to the city. The 'younger' children's cinema which emerged in the mid-1960s was, in quite a different manner, targeted at young audiences and their needs for fantasy. A predecessor of such films was *Sleeping Beauty* (*Prinsessa Ruusunen*) (Laine, 1949), an expensive and excessive prop fantasy which builds upon the beloved Finnish storyteller Zacharias Topelius's modification of the Grimm Brothers' well-known fairy-tale. *Prinsessa Ruusunen* was the first film for twenty years to be free from taxes because of its 'edifying message'. Worth mentioning in this context also is the film adaptation of a ballet based on the author Yrjö Kokko's fairy tale *Pessi and Illusia* (*Pessi ja Illusia*), a love story between the troll and pessimist Pessi and the fairy illusionist Illusia, directed by Jack Witikka in 1954.

The new teen culture found its way to Finland too, and the film industry did its best to exploit this phenomenon, perhaps because of what was beginning to look like another crisis in the industry. Along with increasing competition from other entertainment forms, the cinemas began to lose audiences and companies looked for new subjects to exploit in order for domestic film to survive. Thus, for instance, the popular ballad films were replaced by musicals (but which had no coherent plot).

The standard model of a ballad film retold and illustrated the contents of the song itself. The singing often arose spontaneously from a certain (emotional) situation in the plot whereas the hit cavalcades focused on the music and took place in a studio or on a stage. The narrative consequently concentrated on the professional lives of the artists in films such as *A Big Hit Parade* (*Suuri sävelparaati*) (Witikka, 1959) which dealt with rehearsals for an important charity concert. The quite rudimentary plot of these films focused, then, on conflicts between the different divisions within the music business, for example, *Hit Parade* (*Iskelmäketju*) (Häyrinen, 1959).

Jack Witikka directed another film, *The Virtanens and Lahtinens* (*Virtaset ja Lahtiset*) (1959), a comedy which focuses on a materialistic competition between two families in a modern suburban neighbourhood. The film was based on a popular play, written by Leena Härmä. The film critics reacted unanimously against *Virtaset ja Lahtiset* and its gang of teenagers. The 'liberated' attitudes and lack of table manners of the youngsters were a source of annoyance for many of them. However, in their indignation most of the critics seem to have missed the real idea of the play which was to criticize the modern and superficial way of life.

TOWARDS A MODERN WELFARE STATE

In 1959 the country was hit by a general strike and as a consequence, people had little spare money for entertainment. The film they eventually saw was *Tuntematon sotilas*, and there was neither money nor sufficient audiences to consume the excessive productions that were initiated at the beginning of the decade. The large amount of 'shelf films' contributed to the increasing problems in the industry, as did the new tax legislation, the advent of television and escalating prices. The strike, which lasted for nineteen days and involved 430,000 people, led the country into a severe depression, and the possible benefits that some might have won by it disappeared rapidly in the general inflation.

The year of 1955 had brought with it a change in Finland's position in the eyes of the surrounding world, in that it was accepted as a member of the Nordic Council and United Nations, whereupon it at first adopted a cautiously observant and neutral political line. The Soviet occupation of the Porkkala peninsula ended, which made the neutrality of the country even more plausible. Urho Kekkonen was elected President for the first time in 1956, a position that he was to keep for twenty-five years. The Soviet Communist Party confirmed a resolution which underlined the politically neutral position of Finland and the country began to direct its economic interests towards the Western world. A trade agreement between EFTA and Finland was made in 1961 and fourteen years later Finland signed the EEC's treaty for free trade.

The difficulties in the mid-1950s had brought with them a significant emigration to Sweden, where there was a shortage of industrial labour and the standard of living was higher. During the 1960s the standard of living grew even in Finland, thanks to the improved trade channels to the West. The transition to the 'information society' was laid during this period with the expansion of the education system. Increasing numbers of young people entered higher education and the annual figure of student exams leading to university studies, which had been 4,100 in 1950, had quadrupled twenty years later. In 1987 the figure had reached 31,000 students, 60 per cent of whom were women. This state of affairs was most certainly due to the 1970 school reform, when the standard school system was introduced. Towards the end of the 1980s the country's seventeen colleges and universities were educating four times as many students as during the 1960s. Young people became a visible and important group in society in other respects, too: in the 1970 election the people's representation was rejuvenated significantly in that for the first time it was possible for an 18-year-old to vote in parliamentary elections.

Television was introduced in 1955 and had become nationwide nine years later. The medium was state-owned through the Finnish Broadcasting Company and financed by the licence fees paid by private households. The 1966 general election is considered to be the first in which television played a significant role, since the political parties were given the opportunity to broadcast their message directly to the electors. It also caused major changes in the power relationships between the political parties: the Social Democrats, who had been a rather insignificant party in the shadow of the large communist party (the People's Democratic Party of Finland (SKDL) became more prominent. A people's democratic coalition government was constituted for the first time; the leftists had been in opposition for the last eighteen years. Thanks to these shifts in the power balance and increased standard of living, several important social reforms were realized during the next two years, among them one concerning the school system and another dealing with universal health insurance. A devaluation of more than 30 per cent made the country a stronger competitor on the foreign market and a stabilization programme was initiated between the parties on the labour market. Unfortunately, the devaluation contributed to problems in the film industry.

From the time that Finland developed the same kind of welfare state as neighbouring Sweden, the country's film industry was in trouble. Feature film production had dramatically decreased by the beginning of the 1960s: a total of twenty-nine feature films was made in 1955, and only five years later the amount had decreased by half. Even though production statistics improved somewhat during the following two years, the fact remained that the year 1963 saw but eleven domestic film premières, the closest equivalent to which could only be found in the 1930s.

Several reasons contributed to this decline, as it did in every other country during this period, such as competition from other entertainment forms, changing leisure habits and, of course, television. It was significant for such circumstances of structural change that large companies perhaps suffered most. Suomen Filmiteollisuus (SF), the largest and most productive company for many decades, filed for bankruptcy as a result of a rapidly accelerating process of decline. Interestingly enough, when the company ceased film production in 1963, it created a vacuum that was filled quite rapidly by a small number of new companies, but these did not succeed in producing more than one or two films each. One of the most productive among the new companies was FJ-Filmi, which later merged with Jörn Donner's company Donner Productions.

In spite of the troubles, three new directors made their debut in 1961 and a further six had their premières only a year later. Among these, several would prove to be important names in what might be called the new wave of Finnish film: for example, Risto Jarva, Jaakko Pakkasvirta and Mikko Niskanen. Two of the new directors were women: Ritva Arvelo and Veronica Leo-Hongell.

Another factor that seemed to contribute to the production crisis of the early 1960s was a strike initiated by the Actors' Union. Even if the strike was directed against the film industry, it did not halt film production because the companies hired freelance and amateur actors for their productions instead. The strike lasted for two-and-a-half years and the question as to whether it benefited anybody still remains unanswered. Yet, in terms of a generation shift among the actors in Finnish cinema this strike functions as a sort of a landmark.

During the 1950s it was still possible for the first lady of Finnish cinema, Ansa Ikonen, to play the role of a young girl (for example, *The Girl from the Moon Bridge* (*Tyttö Kuunsillalta*)) without upsetting the audiences' eventual demands for realism. In the 1960s both Ansa Ikonen and many of her female colleagues were inevitably assigned to the roles of grandmothers in family series on television, so in those cases they did continue their careers. The male actors had, as we know, fewer problems in this respect, and an actor such as Tauno Palo was able to play the star part of the lover in spite of his age for a few more years. This was most certainly not the case for many of the leading actresses. Several of them, for example, Helena Kara and Regina Linnanheimo, had withdrawn from the silver screen during the 1950s. Even if this was not always apparent, one of the main reasons was the insensitive and at times cruelly sexist reviews written by the film critics, who focused on the female artists' changing looks instead of evaluating their professional skills.

The new generation of actors in the 1960s lacked the glamour and glory created by the star industry; the faces which came to represent the film acting of the period belonged in the first place to the young drama students such as Kirsti Wallasvaara, Kristiina Halkola and Eero Melasniemi. Engagement in political and societal questions by the young actors was new too, and it is possible that this generation of actors became less known for their professional work than for participation in political debate.

Television was of course not popular among the professional film workers, since it was understood to be one of the factors contributing to the decline of the film industry and was regarded as a downgraded version of the cinema. Kari Uusitalo, in his book *Suomen Hollywood on kuollut*, compiled statistics that show an increase in the amount of television licences from zero to nearly half a million in six years, while the number of cinemas nationwide decreased from 612 to 529, or almost 10 per cent during the same period. This tendency accelerated, and in 1969 the number of cinemas had decreased to 341, and the audiences had reduced to 60 per cent between the years 1955 and 1963.

The death of the cinemas was not only caused by competition from alternative entertainment forms, but also by the obvious fact that cinema did not have the same appeal to the audiences as before. During the 1930s and 1940s and, to a lesser degree, the 1950s, there had been an apparent contradiction between the preferences of the actual audiences and the taste of the professional critics. At the beginning of the 1960s the situation was that the critics, in their appreciation of the artistic values of European cinema, castigated the Finnish film industry for its lack of spirituality and artistic stature, and the audiences started to abandon their former favourites. A possible reason for this might be changes in the structure of the population. The modernization of agricultural production and its consequences – the increasing urbanization – changed the life patterns and values of the people. The domestic film had always had its largest support group in the countryside, the very group which was constantly diminishing. When the people living in the towns were offered a possibility to choose between a Finnish film and a foreign (i.e. American) film, the former would lose. Audience displeasure was initially directed towards the more recent films because, when SF sold the rights of all its films to Finnish television for a bargain price, it showed that the spectator rates for the older feature films on television remained surprisingly high, even up to the present day.

The importation of foreign films continued to be a rather lucrative business since these films were approximately three times more popular in the towns than in the countryside. In the mid-1960s the percentage share of domestic films shown in relation to all films had decreased to 3 per cent. American film occupied 45 per cent of the market, French film 13 per cent, and number three was British film at almost 10 per cent. It is important to note that the most popular film in the mid-1950s was the Danish soft porn movie *The Goat in Paradise* (*Bocken i Paradiset*), whereas the second and third positions were occupied by films such as *Zorba*, *My Fair Lady* and *The Sound of Music*. (It is also important to note that even if the share of domestic film was rather small in relation to the total amount shown, it was still seen by more spectators than one might suppose from the size of this share.)

The Finnish film that was seen by the largest number of film-goers during this period was Edvin Laine's *Here Beneath the North Star* (*Täällä Pohjantähden alla*) (1968), based on a rural trilogy written by Väinö Linna. Number two was *Under Your Skin* (*Käpy selän alla*), and its sequel *Akseli and Elina* (*Akseli ja Elina*) (Laine, 1970). It would appear that by this time the Finnish spectacle genre with its literary background had died out. Not many films demanding large crowd scenes and monumental direction were made after this; Pekka Lehtos and Pirjo Honkasalo's *Flame Top* (*Tulipää*) (1980) and Pekka Parikka's *The Winter War* (*Talvisota*) (1989) as well as Rauni Mollberg's remake of *Tuntematon sotilas* (1985) could be included in this genre.

REALISM–MODERNISM

The film industry attempted new themes for films during the production boom of the early 1950s. At the beginning of the 1960s there were a few films that were inspired by Italian neorealism and the French new wave, but it was not until the film *Käpy selän alla* was made that the director Mikko Niskanen and the script writer Marjaana Mikkola seemed to find a cinematic story form that corresponded to the sentiments of the period and paid dividends not only in the form of positive reviews but also in economic terms. During this period, when almost every domestic film turned out to be an economic failure, the audiences for *Käpy selän alla* were quite large, at around 600,000.

Mikko Niskanen made his debut as a film director in 1962 (the same year as Risto Jarva) with *The Boys* (*Pojat*), a film that received much attention in its time. Niskanen, himself an actor, had used young amateur actors in this film and even for *Käpy selän alla* he engaged unknown actors whom he discovered at the Theatre College in Helsinki. Script writer Marjaana Mikkola initiated her career as author of the film script and reportage prose typical of the period, expressing the views of the dominant leftist radical intellectuals.

Not surprisingly, the story of *Käpy selän alla* takes place over a few days, and is set against a background of white birch trees, a glittering lake and early summer greenery. The film has a rhapsodic character and describes the relationships between four young adults: Santtu, Timppa, Leena and Riitta, who erect their tent in a grove. The agile camera work still captures, after thirty years, the fluidity of the relationships and the private feelings of the characters in a spontaneous way.

The summer beauty of nature corresponds gracefully with the Scandinavian fantasy world that is always associated with freedom, youth and sentimentality. But *Käpy selän alla* also breaks the illusion of reality of the narrative cinema on several levels, and the focus of the camera goes beyond the confines of the narrative, and draws in the audience. When Riitta suddenly bursts into song, the notes, composed by Kaj Chydenius, are new, naked and raw, and the lyrics are directed as a protest towards contemporary society. The acting style is based on improvisations reflecting the arbitrary character of life, a randomness that is possible to distinguish at other levels of the story as well.

Käpy selän alla was awarded six Jussi statues. The Jussi Awards, the Finnish equivalent of the Academy Awards in the USA, had been given for acting, directing and other achievements in film production since the mid-1940s. A few Finnish films such as *The White Reindeer* (*Valkoinen peura*) (Blomberg, 1952) and *Stolen Death* (*Varastettu kuolema*) (Tapiovaara, 1938) had attracted some attention at the international film festivals, and it was perhaps on behalf of these successes that the importance of the domestic film as an international PR item was eventually recognized in Finland. National cinema as a value on its own thus became part of a more general ideological project, namely that of establishing Finland, particularly its culture and politics, as an independent nation in the international consciousness after the Second World War.

The idea of a national cinema, as discussed above, had been important from the very inception of the country's film industry, due to the initiative of individual patriots. During the 1960s it was instead formulated as one of those societal projects for which the government was expected to share responsibility. The existing public debate initiated a quest for organized state support of the film industry. It was thanks to the resolute efforts of a small number of devoted individuals that these ideas were finally realized.

The first step in the direction of state subsidies for domestic film was taken in the spring of 1961 when Parliament decided upon an annual grant for the State Film Prize. The stipulated amount of 15 million marks was modest to begin with, but according to Kari Uusitalo this initiative encouraged several interesting new productions in autumn 1961, such as Mauno Kurkvaara's *Darling . . . (Rakas . . .)*, and Ritva Arvelo's *The Golden Calf (Kultainen vasikka)*, based on Maria Jotuni's strong and excellent production. Ritva Arvelo, an actress and script writer early in her career, was now to be one of the first female film directors in the country. *Kultainen vasikka* was unfortunately her only feature-length film, as she was to continue her work within Finnish television.

At the end of the 1960s another support measure was taken; a grant for individual film workers who made short films and who were under the age of 30. After 1970 yet another kind of grant system replaced this support for young artists. During the five years of this grant's existence it was assigned to thirty individuals, five of whom were women. According to Kari Uusitalo this encouragement proved to be valuable for the new generation since many of the grantees actually continued as active film artists into the 1980s.

The older generation of film workers seem to have considered themselves as masters of a craft, keeping themselves within the industry, basically directing their films according to the standard rules of the mainstream narrative film production. In opposition to them the younger generation, especially directors, participated actively in the public debate concerning the film politics of the day. The older generation did not have any obvious reason to do this since many of them were employed on a long-term basis by the production companies, and moreover were often involved in their leadership. In spite of the endless complaints and talks about a crisis within the industry, the economic prerequisites always seemed good enough to ensure the independent survival of production companies during the earlier days. The state was perceived as an antagonist to the industry due to its constant regulation of box-office prices, control from the censorship authorities and, last but not least, taxes at several stages.

The new attitudes of the 1960s saw it as self-evident that the state would support film production in a similar manner to its support of other art forms. In addition to increasing cultural appreciation, film was more and more often associated with the traditional art forms. Consequently, it was considered important that the state would protect the eventual artistic development of domestic cinema against the increasingly commercialized materialistic models. The film workers, who now wished to identifiy themselves as artists (among other things due to the changing educational climate), tended to consider the production companies as their antagonists. Many film workers felt that the producers, in order to protect their commercial interests, tended to confine all artistic ambitions that the aspiring directors might be capable of. Under such circumstances it was natural to look for support from the state, which was now perceived as a 'neutral' quarter. Thus the scope and circumstances around the film industry were, in a rather short period of time, transformed from a private economic enterprise and an entertainment industry into a state concern over fine arts and highbrow culture.

THE ESTABLISHMENT OF NATIONAL FILM POLITICS

In the summer of 1964 a new bill concerning film tax was passed in Parliament, a bill which was historic in that it made domestic and imported films equal: the domestic films had earlier been favoured either by freedom from taxes or by a lower tax percentage. The law ruled that all films shown in public would have an entertainment tax ranging from zero to 30 per cent depending on the quality of the film in question. Another important change in the law was that small cinemas were to escape taxes altogether; the state thus wished to prevent or at least slow down the accelerating death of cinemas which had become prevalent, especially in the countryside. The new bill did not favour short films, which now lost their ability to qualify for lower taxes. This in turn suffocated the entire production of short film in Finland.

The new bill contained another item that underlined the changing attitudes of the state towards the film industry: it was ruled that the producers would be offered the possibility to apply for a reimbursement of the tax money. The censorship authorities were once again appointed as judges with the task of deciding whether the films in circulation corresponded to the artistic, technical and moral criteria required for tax deduction or exemption.

The Danish Film Institute was established in 1964, inspiring a public discussion concerning the future of domestic film, a discussion that was further influenced by the ongoing debate in Sweden (the founding of Svenska Filminstitutet took place in 1963). Several propositions were made in the Finnish Parliament which had set up the State Culture Committee to examine the problems concerning future film production in the country. Three years later the committee published its report which resulted in the proposal concerning the promotion of art. The proposal suggested that the State Art Board, the organ for issues concerning art and artists, would be replaced by seven councils, of which one would be the Camera Art Council. The task of this state body would be to support the Ministry of Education in issues that dealt with photo, film and television culture.

The newly founded Camera Art Council presented a general plan in 1967 which recommended the establishment of a film foundation that would have an annual budget of around 5 million marks. The following year another council was appointed according to the proposition of 1965.

The team included the elderly Eric Blomberg and Jerker A. Eriksson, and its composition was widely discussed and disputed. Many film workers considered that those appointed to the council had no knowledge whatsoever about the current situation of Finnish film production. Yet the protests had no effect and the appointed members remained in their posts.

During the 1960s several different kinds of councils were established; in 1968 still another was appointed to scrutinize the 1964 film tax bill. The following year it published a report to recommend the establishment of the Finnish Film Foundation. According to the proposition 4 per cent of income from the box-office should be directed to the activities of the foundation. The state would consequently relinquish the film tax income for the benefit of the Film Foundation. The agreement to seal the establishment of the Foundation was made between the state and representatives of the film industry in 1969, the board was appointed and the activities were set in train three months later.

At this point it was evident that a state body for film production was necessary in order for domestic cinema to survive. The competing entertainment forms, increasing costs and a crisis in artistic production all troubled the film industry more than ever. In 1967 only three feature films were produced and, even after this low number, annual production seldom exceeded a dozen. The worst rates ever were supposedly reached in 1974 when only two films had their premières.

The newly founded Film Foundation was immediately blamed for this recession. Among its many critics was the well-known film reviewer Sakari Toiviainen, who directed harsh words against the Foundation in his book *Uusi suomalainen elokuva* published in 1975. According to Toiviainen, the leadership of the foundation comprised representatives of companies which received their main income from the distribution of foreign films, a fact that made them more or less indifferent to the survival of domestic film production. He maintained that the Foundation was paralysed, looking for compromises and lacked ambition for any artistic production. In retrospect it seems rather that the initial passivity of the Foundation was due to certain inflexible characteristics of many newly established organizations.

Another important step in further engaging the state to institutionalize film production had taken place twenty years earlier, even before the discussions concerning the Film Foundation. This was when the initiative for a national film archive was taken. The proposal came from a private source. At the beginning of the 1950s two film clubs had been founded in Helsinki: the Academic Film Club (Akateeminen filmikerho) and Studio. A group of future decision makers was recruited from among the members of the former club who, with barely any funds, laid the foundations for the Finnish Film Archive in 1957. The previous year a certain Jörn Donner, a future author, film director and executive director of the Swedish Film Institute, had participated in the annual meeting of the international organization of film archives (FIAF), which accepted the Finnish Film Archive as a member in 1958.

The idea of a film archive itself was nothing new: during the 1920s a handful of individuals had lobbied for one, and from the Second World War, the film archive for national defence was in very good shape. Plans to file all material dealing with Finland's participation in the Second World War led to the filing of 35,000 metres of film stock, especially from the Continuation War. This archive was further supplemented by material from the Archives of Ethnographic Film that had been collected during the 1930s.

During the first days of its existence the Finnish Film Archive was managed as a society where interested volunteers worked during the evenings without any kind of compensation until the year 1962, the first year the governement granted state support on behalf of a proposal from the Communist Party. The grant sufficed for proper machinery and some-what better facilities. After five years of activity a salaried part-time worker was employed to run the archive. Another important measure was taken in 1972 when the Film Political Committee, led by the film director Risto Jarva, supported a proposal concerning the rescue of the early domestic film; the nitrate-based film was decomposing in Finnish archives as it had been all over the world. Initially, the rescue work was begun in the autumn of 1972 as a ten-year project separate from the other archive activities. A few years later restoration work was finally established among the regular activities of the archive. To date, 90 per cent of existing old film stock has been rescued, including old colour film stock from the 1950s and 1960s.

In the spring of 1979 the decision was made to nationalize the Film Archive, thus putting an end to its insecure existence. The archive came under the jurisdiction of the Ministry of Education, and is now governed by a board consisting of representatives from museum archives and the film industry. Today there exist three film archives in the country, those belonging to the National Defence, the Finnish Film Archive and commercial television. The obligation to archive domestic moving images aimed at public showing (video and film but not television) as ruled by law did not take effect until 1984.

The ambition of the Film Archive was initially to encourage the film distributors to dispose of those foreign films whose showing rights had expired. Those foreign films with Finnish subtitles held barely any value for their originators, who consequently seldom wished them to be returned. Instead, it was customary for these copies to be chopped up with an axe in the presence of *Notarius Publicus*. Fortunately this barbaric activity has now almost entirely ceased and the archive, thanks to an agreement with the distributors, has access to 95 per cent of all foreign films shown in the country. Today the Archive deposits approximately

1100 foreign titles and all preserved feature films produced in Finland. When the archive obtained a cinema of its own, (the Orion in Helsinki) at the beginning of the 1980s, regular showings were arranged, an activity that has extended to other college and university towns. The Film Archive moved into new and modern facilities in 1986 and within two years it had also obtained suitable storage facilities for both acetate and nitrate film.

CHANGING VALUES

Over a short period of time the responsibility for film production had become a cultural political question that concerned everyone. At the same time it was possible to note politicization of the production side, especially among the younger directors who eagerly gave expression to their personal political opinions through their films. The political climate in society was dominated by an interest in the working class, its habits and culture. In addition, a revision of recent history also occurred. The film-makers as well as other artists were now looking for subjects that dealt with the period immediately before and after the Civil War, long called the War of Independence. Now the war was called the Class War and was seen from the side of the losers, the Communist revolutionaries.

A series of films that probably had their beginning in the urbanization of the 1950s and the adaptations of contemporary 'problem' stories, such as *The Moon Is Dangerous* (*Kuu on vaarallinen*) (Särkkä, 1962), was succeeded by films directed by Mikko Niskanen, Maunu Kurkvaara and especially Risto Jarva. Jarva had already become established as a film director when his film *A Worker's Diary* (*Työmiehen päiväkirja*) (1967) contributed to a new type of film labelled by the critics 'Participating Cinema'. Characteristic of the aesthetics of films from that period is clean surfaces and bare interiors *à la* Antonioni in which the characters speak in monotonous tones without addressing each other. Their explicit purpose, with central themes such as the arbitrariness of life and the rootlessness of people, was to describe the isolation of modern man in a hostile, industrialized setting.

One of the most important words of the debate was 'alienation', and in their best moments films such as *A Worker's Diary* (*Työmiehen päiväkirja*) and *The Asphalt Lambs* (*Asfalttilampaat*) (Niskanen, 1968) not only succeeded in mediating a disconsolate feeling of the 'outsiderness' of the people, but also their awkward attempts to make contact with each other. An interesting film from this period is *Rally* (*Bensaa suonissa*) (1970), a story which rotates around a core of a 'ménage à trois' comprising a well-established but ageing car rally driver, his wife, and a young mechanic with a claim to the championship as well as to the wife. This emotional theme is expressed through action and dialogue, while the visual images express a critical attitude towards the commercialized and mechanized lifestyle in itself and motor sports in particular. The narrative story-line is accompanied by a neutral voice-over and documentary shots of commercial advertisements and of materialism as well as motor sports. As a result, the representatives of sports organizations gave indignant interviews in the newspapers, accusing the film of promoting an inaccurate image of motor sports and the people involved in it.

From the realistic and low-key 'commonplace' style of the 1960s there developed a sort of naturalist aesthetics, a style with outlandish elements that has become characteristic of recent Finnish national cinema. One of the first naturalist films was Rauni Mollberg's *The Earth is a Sinful Song* (*Maa on syntinen laulu*) (1973), one of the greatest international successes in the entire history of Finnish cinema. The film is based on Timo K. Mukka's (1944–73) novel of the same name. The action takes place among the impoverished inhabitants of northern Finland where religious pathos together with sexual undercurrents and the rough conditions convey the lives of its people. *Maa on syntinen laulu* contrasts the barrenly beautiful landscapes and the primitive circumstances with luscious colours that show the blood pulsating, steaming and dark red, the frost glittering white on the wilted grass, and the arctic darkness spreading itself protectively around the mating animals and people.

One of the most worthy examples of the aesthetic naturalism of the period is Pirjo Honkasalo and Pekka Lehtos's *Flame Top* (*Tulipää*) (1980). The film tells the story of the proletarian author Algot Untola (1868–1918). Untola is one of the most fascinating characters of Finnish literary history; for example, he used several pseudonyms, and when he changed his name he also altered the literary style he was using. His most famous pseudonym is, interestingly, the female name Maiju Lassila, used during a period when women authors preferred to use male pseudonyms. Untola/Lassila described the life of the poor people in the countryside in comedies that are staged even today. In his other guises he was either a romantic and idealist poet or in his newspaper articles a socialist, and a devoted critic of the prevailing class society. He was, as a consequence, executed during the last days of the Civil War.

Tulipää opens with a dawn scene, followed by the camera sweeping across a number of objects in a shabby room, among them part of a letter announcing a memorial ceremony for the author, who died two decades earlier. The camera glides past the forehead of a sleeping woman in order to focus on a glass of wine on the table. The lamp is lit and the red wine glitters, and next to it is a decanter and a handful of dried roses, decoratively arranged; the image reminds the spectator of an oil painting at the turn of the century. In the light of the lamp it is also possible to distinguish a dental plate in the wineglass, and when a hand stretches towards it accompanied by the sound of heavy breathing, it is hard for the spectator to avoid feelings of disgust. The sound of quick swallowing moves over to images of inhaling narcotics, and when the glittering glass is placed back to the table, only the brownish plate is left in it; a perfect metaphor for this story about beauty, high ideals, and in the background the constant presence of death and mortality.

Films such as *Tulipää* filled aesthetic demand and the expectations of social engagement of the period and regularly won state awards and applause from the critics. Besides these artistically ambitious films dwelled another kind of film: from the mid-1960s there had been a steady stream of comedies, basically produced by the comedian Pertti 'Spede' Pasanen. Pasanen's production company, Filmituotanto Spede Pasanen, was established in 1967 and the producer himself played the leading character in his films full of gags, crazy humour and situation comedies. Popular as his films are in Finland, it is impossible to persuade foreign audiences to understand them. The loose plot often links up with current politics or popular faces, which presupposes knowledge of the real actors in Finland's cultural-political arena. The critics were frequently lost for words to express their contempt for these films, although audience interest was great, as was the income.

During the 1970s, Spede Pasanen introduced a character who in his studied vulgarity and bad taste was to transgress all limits: *Numbscull Emptybrook* (*Uuno Turhapuro*), starring Vesa-Matti Loiri. Uuno is a beer-drinking, burping and farting character who lies on a couch yelling and fighting with his wife (who supports him financially) in such an outrageous manner that one suspects, in order to understand the phenomenon at all, it to have some kind of cathartic effect on the Finnish audiences. The first *Turhapuro* film was made in 1973 at almost no cost, with the equipment and facilities borrowed from Finnish Television. It became an immediate success with an audience of more than 500,000.

The most popular *Turhapuro* film hitherto has been *Uuno Goes Military* (*Uuno Turhapuro armeijan leivissä*) (1984). The film exploited an old popular genre, the military farce, and was seen by an audience of 750,000. The success of Uuno has been enigmatic for many. Perhaps it dwells somewhere in the ambiguity of the character itself, its exaggerations and grotesque behaviour that on the whole has become one of the most distinctive features of contemporary Finnish cinema. In an interesting analysis, a group of Finnish film scholars considered the Uuno films as part of the national counter-culture. Since the films neither adjusted to the demands of the young leftist radical establishment nor to the traditionally conservative circles' needs for national themes to support traditional values, they speak to the different subcultures outside the established opinion-building groups. Whatever the reason, the fact remains that when looking back at the period between 1984 and 1992, eight out of the ten most popular films are *Turhapuro* movies. The two others – the Mollberg remake of *Tuntematon sotilas* and Pekka Parikka's *Talvisota* – deal with the traumatic experiences of the war.

The video explosion took place during the 1980s, and in 1980 there were 8,500 video machines in the country; eight years later the amount had increased by nearly a hundred times. That year the Finnish people made an average of 1.35 visits to a cinema. American film ruled alone with 58.5 per cent of the market. The statistics kept by the Finnish Film Foundation show that during the first sixteen years of its existence (1972 to 1988) the most popular film was Milos Forman's *One Flew over the Cuckoo's Nest* (1976), number two was *Papillon* (1974), and after that the above-mentioned *Uuno Goes Military*. Other popular foreign films during the ten-year period from 1983–92 were *Amadeus* (Forman, 1984), *ET* (Spielberg, 1982) and *Pretty Woman* (Marshall, 1990).

As time passed, another sign of, if not lightening then decreasing darkness, was that the extensive closing of cinemas ceased and, instead, a small number of new cinemas were registered. In 1987, the amount of domestic film premières was fifteen, which was 14.8 per cent of the total amount, and the audience rates increased for the first time during that decade. It was as if the Film Foundation had found itself and its role in the production cycle. The Foundation also extended its activities by initiating different projects apart from granting production subsidies. In 1986 a two-year cinema project was initiated, the purpose being to stimulate the screening activities in small locations around the countryside. The project offered education in cinema techniques as well as in public relations. At the end of this project period the Foundation also decided on showing subsidies for children's films and what was perceived as 'quality-film'. The cinema project was succeeded by a documentary film project, the aim of which was to stimulate the production of this genre. The project was quite successful and resulted in eighteen new documentaries and was therefore extended for another year.

By 1989 twenty years had passed from the inception of the Finnish Film Foundation. Its activities now turned over more than 27 million marks, the major part of which consisted of state support, and the Foundation had twenty employees. Of the ten feature films that had their premières in the same year, all had received some kind of support from the Foundation. A new development programme was also presented, the aim of which was to change the decision process that led to the support grants. At the beginning of the enterprise the board of the Foundation was the deciding factor when it came to feature film support. Now it was suggested that the right to make decisions concerning the different support forms would be transferred to the executive director, a newly appointed production board, and one producer, who was to be appointed. The following year this assignment was shared between two producers, one of whom was responsible for feature film production and the other for the production of documentary films. A new form of fixed production support was made permanent, too; if the rest of the financing of a film was guaranteed, the Foundation would secure one-quarter of the net production costs. Apart from this the Foundation distributed support for script writing and pre-production.

In 1988 nine films were produced, eight of which received production support. During recent years all films that have been completed and premièred in a public cinema have been dependent on the Film Foundation in one way or another. Even the *Uuno Turhapuro* film *Double-Uuno* (*Tupla-Uunot*) received support to develop more copies. However, another film produced by the company of Pertti Pasanen (the company had now changed its name to Spede-team), '*Has Anybody Seen Viljo?*' ('*Onks Viljoo näkyny?*') was not considered 'culturally valuable' enough to receive support from the Foundation. Yet two years later even the *Uuno* films were granted regular subsidies together with other films, a fact which shows that either the evaluative tastes or other elements behind the distribution of the production support had changed radically.

A new generation of film directors of the 1980s is best represented by two brothers, Mika and Aki Kaurismäki, who founded the production company Villealfa in 1981, when Mika finished his film education in Munich. The brothers Kaurismäki are the Finnish answer to the American 'movie brats', a generation of film directors who have grown up not only with film matinees but also television, and are thus in possession of a respectable amount of knowledge of film history and cinematic narration as well as a detatched attitude towards the medium and its means for expression. An eloquent example of this attitude is a description of Aki Kaurismäki's film *Ariel* (1988) found in a brochure: 'A film that begins as an unemployment story, turns into a hanging-out movie, has a touch of a love story about ordinary people, becomes a crime and prison film before ending up as an over-romantic melodrama. Contains truth about life in a typical western "Everything-For-Sale" society. Some drama included' (literal translation).

In the 1960s and 1970s the dominating circles in Finland considered the Winter War, and participation in the Second World War on the whole through the Continuation War, to have been unnecessary. The leftist oriented cultural elite had an especially warm relationship with the Soviet Union, and the common understanding for many was that the Finns should have accepted the Soviet demands in the autumn of 1939. Thanks to Glasnost, the real plans Stalin had for Finland were revealed, and it was proved that his aims were not confined to renting a few islands in the Finnish archipelago. When the Soviet Union finally admitted its culpability at the outbreak of war, it was possible to re-evaluate the significance of the Finnish resistance and the sacrifices that were made in 1939 to 1944. The film director Pekka Parikka has paid homage to everyone who experienced the war with his film *Winter War* (*Talvisota*) (1989). The film, where the war scenes are so realistic that the audience experiences a certain amount of revulsion and shock, is based on Antti Tuuri's novel of the same name. The author himself contributed to the script and the dialogue, which is quite obviously from his pen: cunning, well balanced and full of humour. The slow Ostrobothnian dialect is exceptionally natural and contrasts with the 'alienated' literary style of dialogue that has become a convention in Finnish cinema since the 1960s. The camera work in the film often consists of slow, sweeping, sideways movements, as if the spectator is allowed to share the soldier's watchful gaze.

Pekka Parikka's film tells a tale about brothers at war, and is a man's story about men's war; there are only a few female characters, each of them quite marginal. In this film a woman is good only for casting lustful glances after the marching soldiers and to stand naked at a window asking questions about life in the front lines. *Talvisota* is a touching and well-made, realistic film, whose scrupulous realism and quest for generalization leaves it open to criticism, since the female image it portrays is completely false. The seldom admitted fact is that Finnish women, through such mediums as the Women's Voluntary Defence Service, contributed to the war efforts just as much as men. Thus even Parikka's film contributes to an interesting (and unfortunate) syndrome in Finnish war fiction, one that totally ignores this enormous contribution and instead describes a woman's function during war as that of a prostitute. The misogyny so typical of post-war cinema in Finland lies deeply embedded in history: from the beginning the female characters in film fiction were described as strong and independent or at least rebellious. After the war, parallel with the monumental mothers of the fatherland, the matrons *à la* Wuolijoki and witty comedy heroines embodied by Lea Joutseno, develop the image of the female body stigmatized by sin, contaminated by venereal disease and impregnated by alcohol. The clinical attitude of the 'syphilis films' of the late 1940s was continued, for instance, in the 1960s voyeurist camera eye of Jörn Donner's films, where naked and promiscuous young female bodies are put on display for closer scrutiny, preferably in gynae-cological chairs, the film director himself playing the role of the gynaecologist. Nothing much was left to the imagination as regards the female body for the later generations of film directors except perhaps the anorexic murderesses in the brothers Kaurismäki's films such as *The Match Factory Girl* (*Tulitikkutehtaan tyttö*) (1990), or Pekka Lehto's psychotic mothers whose miserable existence forces them to drown their offspring in a well one misty, freezing morning (*The Well* (*Kaivo*) (1992)).

The scary imaginary woman of Finnish fantasy has obviously had its impact on reality, too, since it has been exceptionally difficult for women to make their way as directors and photographers within the film industry in Finland. Apart from the 'heyday' of the 1980s when a handful of women film directors had their debut, not many have been able to make a second film. In the spring of 1995 the first full-length feature film in nine years directed by a woman had its première: Kaisa Rastiomo's *Bittersweet* (*Suolaista ja makeaa*).

One of the most enduring female film directors has been Pirjo Honkasalo, whose artistic integrity and stubborn nature has resulted in interesting and impressive documentaries, such as *Mysterion* (1991), a film that in concrete terms tells of the daily life among the nuns in a Russian Orthodox monastery in Estonia. But at the same time in its palpable everyday description the film transgresses its limits and reaches towards the ineffable: the mystery of a religious experience.

Yet the founding of the production company Villealfa signifies the beginning of a flow of films, not only produced by the Kaurismäki brothers Mika and Aki, but also other young directors: Pauli Pentti, Veikko Aaltonen. and a woman, Marjaana Mykkänen. The films produced by Villealfa are characterized by a sort of 'aesthetics of meagreness' as opposed to the earlier extravagance of the 1970s seen in Mollberg's films, for instance. In these films the audience is confronted with outlandish characters whose feelings are described in all possible means except words; with some exaggeration one might characterize contemporary Finnish film as studies of the folk soul, or Finnishness itself. It is quite often that the contemporary film, including the *Uuno* films, makes an effort to express the essence of these strange people on the outskirts of Europe. When Finnish cinema, less than a hundred years ago, was begun as part of a national project to introduce the country and its people 'to the whole wide world', it seems as if the medium still continues the project in its efforts to dissect this people, the arctic hysteria and the isolation of the inhabitants. Of course, by doing so the films contribute to the building up of a national fantasy and myth of seclusion and loneliness.

Film landscape in recent decades has polarized into two scenes: either the camera eye looks for the solitary northern wilderness and describes it as the goal of the longings of man, or it has registered the concrete parks of the urbanized world. Finnish fiction has always ascribed many positive values to the countryside and nature, but in accordance with the increasing urbanization this frontier land has retreated further and further to the north. Risto Jarva's last film, *The Year of the Hare* (*Jäniksen vuosi*) (1977) may be seen as an archetypical reflection upon the contemporary split in the soul of the Finnish people: the film is about a civil servant who one day observes his narrow existence, leaves his office and, together with a hare that has given the film its name, begins his travels to the north, to freedom and peace.

SELECT BIBLIOGRAPHY

Cowie, Peter, *Finnish Cinema*, Suomen Elokuvasäätiö, Helsinki 1990.

Chapter 4

Iceland

Astrid Söderbergh Widding

The year 1979 marks the start of Icelandic film production in its proper sense, when there was the breakthrough of a new national film, also much discussed internationally, and the onset of a period of intense and still increasing production. This late date, however, also has its prehistory, simultaneous with the film history of the other Nordic countries. But the lack of a national production makes the Icelandic case unique. Its earlier film history is characterized by a number of co-productions, above all with the other Nordic countries. To study this prehistory thus means that the notion of 'Nordic film' is focused on in an interesting way, as before 1979 Icelandic film existed only in the sense of Nordic film.

In 1903 the first documented screening took place in Iceland, during the period when Reykjavik was developing into a kind of capital. The population in the smaller coastal towns was increasing as people moved in from the countryside, and the resulting greater demand for amusement and culture made the modern form of culture represented by film extremely popular. In 1906 Reykjavik Cinema Theatre was inaugurated, and in 1912 a rival cinema opened. Remarkably enough this did not lead to any drop in attendance at the original theatre: thus the number of visitors almost doubled in a town that by this time had only 11,600 inhabitants. Cinema statistics in Iceland have always been and still are topmost among the Nordic countries.

There were, however, experiments in film production, resulting in simple attraction films celebrating the new technique. A production of short documentaries and newsreels based on foreign models was gradually introduced, and these were shown in those cinemas featuring the imported programme. This kind of production has occurred constantly through the decades, apart from the 1930s when it almost completely disappeared due to the economic crisis. In surveys of Icelandic film you will generally find – in addition to the type of films mentioned above – foreign films with a connection to Iceland, such as *The Outlaw and his Wife* (*Berg-Ejvind och hans hustru*) (1918) by Victor Sjöström, based on a play by Jóhann Sigurjónsson, or the Danish films *The Story of the Borg Family*

(*Borgslægtens Historie*) (1920) based on a novel by Gunnar Gunnarsson, and *Hadda Padda* (1923–24) and *Sleeping House* (*Det Sovende Hus*) (1926), both with an Icelandic director (the author Gudmundur Kamban) and produced by the Danish company Nordisk Films. One of the Icelandic film pioneers was Loftur Gudmundsson, with the silent film comedy *The Adventures of Jon and Gvendar* (*Ævintyri Jons og Gvendar*) (1923).

In 1944 Iceland became independent of Denmark, which led to a strong national conscience. In 1949 Loftur Gudmundsson made the first Icelandic sound film, *Between Mountain and Shore* (*Milli fjalls og fjöru*), moreover in colour. In this film Loftur made use of documentary material that he had filmed in the 1920s. This time, however, he made a fiction film: a love story from the nineteenth century, based on reality.

During the 1950s Óskar Gíslason made a number of 16 mm films characterized by national feeling, half documentary, half fictitious. One of them, *A New Role* (*Nytt hlutverk*) (1954), describes an ageing docker's problems in accepting his role as a senior citizen after he has finished work, and at the same time gives a vivid picture of one of Iceland's foremost trades, that of herring fishery.

At this point a few co-productions from the same period should be mentioned (with Sweden, Germany and Denmark respectively). The Swedish film, *Salka Valka* (1954), based on a novel by the Icelandic Nobel prize winner Laxness and partly filmed in Iceland, was filmed by Sven Nykvist. In 1966 a German film was made based on the *Niebelungen* tale, and in 1967 Gabriel Axel's *The Red Mantle* (*Den røde kappe*) appeared, an Icelandic-Danish-Swedish co-production based on an Icelandic saga. The idea of co-productions will later be used as a model. This afforded an opportunity for Icelandic directors to make films in spite of the financial problems due to the country's size.

The first Icelandic television company, RUV, was established in 1966. To begin with, however, this had barely any effect on film production and the situation of the film-makers. Instead of using Icelandic film-makers, RUV imported people from abroad. The emphasis was on technical skill rather than competence. Commercials, however – which were from the beginning part of television programming – offered certain opportunities for practice to the directors. As RUV began to produce its own feature films and also faced competition from two further television companies, the situation gradually changed in favour of the film-makers.

In 1972 the Icelandic cultural fund began to support the country's film production for the first time, which in turn led to the creation of a separate film fund in 1978. Icelandic film-makers had for some time been working hard for the acceptance of film as an art form and accordingly for national support of film on the same terms as other forms of art. The creation of the film fund and the breakthrough of Icelandic film at the end of the 1970s had to do with the fact that a new generation of young film-makers returned home after having been educated at film schools in other countries. Among them, several had chosen to go to film schools in other Nordic countries: for instance, Sweden and Denmark. These young directors now started to make the new Icelandic films.

MODERN ICELANDIC FILM

The creation of the film fund had an immediate impact; modern Icelandic film began with three national productions in 1979: *Land* (*Land og Synir*), *The Chase* (*Veidiferdin*) and *Father's Estate* (*Odal fedranna*). These films had audiences of between 60,000 and 70,000, i.e. 35 per cent of the population: an almost incredibly high figure, which led to the launching of a number of new productions. The interest in national film production, however, soon waned and the least popular of these new productions were seen by only 6,000 to 8,000 people, i.e. 4 per cent of the population. In the other Nordic countries such a result counted at a percentage would be considered good, but in view of the small base of spectators in Iceland it was commercially disastrous.

The fund, however, was made more effective on two occasions: in 1984 by changes in cinema taxes, and in 1986 by additional governmental support for the fund. At the same time Iceland had been highly dependent on foreign film funds. Above all, the Nordic film and television fund had been of crucial importance. In order to minimize the economic risks, Icelandic film has also often been linguistically adapted for distribution abroad, for example, using minimal dialogue or by also recording the dialogue in an English version. The orientation towards the Anglo-Saxon countries was much greater in Iceland than in the other Nordic countries. The attempts at defending oneself particularly against the dominance of American film that was prevalent elsewhere is completely lacking in Icelandic film history. The import of Anglo-Saxon film that had earlier already been dominant, increased dramatically during the Second World War and the Occupation. The American and British military forces also built new cinemas in Reykjavik, which were taken over by Iceland after the war.

In a national production as small as the Icelandic one it is convenient to talk about trends or tendencies rather than genres. A particular tendency, also to be found in the other Nordic countries, is for films to allude to established, mostly American genres. There was often only one film that was presented in an Icelandic context. Thus in 1987 Fridrik Thór Fridriksson made an Icelandic film noir, *White Whales* (*Skytturnar*), which is a hardboiled thriller set in city surroundings. The musical comedy *On Top* (*Med allt á hreinu*), directed by Ágúst Gudmundsson, is another genre film of the same type. A few more comedies have also been produced, but they lack the light comedy character typical of, for example, Sweden.

Plate 4.1 Modern Icelandic film *Land* (*Land og Synir*) (Gudmundsson, 1979)

Plate 4.2 The saga tradition *When the Raven Flies* (*Hrafninn fly´gur*) (Gunnlaugsson, 1984)

The comedy *New life* (*Nýtt líf*) (1983), with a male pair of comedians taking the leading parts, was a runaway success, and two sequels were produced. In addition to these examples of genre film, there are groups of motifs and films rather than genres. This is also the case in the other Nordic countries.

What is most typical of Iceland, at least as seen through foreign eyes, are films inspired by the medieval Icelandic sagas; the filmic character of the laconic utterances in the sagas has often been mentioned. You find direct transformations of sagas into films, for example, Ágúst Gudmundsson's *Viking Outlaw* (*Útlaginn*) (1981), following *Gísle Súrssons saga* – where Gísle becomes an outlaw through a twist of fate. Other films are more loosely connected to the saga tradition, such as Hrafn Gunnlaugsson's two films *When the Raven Flies* (*Hrafninn flýgur*) (1984) and *In the Shadow of the Raven* (*I skugga hrafnsins*) (1988). The filmic language developed by Hrafn is vehement and brutal, with visual violence and a very marked cutting rhythm often reinforced by sound effects. Other national literature has also been used for film, including two Laxness novels: *Atomic Station* (*Atómstödin*) (1984) directed by Thorsteinn Jónsson, and *Under the Glacier* (*Kristnihald undir jökli*) (1989). The former was the most expensive Icelandic film ever made, and despite its success at film festivals it was badly received in Iceland and was an economic fiasco.

The mythical history and the barren Icelandic landscape that is so full of contrasts are two factors which have been used in Icelandic film to make it unique. Of all the Nordic countries, Iceland has perhaps made the most effective use of nature, which has become an emblem of Nordic film in general. Mysticism and symbolism related to nature are also the theme of a remarkably large group of films made in Iceland, among them the experimental and dreamlike *Rainbow's End* (*Á hjara veraldar*) (1983) directed by Kristín Johannesdóttir, and quite obviously inspired by Magritte. Some of her examples are psychological thrillers with supernatural features, such as Egill Edvardsson's *The House* (*Húsid*) (1983) or Thráinn Bertelsons's *Deep Winter* (*Skammdegi*) (1985).

Nature also plays an important part in the thematically most distinctive group of films which describe the process of urbanization in Iceland and the development of the modern world. This process has been achieved much more quickly in Iceland than in any other European country – during the 1930s and 1940s the development was explosive and Iceland made the leap from a social structure that had remained almost the same since the Middle Ages to a modern society. In the process of modernization, one-third of the population moved from the countryside to Reykjavik. The resulting conflicts between town and country, between Iceland and the outside world and between the different generations have been a rich source for film-makers to draw upon. Within this group there are films as different as the quietly epic *Land* and the comedy *Golden*

Sands (*Gullsandur*) (1984) directed by Ágúst Gudmundsson, a film branding the Icelandic gold digger mentality but above all a comedy criticizing NATO's military base in Keflavik.

In Iceland as in Denmark, many high-quality films for children and teenagers have been produced, such as Thráinn Bertelson's *The Twins* (*Jón Oddur og Jón Bjarni*) (1981), or *Dot, Dot, Comma, Dash* (*Punktur, punktur, komma, strik*) (1981). The latter, which was Thórsteinn Jónsson's debut based on a novel by Pétur Gunnarsson, had a quite obvious documentary film style. Thórsteinn has also been working as a documentary film-maker for some years and he was educated in the documentary department at the Film School of Prague.

The stylistic diversity among Icelandic directors is evident – thus it is difficult to identify a generation of directors. This has partly to do with the lack of a national film tradition, but also with the fact that many of the directors have had quite diverse educations in different film schools abroad. As far as a homogeneity in Icelandic film may be distinguished, it is rather to be found on the thematic level. The old and dominating tradition of literary story-telling in Iceland appears through all its stylistic diversities.

SELECT BIBLIOGRAPHY

Cowie, Peter, *Scandinavian Cinema*, London: The Tantivy Press, 1992.
Thorsteinsson, Eiríkur (ed.), *Icelandic Documentaries, Shorts and Animated Films 1966–91*, Reykjavik: The Icelandic Film Fund, 1991.

Chapter 5

Norway

Gunnar Iversen

INTRODUCTION

The year 1920 marks the beginning of professional, continuous film production in Norway, when a 'national breakthrough' took place. Calls for a national cinema had been made against the popular Swedish adaptations of famous Norwegian authors like Henrik Ibsen and Bjørnstjerne Bjørnson – Victor Sjöström's *Terje Vigen* (1916) is the most famous example – and Norwegian film-makers sought a new style and content, and started to explore the sense of national identity, through national romanticism and films set in a rural environment.

These new national romantic films enjoyed great domestic popularity. The popularity of these films is to a certain extent related to the fortunes of the nation, and since that time most Norwegian films have been judged against the international imports, especially the American films that have dominated Norwegian screens. Its small and marginal film culture has always met with public acclaim in Norway, where films reflected an interest in genuinely national topics or used the landscape of Norway as an integral part of the story. Norwegian national cinema has to a large degree been a cinema of opposition.

Norwegian cinema has always been tempted to use the generic modes established by the classical Hollywood cinema, but at the same time always tried to adapt these modes to meet the demand for something genuinely 'Norwegian'. This culture of opposition is also reflected in a singular system of cinemas in Norway; the municipalities have held power under law to licence cinemas, thus effectively regulating the number of cinemas, ownership structure and film content shown in Norway.

This resistance has been triggered by the smallness of Norwegian cinema, and the aggressiveness of foreign imports. The resistance to bigger national cinemas – Sweden in the 1920s or the United States in more recent years – is visible in almost every aspect of Norwegian national cinema, from the country's cinematographic production to screening practices. To understand the development of Norwegian national cinema one must start at the very beginning.

THE PIONEER ERA

The first exhibition of 'moving images' in Scandinavia took place in Norway's capital Kristiania – later renamed Oslo – on 6 April 1896, just a few months after the Lumière brothers' first public projections in Paris. Director Jacobsen at Circus Variété – a music-hall and circus – had seen the German pioneers Max and Emil Skladanowsky present their Bioscop films at the Wintergarten in Berlin in November 1895, and booked the brothers and their films for his music-hall. Between 6 April and 5 May 1896 the Skladanowsky brothers showed their programme of nine films as part of the entertainment at Circus Variété in Kristiania. After Norway the German brothers travelled to Denmark and Sweden.

For the next ten years itinerant cinema exhibitors roamed Norway, setting up their equipment at fairs or music-halls. Most of these early pioneers were foreigners, and so were their films. French and German, and especially Swedish, showmen travelled in Norway presenting their programmes. Film-viewing was in the beginning predominantly an activity for the bourgeoisie. Only the middle classes could afford the ticket prices in this nomadic period, when films were a part of music-hall entertainment. All this changed when cinema became a permanent entertainment attraction in its own right in the larger cities. On 1 November 1904 the first permanent cinema – Kinematograf-Theatret – opened in Kristiania. Before the year ended four more cinemas were opened, and ten years later, in 1915, Kristiania had twenty-one cinemas. A 'Nickelodeon-boom' swept across Norway, and cinema-going became a popular urban form of entertainment that attracted all classes. The largest groups of cinema-goers were women and children.

The most popular genre in these early years was comedy. The French and Italian comedies were particularly popular in Norway, and film comedians like André Deed – his comic persona Cretinetti or Foolshead was called Lehmann in Norway and the rest of Scandinavia – and Max Linder were the most popular 'stars'. During the 1910s the Norwegian audiences slowly but steadily became more and more fascinated by American films. Vitagraph westerns were popular, and Chaplin became the new comic favourite of the cinema-going audiences. Danish films also enjoyed great popularity. The Danish erotic melodramas became infamous in Norway in the early 1910s.

Besides the comedies and erotic melodramas – and later American westerns – actualities were important. The British Boer films in particular played an important role in the early programmes of short films. Domestic actualities enjoyed a special popularity, the first being produced in Bergen in 1897. In around 1900 the production of actualities increased in Norway, and the themes of most of these first actualities were winter sports.

At the turn of the century Norway was still a part of Sweden. In 1814, after centuries of Danish rule, Norway had been handed over from

Denmark to Sweden. Full sovereignty from Sweden was achieved in 1905, and films played an important role in the building of a national identity in that year. Actualities depicting the coronation of the new king, and his journey through Norway, were enormously popular. The coronation became a media event, which sparked renewed interest in the new visual media as well. Many photographers filmed the new king arriving in Trondheim, among them Charles Magnusson, who later became a movie mogul in Sweden.

At this time individuals seized the initiative in Denmark and Sweden, building big production and distribution companies. Ole Olsen's Nordisk in Denmark and Charles Magnusson's Svenska Bio in Sweden had no counterpart in Norway. Hugo Hermansen in Kristiania came closest to becoming a mogul. He owned twenty-six cinemas, produced many actualities and the first Norwegian feature film, but he suffered a stroke in 1909 and disappeared from the business. The other Norwegian film producers stuck to actualities and an occasional feature, and regarded the new visual medium as a pastime pure and simple.

The first Norwegian feature film was the short *Dangers of a Fisherman's Life – An Ocean Drama* (*Fiskerlivets Farer – Et Drama paa havet*), made by Hugo Hermansen sometime between 1906 and 1908. This one-reeler tells the story about a fisherman whose son falls overboard in high seas. The son is pulled on board, but too late for him to be saved. On the shore the mother sees the accident and tears her hair out. A dramatic intertitle ends the film: 'DEATH'. This first Norwegian fiction film has unfortunately been lost, and the written sources regarding the film often contradict themselves, so it is a mystery still waiting to be solved. One thing is clear, though, and that is that the photographer was another Swede: Julius Jaenzon, later to become the master photographer for Victor Sjöström and Mauritz Stiller's famous Swedish films in the late 1910s and early 1920s.

By 1910 film-going had become a major popular entertainment form in Norway, but domestic film production was small, mainly actualities. Between 1906 and 1919, seventeen feature films were made, and reached a limited audience in Norway. These films seem to have taken their strongest inspiration from the Danish erotic or 'social' melodramas, showing either flirtation among the rich, or the temptations and dangers of lower-class city life. These Norwegian films were made by many different directors and production companies. They did not get the best of receptions, and were not widely distributed in Norway.

The most important of these early pioneers was Peter Lykke-Seest. He was a prolific author of popular novels, and began a career as a script writer in Denmark and Sweden in 1912. At Svenska Bio in Sweden he wrote most of the early films of Sjöström and Stiller. He returned to Norway, and established his embryonic studio – Christiania Film

Compagni – in 1916. This was the first film studio in Norway, and Lykke-Seest directed six films between 1917 and 1919. His most popular film was *The Story of a Boy* (*Historien om en gut*, 1919). In this film young Esben is accused of stealing his teacher's watch. Disappointed that nobody believes he is falsely accused, he sells his clothes and books and runs away from home. In several episodes he is shown roaming around the country, until he finds out that the real thief has been found, and he can safely return home. The film ends with his return to his parents, who embrace him warmly. This film was Lykke-Seest's greatest success, both artistically and economically. *The Story of a Boy* was exported to several countries. It found a good reception in Sweden, and recently a copy of the film was discovered in Czechoslovakia.

Lykke-Seest's production company represented a most promising start to extensive and serious feature film production in Norway, but it was discontinued when the efforts to market films in the USA met with failure. Another obstacle to Lykke-Seest's ambitious plan was government legislation. The passing of the Film Theatres' Act in 1913 would change the situation in Norway, regarding exhibition practices as well as the production of films.

Before 1913 local communities were themselves responsible for films showing at their cinemas. The local police authorities controlled the cinemas, from a rudimentary censorship to building and safety regulations. Control measures varied greatly between communities, and many voices were raised against the new and powerful media. The first reaction came from teachers. Letters from teachers were sent to different newspapers, complaining about the cinema's harmful effect on learning and upbringing, and damning it for corrupting the younger generation. These local initiatives by teachers and school authorities were followed by attacks on a nation-wide scale by the Society for the Promotion of Morality (Foreningen til Saedelighetens Fremme), a national body established in 1880.

In 1910 the Kristiania division of the Society passed a resolution, calling for municipal by-laws to limit the number of cinemas and recommending that a municipally appointed committee should oversee programming. Many citizens were concerned about the supposed effects on children. Sweden and Great Britain already had centralized censorship of films, and pillars of society now advocated that the same measure be established in Norway.

The idea that the municipalities should take over cinema operations was symptomatic of the times. An upsurge in all forms of mass enlightenment came in the early years of the century, and the notion of public control over the instruments of persuasion and instruction tied in well with the platforms of the two largest political parties: the growing Social Democratic (Labour) Party and the ruling Left (Liberal) Party. The

Norwegian peculiarity of local licensing – since 1837 Norwegian municipalities had won a fair measure of local self-determination, guaranteed by law – tied in perfectly with the call for control.

In 1913 Parliament passed The Film Theatres' Act, which brought together political expediency and constitutional tradition. The Act stipulated that the municipal councils were to license all public showings of films within the area of their jurisdiction – thus controlling the rapidly growing cinema interest – and established a Central Board of Film Censors in Kristiania, which was to process all films destined for public screening. From 1913, through national legislation and local initiative, film screenings was subject to the controlling will of public powers through municipal ownership of cinemas. This municipal cinema system was – and still is – a Norwegian peculiarity; a unique break with the predominant Western, capitalist paradigm of the cinema. The municipal cinema system may be seen as one of a number of instances in Norwegian society where public involvement and control has supplemented, and supplanted, private initiative. Thus considered, the municipal cinema system may seem to epitomize the pacifying tendencies of the 'welfare society'.

Shortly after the Film Theatres' Act had been passed, local municipalities started to take over the cinemas by buying out the private owners. The municipalization could be restricted to give licences to private owners, but many local authorities were moved by reasons other than just moral anxiety. They saw the financial possibilities in running the cinemas themselves, thereby both controlling the new and powerful media, and at the same time earning a profit that could be used for other cultural purposes.

The first municipal cinema was established in Harstad – in the north of Norway – in 1913, and after a two-year lull a spate of local authorities moved to municipalize screenings during the years 1915 to 1917. This important phase ended with the foundation of Kommunale Kinematografers Landsforbund – the National Association of Municipal Cinemas – in 1917. The definitive breakthrough of municipalization came in around 1920, and the establishment of municipal cinemas in the capital – now renamed Oslo – in 1925 saw the end of private ownership of cinemas in the big cities, or on a large scale, in Norway. Some private cinemas continued their business – and still do – but in the smallest of municipalities, and all the cinemas in the bigger cities in Norway are still municipally owned.

The private cinema owners tried to resist municipalization, but without success. The private rental companies boycotted the municipal cinemas for a short period, but the establishment of Kommunernes Filmscentral A/S – the Municipal Films Exchange Ltd – between 1919 and 1920 broke the boycott. Thus, by 1925, most cinemas in Norway were owned by the municipalities, but film rental and film production were left to private initiatives.

The municipal cinema system displays some undeniably attractive features. Owned by the municipalities, cinemas are supposed to operate for the common good of the local community, its profits used for local purposes, its programmes tuned to local needs and wishes. The municipal cinemas are run by directors who make their own individual decisions as to which films to screen, for how long, and at what ticket prices and hours. This system has effectively counteracted the establishment of any centralized cinema circuits. Being a local institution in the true sense of the word, a municipal cinema is thus seen less as a commercial enterprise and more as a cultural service institution, as part of local cultural life.

The municipal system nevertheless has one serious flaw: it does not generate production capital. No more than one-third of box-office receipts are returned to film production today, and in previous years virtually no money was invested in the production of Norwegian films. The municipal system broke the circular economy inherent to film industries elsewhere, and the municipal ownership of cinemas in Norway has no doubt seriously hampered the development of a national film industry. Finland, a country of much the same size and with an economy comparable to that of Norway, has produced about double the number of feature films over the last eighty years. The horizontally integrated cinema system in Norway – with the cinemas municipally owned, and film rental and film production privately run – has its obvious flaws. A vertically integrated corporation – like that of Hugo Hermansen before 1910 – became impossible after 1920. The municipalities used the profit from film screenings to build hospitals and schools, to subsidize the theatre proper, and to build art institutions. One municipality even built a hotel! To illustrate the problem of municipally run cinemas, it has been suggested that Norwegian film production lies buried under the largest statue in the Gustav Vigeland Sculpture Park in Oslo, a park financed by the profits from film showings in the 1920s.

Thus, the municipalization of the cinemas made it harder to produce films in Norway, as pioneers like Peter Lykke-Seest soon found out, but it secured a high standard in cinemas and the films shown there. The municipal cinemas realized the importance of domestic film production, and on a small scale they tried to initiate film production by subsidizing some privately produced films. This led to a 'national breakthrough' in the early 1920s.

THE NATIONAL BREAKTHROUGH

In 1920 film production in Norway was more unstable than ever. Private capital was limited, and investors were not interested in film production at a time when cinemas were being taken over by the municipalities. Only two feature films were produced in 1920, but these two films signalled a national breakthrough in film. In an apparent response to Swedish film production in previous years that had enjoyed great popularity in Norway, domestic feature films for the first time explored the countryside in depth.

The feature films made in Norway between 1906 and 1919 had a vaguely international tone. They were erotic melodramas exploring modern city life, and could have been made in almost any Western city. After 1920 the countryside and rural romanticism became the centre of attention in Norwegian film production, in films with a new and distinct national, local and 'Norwegian' look. Of the twenty-nine feature films produced between 1920 and 1930, only five were set in cities. This new national tone in film production met with great interest, and these films enjoyed domestic popularity, unlike the earlier erotic melodramas.

A vital turning point in Norwegian film history was the first of these rural films: *Anne, The Tramp* (*Fante-Anne*) (Rasmus Breistein, 1920). This was the first Norwegian feature film to be adapted from literature, being based on a novel by Kristofer Janson written in 1879. The film was also the first to make use of only professional actors. *Anne, The Tramp* was privately produced, by the director Breistein himself, who took out a mortgage on his house and invited some fellow-actors to spend a holiday in the beautiful village of Vågå and make a feature film there, but the film received both moral and financial support from the newly established distribution company for the municipal cinemas, Kommunernes Films central A/S. In more ways than one, *Anne, The Tramp* is typical of Norwegian film production for more than a decade, being an adaptation of a well-known literary work, and set in a rural milieu.

Anne, The Tramp is the story of a gypsy girl, Anne, who has been brought up as a foster-child on a large country estate. Her childhood sweetheart, Haldor, is the son of the estate-owner, and the first part of the film shows how Anne constantly creates funny but precarious situations. The weak Haldor always follows the unruly Anne, and gets into trouble. When they grow up Haldor is not allowed to marry Anne. In a fit of jealous fury, she sets fire to the house Haldor is building for his future wife. Parallel to this tragic love story is another, equally tragic story of love. One of the estate workers, the good Christian cotter Jon, has come to love Anne. He justifies his secret affections for Anne by assuming blame for the arson. He is found guilty and sentenced by the court, and has to go to prison. Anne quits her job as a milkmaid and moves to the city, so that she can visit Jon. Years later he is released. Jon is seen on a big ship going to the USA with Anne and his mother. The last intertitle informs us that they are leaving Norway, and travelling to the United States, 'the land where every man can be himself, independent of rank and prejudices'.

The director Rasmus Breistein made the film with the photographer Gunnar Nilsen-Vig, who was responsible not only for the photography, but for the decor and the editing. Breistein himself wrote the script. He also played the violin when he screened the film in community houses all over Norway, and in Norwegian settlements in the USA. In that way he raised money for new film productions. Breistein is one of the few Norwegian directors who has made a profit on every film, and he made several romantic melodramas in the 1920s. Ten years after *Anne, The Tramp* he demonstrated his skill in his fifth feature film, *Kristine, the Daughter of Valdres* (*Kristine Valdresdatter*) (1930), the last silent film in Norway, where a woman from the country is made pregnant by a visiting British aristocrat. She abandons her baby, who, like Anne in his first film, grows up ignorant of her parents' identity. Unlike *Anne, The Tramp*, however, this later film by Breistein closes with a happy ending, a reconciliation between youth and age, as the dying British lord reveals himself to be Kristine's long-lost father.

Breistein was the most important Norwegian director in the 1920s, and his films became a vital turning point in domestic film production. *Anne, The Tramp* portrayed the countryside in a less idyllic, more naturalistic and critical way than the later films. Films like *The Magic Elk* (*Trollelgen*) (Walter Fürst, 1927), about a magic elk that is a reincarnation of·a dead man, or *The Bride of Glomdal* (*Glomdalsbruden*) (Carl Th. Dreyer, 1926), are more romantic, and paint an idyllic portrait of the countryside. The popularity of these new 'national' films can be partly explained by their classic, melodramatic structure, but also because they showed the Norwegian countryside as an idyllic reservoir of the past, suitable for romantic recreation, in a time of difficult modernization, when Norway was being transformed into a modern, industrial nation.

In a recently urbanized country like Norway many people shared a rural homesickness. This may be one reason why Norwegian films became so popular. These films, with the use of rural scenery and national symbols, were melodramas that related strongly to the themes and structures of folk-tales and popular literature. The rural melodramas of the 1920s initiated a 'national breakthrough' in film production. For the first time, Norwegian films could – successfully – compete with the popular American films in the domestic market. In 1931 *Kristine, The Daughter of Valdres* was the most seen film in Norway's capital Oslo, even though it was a silent film, and more popular than sound films like Chaplin's *City Lights* (third place in Oslo in 1931) or Lewis Milestone's *All Quiet on the Western Front* (fifth place).

Film had become big business in Norway, and from the year 1920 cinemas had to pay an entertainment tax. In 1920 the cinema owners – by now mainly the municipalities – earned a profit of 23 million kroner, 8 million in Oslo alone. However, during the 1920s profits dropped swiftly, and depression and economic crisis made the film business more insecure than ever. In the period between 1930 and 1935 cinema owners in Norway earned a profit of only 10 to 11 million kroner each year. The number of films produced dropped also, from the peak years of 1926 and 1927 when five feature films were produced each year, to only one feature film produced in the year 1931. All through the 1930s film production remained uneven, from five feature films in 1932 to only one in the years 1935 and 1936. The hard times continued, and the advent of sound made matters worse.

A 'GOLDEN AGE'

The new decade started in the shadow of the economic crisis, but ended in a 'golden age', a revitalization of film production in Norway. One reason for this revitalization was that municipal cinemas had realized the importance of domestic film production, perhaps as a result of the rural films and their large popularity, and tried to boost output by subsidizing privately initiated production on a larger scale than before. With the advent of sound, and the rise of production costs, this intervention was intensified.

In 1932 municipal cinemas financed the production company Norsk Film A/S – Norwegian Films Ltd – by shares offered in subscription to cinema-owning municipalities. This production company played a vital role in revitalizing Norwegian film production during the 1930s, and has been the longest lived and largest production company in the country; it still produces several films each year. Three years after the establishment of this production company, the first real film studio in Norway was built with capital from municipal cinemas. Norsk Film A/S and the studio at Jar, outside Oslo, were owned by the municipalities until after the Second World War, when the government started to support domestic film production and became a co-owner, but it was not until 1971 that the government entered into either Norsk Film or the studio at Jar with a responsibility, i.e. majority, portfolio.

Film production during the 1930s was dominated by the director Tancred Ibsen, who worked closely with Norsk Film A/S which produced his most important films. Ibsen made most of the films in this period, but other directors – like Leif Sinding or Olav Dalgard – also made important feature films. Many of the films produced in the late 1930s are among the most popular in Norwegian film history. These films are regularly shown on the state-owned television, often at special occasions – like Christmas – and have a large following. The Norwegian features of the 1930s have an important place in the country's cultural history.

Tancred Ibsen (1893–1978) dominated film production during the 1930s. He was the grandson not only of the dramatist Henrik Ibsen, but also of the Nobel-prize winning author Bjørnstjerne Bjørnson. As the famous 'double-grandson' it was expected that something great would become of him, and these high expectations made his early years miserable. He joined the cavalry, becoming an officer and then a pioneer in military aviation. Military life depressed him, but he did not know what to do as a civilian, so when he accompanied his famous wife Lillebil – famous as an actress and a dancer with Max Reinhardt – to New York in 1923, he had no idea what the future would bring.

While Lillebil rehearsed *Peer Gynt* for the Theatre Guild in New York, Tancred went to the movies. Film-going was just a pastime, a way to kill time until Lillebil was finished for the day, but one day he saw a re-run of Griffith's *Orphans of the Storm*. This film changed his life, and he made big plans to 'Ibsenize' cinema. This led him to Hollywood and Metro-Goldwyn-Mayer. He worked as a handyman or electrician for MGM on several films, among them King Vidor's *His Hour* (1924) and Victor Sjöström's *Tower of Lies* (1926). He eventually got a job at MGM as a scriptwriter, probably because of his famous surname, but none of his scripts made it into production. After two years in the USA he returned to Norway, a little disappointed, but with practical experience and great plans for the future.

In the early 1930s the rural melodrama was still the dominant generic mode in Norwegian feature film production. Tancred Ibsen's debut, *The Big Christening (Den store barnedåpen)* (1931), co-directed with the actor Einar Sissener and the first Norwegian talkie, broke new ground and gave the audience a fresh view of the big city. Ibsen went against the grain, and his first film signals a new realistic vein in film production. The focus on city life, the use of the new sound technology, and the new realism, all these novelties are apparent in the film's opening sequence, which emphasizes the rhythmic sound of the machines as they start up in a textile factory. The industrial worker, not the farmer, was the focal point of the film.

In Ibsen's first film, the unemployed Harald cares for the lonely Alvilde's baby, whose sailor father has perished in a storm at sea. Harald looks after the baby while Alvilde goes to work in the textile factory, and he finally wins her affections. A parallel plot deals with the church, which denies Alvilde the right to christen her baby, but in the end allows unmarried mothers to christen their babies. Although the film portrays ordinary workers and their lives, the tone of *The Big Christening* is light and lyrical. The grim reality of factory life, and the poverty of the rooming-house where the main characters live, is mitigated by the cheerfulness of the people and the lively music. The workers are viewed with intense sympathy, and the film is not unlike French films from the same period. As in René Clair's filmic world, a smile is never far away, and poverty assumes a romantic aura.

The Big Christening was a success, both artistically and economically, and Ibsen was contacted by a Swedish film company. During the 1930s Ibsen worked both in Sweden and Norway, directing seven Swedish and five Norwegian feature films, thus being by far the most productive Norwegian director. By 1934, Ibsen was directing Victor Sjöström in Sweden, in a new version of *Synnøve Solbakken* for the independent Swedish company, Irefilm.

In Norway Ibsen made several elegant comedies, but not until 1937 was his promising start in 1931 brought to maturity, when he made two feature films in Norway, both extremely successful and innovative. Both films were made for Norsk Film A/S, and thus Ibsen began a collaboration with this municipal company that was to result in several masterpieces and lasted into the 1960s. *Two Living and One Dead* (*To Levende og en Død*) (1937) was a psychological thriller. The film tells the story of a post office employee who, on the verge of advancement, is robbed and loses his chance of a better job. Later, he meets the robber, befriends him, and finally shows his superiors that he was no coward when the office was robbed. The film is based on the novel by Sigurd Christiansen; a Czech film of the novel was made in 1949, and a British adaptation in 1961.

Ibsen's second film in 1937 was even more accomplished. In *Tramp* (*Fant*) he made a beautiful and moving but dark version of Gabriel Scott's novel about fishermen and sea gypsies. In the film, young Josefa escapes from her uncle, who lusts after the young girl, and hides in the boat of a young gypsy, Fendrik. He forces her to sleep with him, and to try to beg or steal on their behalf. She longs for the return of her fiancé, Oskar, a fisherman who is at sea, while Fendrik quarrels with his family and relatives. The film ends with Fendrik drowning, after nearly killing Oskar, and the union of Josefa and Oskar.

As this extremely condensed resumé of the film's action indicates, the films of Tancred Ibsen are conventional melodramas. The model for his films in the late 1930s was the classical Hollywood cinema, and for the first time a Norwegian film director completely mastered that much imitated style. The narrative of the film is built around intensely melodramatic confrontations. The audience is 'sutured' into the narrative through a shot/reverse-shot technique in these confrontations. The technique, developed to perfection in American talkies, is used effectively by Ibsen, to present facial expressions and reactions in close-ups. One obvious reason for the popularity of *Tramp*, not only in Norway but also in Sweden and Denmark, was that it mastered the Hollywood way of telling a good story. It resembled any film from Hollywood, but still contained something Nordic.

American films were popular in Norway at an early stage, and the advent of sound strengthened the US hold on Norwegian audiences. In 1939, 362 films were shown on Norwegian screens, 220 of which came from the USA, i.e. 60 per cent were American films. No wonder the Norwegian producers and directors looked to Hollywood as a model for film narratives. At the same time production in Norway climbed to six feature films in 1939, and the market share for Norwegian films reached 10.4 per cent, compared to just 0.6 per cent three years earlier. Even if American films dominated the screens, a revitalization had taken place in Norwegian film production.

In the late 1930s Norwegian audiences expected a feature film to be like the American movies. The US output was their horizon of expectations. This is one reason why a film like *Tramp* was so popular. Another reason may be the use of the Norwegian seascape, the Norwegian language and the popular actors. Alfred Maurstad, the leading male actor in *Tramp*, was one of the most popular stage actors in 1937, and his portrayal of the lovable rogue Fendrik is unforgettable. Ibsen wrote his next film with Maurstad in mind, and in *Gjest Baardsen* (1939) he plays a nineteenth-century folk hero, a blend of Robin Hood and Harry Houdini. Gjest represents the ordinary people's cause in the face of the arrogance and corruption of the law. Again, Ibsen had made a tremendously popular film.

The most important single director in the late 1930s besides Ibsen was Leif Sinding, who made several realistic and popular films. In *The Gipsy* (*Fantegutten*) (1932) he brought into sharp focus the prejudice with which outsiders were treated in Norwegian society and, adopting a sombre and more realistic tone, he returned to this theme in *The Defenceless* (*De Vergeløse*) (1939). In this film, Sinding exposes the abuse of child labour at a farm where orphans are placed by the government. This feature film adopts a bitter tone, but ends with a melodramatic happy ending. Even more realistic in style were the films of Olav Dalgard, who focused on working life. Inspired by workers' films in Germany and France, Dalgard made several feature films for the National Union's Congress. In *Dawn in the North* (*Gryr i Norden*) (1939) Dalgard reconstructs the match-makers' strike of 1889.

Looking back at the feature films of the late 1930s, and especially Ibsen's films, many historians have named this period a 'golden age' of film production in Norway. The number of films produced rose, and Norwegian films successfully competed with foreign – mostly American – imports. The realistic vein that a film like *The Big Christening* signalled started to dominate film production. Directors like Ibsen, Dalgard and Sinding made popular films, mainly portraying modern city life and working-class heroes. The nature and landscape of Norway still played an important part in many films, but rural romanticism disappeared. Norwegian film production became more international, more realistic, and with the new big municipal production company Norsk Film A/S, film production achieved a new stability. A revitalization had taken place, only to be halted by the Second World War.

Plate 5.1 Norwegian national romanticism *The Bride of Glomdal* (*Glomdalsbruden*) (Dreyer, 1926)

Plate 5.2 A 'golden age' in Norwegian film production *The Big Christening* (*Den Store Barnedåpen*) (Ibsen, 1931)

Plate 5.3 A new realism *The Big Christening* (*Den Store Barnedåpen*)
(Ibsen, 1931)

Plate 5.4 A new realism *The Kid* (*Ungen*) (Breistein, 1938)

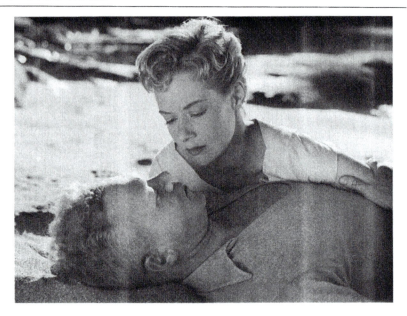

Plate 5.5 Imitating Hollywood in post-war film production *Midsummer* (*Høysommer*) (Brinchmann, 1958)

Plate 5.6 Norway goes international *Orion's Belt* (*Orions Belte*) (Solum, 1985)

Plate 5.7 Norway goes international *Blackout* (*Blackout*) (Gustavson, 1986)

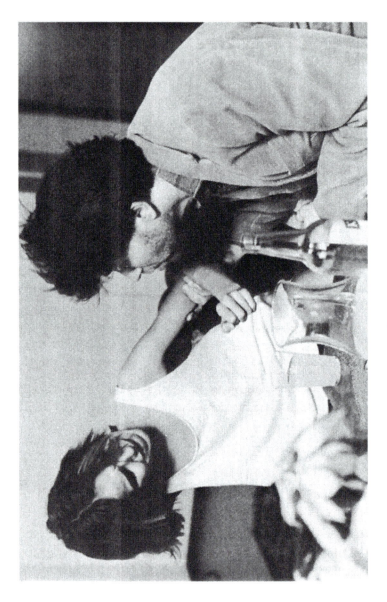

Plate 5.8 Inspired by Antonioni *X* (Einarson, 1986)

Plate 5.9 Current realism *Hard Asphalt* (*Hard asfalt*) (Skagen, 1986)

Plate 5.10 Current drama *The Ice Castle* (*Is-slottet*) (Blom, 1987)

THE WAR YEARS

In April 1940 German soldiers invaded Norway, and thus began five dark years of German Occupation. The Nazis took less than a year to exercise control over every aspect of Norwegian film production, distribution and exhibition. The process of controlling the film media started with distribution. The Oslo office of 20th Century Fox was closed in June 1940, and by the autumn all British and American films had been banned from Norwegian screens. The Germans replaced the municipal cinema directors with their own men or Norwegian Nazis, thus effectively gaining complete control over screenings.

The German newsreels – Deutsche Wochenschau – were introduced into Norwegian cinemas as a propaganda effort, and just like in France and other Occupied countries cinemas became a venue for resistance. Audiences sneezed and coughed through the German newsreels, even though German soldiers arrested people who openly showed their dislike of the newsreels. Screenings were run by decree, and admission between the German newsreel and the main feature film was forbidden. The Resistance Movement was worried about the effect the newsreels, or the German and Italian feature films that swamped the market, would have on the audience, and tried to organize a cinema strike, boycotting the cinemas and preventing people from going to the cinema. Even though people went to the cinema less often during the first two years of the Occupation, this call for a boycott was a failure. In 1939 the attendance figure in Oslo was 5,412,434; the number of visits to the cinemas in Oslo dropped to 3,374,848 in 1941, but rose again to 5,777,471 in 1943. Cinema attendance was the one thing that the Resistance Movement could not stop during the Occupation.

From as early as 1940 the Germans controlled film production by means of a film directorate. For two years this directorate was led by the director Leif Sinding, one of the few men in the film business who used the opportunities offered by the Occupation. The film directorate controlled the production companies – including Norsk Film A/S and the studio at Jar – and film content through censorship. Nothing could happen without the sanction of this organization. This situation could easily have resulted in a production of propagandistic Nazi films, but in the total Occupation output only one feature, *Youthful Will* (*Unge Viljer*) (Walter Fyrst, 1943) can be said to have had an ideological slant towards Nazi ideals.

Of all the genres, comedy was the one most evidently on the increase. The cinema of the Occupation consisted of harmless thrillers and comedies. Most famous of the wartime comedies is *The Lost Sausage-maker* (*Den Forsvundne Pølsemaker*) (Toralf Sandø, 1941), a detective comedy about two totally incompetent private detectives and their search for a man who works as a sausage-maker, but whose disappearance baffles everyone. This slapstick comedy, starring the well-known stage comedians Leif Juster and Ernst Diesen, was followed by other comedies. The most popular Norwegian comedy during the Occupation was *A Gentleman with a Moustache* (*En herre med bart*) (1942), a more sophisticated screwball comedy directed by the famous actor Alfred Maurstad.

The most popular Norwegian feature film during the war years was *Vigdis* (Helge Lunde, 1943). Even though the film contains comic relief, *Vigdis* is not a comedy pure and simple. More than anything else it is a modern version of those feature films of the thirties that brought into sharp focus the way outsiders were treated in small communities. The action in *Vigdis* takes place in the countryside, but the main characters are teachers or doctors, not farmers or milkmaids. In the film young Vigdis gets pregnant, but refuses to name the father. This leads to much trouble, but after many plot twists and melodramatic confrontations she finally names the father, whom she then marries. A simple melodrama in more ways than one, *Vigdis* still criticizes small-town narrow-mindedness and discrimination.

During the war years the entertainment tax on film-going rose dramatically. The tax on every ticket sold rose, from 10 per cent to 30 per cent on foreign film, and from 5 per cent to 25 per cent on Norwegian feature films. However, a small amount of this tax now went towards the production of Norwegian features, and the policy of the film directorate laid the foundations for a form of subsidizing of feature films which significantly influenced film production in Norway from the early 1950s up to the present. For the first time the government subsidized Norwegian feature films, through the film directorate. At the war's end, a sizeable residue – 10.5 million kroner – remained in a production fund. In the first post-war years nothing happened to this fund, but discussions about how it should be used resulted in a new government engagement in film production.

THE POST-WAR PERIOD

The German Occupation of Norway ended in spring 1945, and the immediate post-war period saw many changes as regards the cinemas and film production. Attendance rose sharply, and the post-war years were golden years for municipal cinemas. In 1945 the number of attendances were the highest ever: 8,056,665 in Oslo, and 2,099,885 in Trondheim. People went to the movies more often than ever before. One obvious reason was that British and American films were being shown again. The first film from an English-speaking country that premièred after the war was the British feature film *In Which We Serve* (Lean/Coward, 1942), which became a tremendous success. The film opened in Oslo on 17 May, Constitution Day and a national holiday, an emblematic coincidence that signalled the approaching domination of the Anglo-American film, television and the music industry in Norway in the post-war period.

Another reason for the large attendance figures was the need for information about the war, and the new vehicle for this information was the Norwegian newsreel. The first post-war newsreel was produced by Norsk Film A/S, and shown in Oslo (21 May) and in other cities immediately following the German capitulation. Prior to the war, there had been no Norwegian newsreels for national distribution. The municipal cinema organization in Oslo had been inserting locally filmed news into a weekly newsreel programme consisting of various international newsreels, but this newsreel was not widely distributed. During the war, the film directorate had decided that Norsk Film A/S should produce a weekly Norwegian newsreel, to be shown together with the Deutsche Wochenschau, and a subdivision of Norsk Film A/S was organized. Production started in January 1944, and continued until the last days of the war. So-called 'good Norwegians' largely boycotted the newsreel, but the production facilities were excellent, and became the foundation upon which Norsk Film A/S based its national newsreel service after the war.

The first liberation newsreel met with immediate success, and a national distribution system was improvised almost overnight. In Oslo one cinema was reserved solely for newsreel screenings, presenting the Norwegian newsreel – Filmavisen – in a programme consisting of other international newsreels, like Fox Movietone News and the Pathé newsreel. Seven copies were made of each weekly edition of Filmavisen, and dispatched to the biggest cities. The prints were then circulated locally according to a central distribution plan.

In spite of the intention to establish a truly national newsreel, the Oslo district clearly came to dominate the selection of items presented in the newsreel. Oslo accounted for more than 50 per cent of attendance and income, the production units' base was in Oslo and most major events took place in the capital. Although attendance declined after the large numbers immediately at the war's end, it was relatively stable during the 1950s. In 1959 the newsreel was shown in sixty-three municipal cinemas all over Norway, in addition to screenings with the state-financed mobile exhibition units – Norsk Bygdekino – that travelled to those parts of the country which did not have cinemas, and the welfare service of the large Norwegian merchant marines. The newsreel thus played an important part in the circulation of news and information in Norway during the important years of reconstruction and stabilizing of the economy after the Second World War. It became the 'voice of reconstruction', expressing the desire for national unity. The introduction of television to Norway in 1960 signalled the end of Filmavisen. In the years following, attendances fell sharply, and the last edition of the newsreel was made in 1963.

The Second World War had a huge impact on film production in Norway, partly because wartime experiences offered a wealth of potentially dramatic stories that were to result in a new genre of Occupation dramas which dominated Norwegian feature film production for years, but also because of the government's new interest in the media. The war had shown how important film could be as an instrument of propaganda, both by means of the newsreel service and by fictional stories, so the government signalled a new support for film production. This new governmental support took the form of only words and promises for years, but ended eventually in a new state production system, that guaranteed stable national film production from the early 1950s.

After the war a new generation of film-makers made pioneering advances in Norwegian film production, while providing the hungry audiences with authentic stories from the Occupation. A new genre was created – the Occupation drama – often known as docu-dramas. Many of these films were faithful reconstructions of actual events, often featuring some of those who took part in the events portrayed. The most famous of these early Resistance films was *The Battle for Heavy Water* (*Kampen om tungtvannet/La Bataille de l'eau lourde*) (1948). Directed by Titus Vibe-Müller, and supervised by the French director Jean Dréville, the film relates the attempts of the Resistance to foil German efforts to ship a stock of heavy water (Deuteriumoxide) from Norway to Germany, intended for the manufacture of an atomic bomb. Saboteurs are parachuted into the Hardanger plateau, to carry out their mission to blow up the factory where the heavy water was produced. Operation Swallow, as it was known, later attracted the attention of Hollywood, which two decades later produced *The Heroes of Telemark* (Anthony Mann, 1965).

The Battle for Heavy Water was not the first Occupation drama – Olav Dalgard and Rolf Randall dramatized the patriotic Resistance in *We Want to Live* (*Vi vil leve*) (1946), and Toralf Sandø made his *We Leave for England* (*Englandsfarere*) the same year – but the Franco-Norwegian co-production became the model for later Occupation dramas. Films like *The Shetland Gang* (*Shetlandsgjengen*) (Michael Forlong, 1954), *Contact!* (*Kontakt!*) (Nils R. Müller, 1956) or *Nine Lives* (*Ni Liv*) (Arne Skouen, 1957) sought as much authenticity as possible in their dramatic rendering of the Occupation and the Resistance Movement.

These early Occupation dramas focused on the actions, adventures and struggles of a male war hero. *Nine Lives*, which was nominated for an Academy Award for Best Foreign Film, was an adaptation of a story about a Norwegian saboteur and his harrowing escape from Nazi-occupied Norway to Sweden. Like most Hollywood war films, women in these Occupation dramas acted as marginal helpers in the central male character's heroic pursuit of freedom. *Nine Lives* is no different in this stereotyped depiction of gender, but it signalled a new treatment of the heroic saboteur. Early on in the film, when escaping from German soldiers, the hero is wounded and suffers frostbite, and has to cut off nine of his toes while sheltering in a mountain cabin. For the rest of the film he is rendered immobile, and completely dependent on his helpers. The main protagonist of *Nine Lives* is virtually an anti-hero, and the Occupation drama changed dramatically during the early 1960s. The docu-drama tone disappeared, women became more important in the stories, and the hero was shown to have his faults. The heroes were no longer larger than life and perfect, but human beings like everybody else. The revision of these earlier central themes of the Occupation dramas goes on even today, and films like *The Reward* (*Belønningen*) (Bjørn Lien, 1980) or *Over the Border* (*Over Grensen*) (Bente Erichsen, 1987) show a different side of the Resistance spirit, namely the betrayal and deception not only of the Germans or of the Quislings, but inside the Resistance Movement itself.

The years after the Second World War saw many directors making their first feature films, and this new generation of film-makers favoured a highly realistic approach to film style. Not only in the Occupation dramas, but also in other genres Norwegian directors strived for a new realism. In these years of reconstruction many had a dark, realistic tone. The most important of the new directors was undoubtedly Arne Skouen. He is, besides Tancred Ibsen, the most important, original and productive among the Norwegian directors. Skouen has been regarded as Norway's first genuine auteur, because he wrote the screenplays for all seventeen of his films save one. Towards the middle of his career as a film-maker he also established his own production company to ensure himself even greater independence.

Having already been a successful author and journalist in Norway, Skouen worked in New York as a press attaché during the Second World War. Before he left the USA in 1946, he travelled to Hollywood. Just like Tancred Ibsen two decades earlier, Skouen observed the Hollywood way of making movies, and learned a lot from this experience. In Norway he returned to his work as a writer, and forgot his plans about film-making, but one day in 1949 he received an offer he could not refuse. Norway is a small country, with a small film culture, and the anecdotal story about how Skouen came to be the single most important film-maker in the post-war period tells a lot about the Norwegian system of film production.

As before the war, Norwegian feature film production was dominated by short-lived enterprises which seldom managed more than one film before giving up. Norsk Film A/S, the municipal production company, was handed back to the original organization after the war, but lack of capital resulted in the company producing no feature films between 1945 and 1948. During this time the only active part of the company was the newsreel division, which also produced one feature-length compilation documentary about King Haakon VII. In 1948 the company was reorganized, new capital was invested, and in accord with the national economic policy and its new involvement in the national film culture, this investment was made by the government. Since 1948 Norsk Film A/S has been a joint state/municipal venture. Feature film production resumed after the re-organization, and the first feature the company produced after the war was Tancred Ibsen's *The Secretive Apartment* (*Den hemmelighetsfulle Leiligheten*, 1948).

Even though the government invested capital in Norsk Film A/S, the company was still run by the municipalities, and one man within the municipal organization had enormous power. Kristoffer Aamot was not only the managing director of the municipal cinema organization in Oslo, he was also top man within the nationwide organization of all municipal cinemas, and chairman of the board of directors of Norsk Film A/S. In this key position, he often acted on his ideas and whims, and initiated film projects himself. In 1948 Aamot read Arne Skouens' novel *Street Boys* (*Gategutter*) and liked it so much that he wanted Norsk Film A/S to make a film of the book. Aamot also wanted Skouen himself to direct the film, although Skouen had no prior experience of film-making, apart from his trip to Hollywood. One day Skouen received a telephone call from Aamot, who wanted to see Skouen at his office. When Skouen arrived, the novel *Street Boys* was on the desk, and before Skouen could say anything, Aamot just pointed his finger at the book and asked if Skouen wanted to direct a film adaptation of the novel. Skouen said yes, wrote the script, and with the assistance of the experienced photographer Ulf Greber, directed his first feature film in 1949. This led to other projects, and between 1949 and 1969 Skouen directed seventeen films, thus being one of the few Norwegian directors to direct more than one or two feature films. As this anecdote illustrates, film production in Norway has often been dominated by strange coincidences, and even though the government invested money in film production after the war, no proper industry evolved. Just a handful of films were made each year, some produced by Norsk Film A/S, others by short-lived private companies.

Skouen's *Street Boys* (*Gategutter*) (1949) tells the story of a gang of boys. They wore baggy shorts and shirts, with large caps on their heads, as they ran through the streets of Oslo in the 1920s. They all go to school, but eagerly await the time when school's over so that they can get jobs, and start earning money and being a financial help to their poor families. Days are spent on petty thievery, stealing fruit from the harbour boats and copra from trucks passing 'their' street. The film paints a grim picture of broken families, strikes and lock-outs, and domestic poverty. At the centre of this highly realistic feature film stand Karsten and Gotfred, two boys who become rivals. They both want to head the gang. Karsten gets a job after his school days are over, and learns the importance of solidarity and union membership, while Gotfred ends up as a petty criminal who goes to gaol or borstal. *Street Boys* is a stark and realistic picture of Norway during the 1920s, but the film also contains many poetic sequences focusing on the hopes and dreams of these boys, and the growing friendship and solidarity within the group. The film ends with Karsten and his younger friend Sofus wandering home at dusk, after a fight with the police and strike-breakers that nearly lands them in gaol. As they wander, the street-lights are suddenly switched on, bathing the two in a new light; they keep on walking and the film ends.

The ending is apparently a combination of a Chaplin film and the French poetic realism of the 1930s. Skouen himself has often talked about Marcel Carné's *Le Jour se Lève* (1939) as his model and favourite movie, but *Street Boys* resembles the Italian neorealist films more than anything else. It bears a close resemblance to some of Vittorio de Sica's films, for instance, *Sciuscia* (1946) or *Ladri di biciclette* (1948), and Skouen's films share the stylistic traits of the Italian neorealist films. Important is Skouen's use of amateurs in most parts, and the young kids in the film were practically taken off the streets. Many of the boys later pursued a career in acting or directing. The young Sofus was played by Pål Bang-Hansen, who became a film director in the 1960s, and also a popular television commentator with his own programme about films.

With his next feature, *Forced Landing* (*Nødlanding*) (1952), Skouen made the first of four Occupation dramas, the most famous being *Nine Lives*. As is usual in the genre, Skouen's early films are realistic docudramas, but in his later films – *Surrounded* (*Omringet*) (1960) or *Cold Trails* (*Kalde Spor*) (1962) – he creates chamber-plays (*Kammerspielfilme*) about guilt and wrongdoing during the Occupation. To a larger degree he questions the official hero-worship of the Resistance fighters.

Skouen's films often tell the same story over and over again, disguised by genre and locales. His protagonists are outsiders who through their actions and attitudes have excluded themselves from their community. To get back inside, and to be part of a community, they often use desperate measures. In the highly expressionistic *The Flame* (*Det brenner i natt!*) (1955) the main character is a love-starved poet suffering writer's block who turns to arson. Only in this way can he fill his life with a perverse warmth. Skouen's credo may be simple, and his films convey the message that people should stick together and care for each other, but his films are highly complex and assured dramas. Skouen made his last film in 1969. *An-Magritt* is in many ways different from the rest of his films, being an adaptation of another author's book, set in a primitive seventeenth-century community, and having a woman as protagonist. The young An-Magritt, played by Liv Ullmann, is an orphaned girl who has to fight for her basic rights. Her mother committed suicide because she was raped, and An-Magritt is the consequence of that rape. She fights the constant repression and violence, is forced to labour in a stone quarry and, denied even a modicum of food, she clings to life through her friendship to Johannes, a German migrant artist. *An-Magritt* became Skouen's swan-song, and his focus on a woman as the main character heralded a new turn in the history of Norwegian film.

Two other directors emerged in the late 1940s and became the makers of the most popular films. The comedies of Nils R. Müller and Edith Carlmar dominated the Norwegian screen in the 1950s. Edith Carlmar was the first female Norwegian director, but her first feature film *Death is a Caress* (*Døden er et kjærtegn*) (1949) was about masculinity and male melancholia. It is a film noir, the story of a wealthy middle-class woman Sonja and Erik, a garage mechanic. She divorces her husband and marries the younger Erik, but their marriage becomes a series of increasingly violent rows, and Erik finally kills her. The film is told in flashbacks, as Erik awaits the sentence for the murder of his wife. Sonja is a *femme fatale*, and the film has all the stylistic features of film noir. Thus, the first woman director made her debut with a film about male melancholia!

After this film noir, Edith Carlmar made two social problem films before turning to comedy. Her most popular comedy was the enormously popular *Fools on the Mountain* (*Fjols til fjells*) (1957), a situation comedy of mistaken identity set in a mountain resort. The most popular genre in Norwegian post-war film production was comedy. In the 1950s the sub-genre of romantic comedies dominated Norwegian film production. In no other period in Norwegian film history has this sub-genre been so popular with film-goers nor films so numerous. In the years from 1951 to 1963 the number of romantic comedies varied between one and four, of a yearly production varying from six to twelve features.

The first commercially successful Norwegian film comedy after the war was *We are Getting Married* (*Vi gifter oss*) (Nils R. Müller, 1951). This film became one of the greatest box-office hits ever in Norwegian cinema, and was followed by many films that were variations of the same story. Müller's film tells the story about a young, urban couple and their housing problems. They want to establish a home of their own and get married, but they cannot do so without having somewhere to live. Frustrated by this situation, the couple are forced to move from the city to a farm in the countryside. This is a place of hard work and female intrigues, and their marriage seems to be on the verge of collapse, until one day the husband wins a popular music contest. This allows them to move into a house of their own, and saves the marriage. The film ends in a celebration of traditional values, marriage and the middle-class nuclear family.

We are Getting Married takes a social problem – the lack of housing – as a way to paint an idyllic portrait of a romantic couple and their marriage. This blend of social and political issues, and romantic comedy, characterizes feature film production in Norway in the 1950s. Popular films like *A Woman's Place* (*Kvinnens Plass*) (Nils R. Müller, 1956) and *Dust on the Brain* (*Støv på hjernen*) (Øyvind Vennerød, 1959) deal with sex-roles within marriage. By focusing on the female sex-roles, which appear to be under pressure and changing, these films give the female protagonist a more central position in the films than hitherto. *Dust on the Brain* also deals with adultery, or what happens in a marriage when the woman is so immersed in her role as mother and housekeeper that her husband no longer finds her attractive as a woman, and she can no longer keep him at home. In some of these films of the 1950s the man and the woman are not equal, but in others the woman appears to be superior to the man, thus having a dimension of social critique and not only being 'pure entertainment'.

With very few exceptions the most popular comedies in the 1950s were romantic, 'marital' comedies. The married, middle-class couple are at the centre of a story that focuses on the condition of love and sexual desire inside the institution of marriage. The 1950s was a period of rebuilding and recovery after the war, but also a decade of economic growth and social change. In this decade, large-scale urbanization and industrialization were indicative of progress and modernization, and the period was full of optimism. The comedies reflect both this new optimism, and, in dealing with the emerging 'new' society – where the nuclear family was at the centre, and the housewife was given a special role – reflect the changing ways of life and sex-roles.

These comedies were enormously popular all over the country. In earlier years the difference in taste and preferences in individual cities was extensive, but this changed during the 1950s. Comedies like *Fools on the Mountain* or *Dust on the Brain* dominated the screens in Norway the year they were released, and no foreign imports could match their popularity. Even though American movies still dominated the imports, Norwegian films were favoured by the audiences. During the 1950s a homogenization of film taste seemed to take place, but domestic films were still preferred.

Feature film production in Norway in the 1950s and 1960s was dominated by comedies. One obvious reason for this dominance was the popularity of the genre. These comedies allowed both male and female spectators to laugh, both at comic situations and characters, and at themselves and their everyday life in the changing Norwegian society. However, audience popularity was not the only reason for this dominance. Another reason may be the changing production support provided by the Norwegian state.

After the Second World War the government showed an increased interest in film production. The new state involvement in domestic film culture started in 1948, when Norsk Film A/S became a joint state/municipal venture. Two years later, the government launched a generous system of support for feature film production. This revolutionary system, the state production system of 1950, made film production a national project in Norway, and guaranteed continuous domestic film production. The new production system made it much easier for the private producers. If the films they produced had 'a minimum of artistic quality', the state would contribute 300,000 Norwegian kroner – later raised to 350,000 – towards the production. This amount was rather lower than the cost of an average feature film, but this support was extremely important, and the chances of losing money on the production of a film became less. Thus, since 1950 film production in Norway has been a joint venture between private companies and the state. At first, private companies made their films and later applied for support, but this was to change a few years later due to the sinking quality of the films that were produced.

Film production rose in Norway in the first years after the initiation of the production system of 1950, and more production companies dared to make ambitious artistic films. After a few years, while still wanting to make quality productions, many private companies had adapted their production methods to the new state support system. To minimize loss, production companies made their features as cheaply as possible – the goal being to produce a film at the same cost as the state support, thus guaranteeing no loss at all – and as a result, the Board of Review which controlled quality started to worry about film production. A new type of 'kitchen-sink'-production emerged, i.e. films made as cheaply as possible, and these productions jeopardized the whole production system. At the same time the government knew full well that a producer who was denied support would be in financial trouble, so for a few years every Norwegian feature was almost automatically supported by the state.

This situation became more and more of a problem, and in 1953 a film was denied state support because it was not good enough. The film *The Seal-Woman* (*Selkvinnen*) (Jonson, 1953) was considered too primitive, and did not fulfil the demands for 'a minimum of artistic quality'. The man behind the production was Leif Sinding, former head of the Nazi-controlled film directorate during the war, and he believed the government wanted to punish him for his wartime crimes as a collaborator, but this is probably not true. *The Seal-Woman* was a bad film, and simply too bad for the government to sponsor and encourage; thus the speculative way in which private producers like Sinding used the production system of 1950 eventually led to its demise.

In 1955 the old production system was replaced with a new state production system. This system was different, in that it did not endorse the production of 'quality' films but rewarded popular films. From now on a production company received support from the state according to a film's box-office receipts. The more money a film earned, the more money the private production company received from the state. This new system boosted the production of comedies in Norway, and made it much harder to produce films for a smaller segment of the audience.

After 1955, and until the late 1960s, the government's support encouraged the production of popular films. Thus, film production as a national project changed drastically. Film production in Norway in the post-war years may be divided into two periods, the first between 1946 and 1955, when film production was artistically ambitious and the government (from 1950) supported a 'quality' production by minimizing the chance of loss, the second period after 1955, when box-office receipts and popularity were what the government sought to support.

Because of the unique municipal cinema system, and the state production system of 1955, fewer dramas were produced in the 1960s. A few Occupation dramas were made, but comedies predominated. Some social problem films were also produced, films that focused on social problems like juvenile delinquency (*Youth on the Run* (*Ung Flukt*) (Edith Carlmar, 1959)), ecstatic religion (*Brother Gabrielsen* (*Broder Gabrielsen*) (Nils R. Müller, 1966)), or narcotics (*Heaven and Hell* (*Himmel og Helvete*) (Øyvind Vennerød, 1969)), but many of these social dramas were speculative. They focused on social problems as a way of staging scenes of sexual excess, and for all their raising of social problems they ended up confirming, rather than querying, a consensual view of the world.

The early 1950s was the golden age of documentary. Short films accompanied every feature in Norway, and many full-length documentaries were produced. They were very popular, and Thor Heyerdahl's spectacular travelogue recorded in *Kon-Tiki* (Olle Nordemar, 1950) in particular was a huge success, and won an Oscar for best documentary. The director Per Høst also made many documentaries about his voyages to exotic places far from Norway, but his most famous film of this period was about the Lapps in northern Norway: *The Laplanders* (*Same Jakki*) (1957). The introduction of television to Norway in 1960 brought this golden age of film to a close. The Norwegian newsreel ended in 1963, and both short films and full-length documentaries nearly disappeared from the screens during the 1960s. In the 1950s eighteen full-length documentaries were produced in Norway, but a decade later this number was reduced to one-third, only six long documentaries.

The coming of television signalled great changes in film culture in Norway. Attendance fell sharply, and feature films no longer held the same attraction as before. The audience changed and became younger and more educated, and the older generation of film-makers was replaced by a new generation, with fresh ideas about how to compete with television and socio-cultural changes in leisure-time activities.

THE MODERN BREAKTHROUGH

Directors like Tancred Ibsen and Arne Skouen showed that Norwegian film could be both popular and respectable, international and national, by simultaneously drawing upon popular Hollywood cinema and domestic conventions of literature and theatre as well as using the Norwegian landscape. Ibsen and Skouen, or the directors of popular comedies in the 1950s or 1960s, used the conventions of classical Hollywood cinema, but transformed and decoded them in a new national context. Thus, emphasis upon collective or group action in Skouen's films separates his production from classic Hollywood individualism in terms of both ideology and narrative style.

In the late 1960s the relation between Norwegian cinema and classical Hollywood cinema, in terms of style and ideology, shifted from one of similarity to one of outright antipathy. At the same time a new generation of film-makers dominated film production. Edith Carlmar made her last film in 1959, Ibsen his in 1963, and Skouen's last movie came out in 1969. The old generation stopped making movies, while the new young film-makers actively embraced oppositional approaches and alternatives to Hollywood. In Norway, American movies were still popular, but the new generation of domestic film-makers searched for alternative sources of cinematic style and social values.

French new wave films had a profound influence on this new generation. For a short period Norwegian film-makers embraced the French new wave as a model cinema, and a modernist breakthrough took place in film production. The director most inspired by French film-making was Pål Løkkeberg, who became an enormously influential director in Norway. His first feature *Liv* came out in 1967, and was the portrait of a young photographic model called Liv. His next film *Exit* (1970) was even more sharply influenced by Jean-Luc Godard, and resembles a remake of *Pierrot le Fou* (1965). *Exit* experiments with flashbacks, flashforwards, dream sequences and abrupt cutting, while expanding the theme from *Liv* about middle-class alienation. Even more experimental than Løkkeberg, who returned to the theatre proper after his two features, was Lasse Henriksen. His first, and only, feature film, *Love is War* (1970), is based on short stories by the Norwegian author Johan Borgen. This film used infra-red photography and videotronics in order to blend two fragmented stories, about a man and a woman, into a single entity. *Love is War* won a Silver Bear award at the Berlin Festival in 1971, and the film's self-conscious psychedelic effects captured the spirit of the times.

Until this modern, and modernist, breakthrough, few films had been made in Norway that could be characterized as experimental or modernist. Tancred Ibsen made a modernist feature in 1948, the strange *The Secretive Apartment*, a film that resembles Roman Polanski's *The Tenant* (1976). The film tells the story of an elderly man who changes apartments. His new apartment is furnished, and full of modernist art, and at first this scares the conservative man, but slowly his attitudes to life change until he takes on the identity of the previous owner. The film used voice-over to give the audience a chance to hear the character's inner thoughts, and Ibsen experimented with different styles. The end result is not altogether convincing, and it was eleven years before another modernist feature film was to emerge in Norway: Erik Løchen's *The Hunt* (*Jakten*) (1959).

The Hunt was an unusual film in more ways than one. It tells the story of a hunting trip in the mountains. Two men and a woman are isolated, and two old rivals fight over the woman. Male desire generates violence and death, and the film openly criticizes male mimetic desire. *The Hunt* used modernist Verfremdung effects in the Brechtian tradition, to tear the fabric of the film apart, right in the middle of action-oriented sequences, and thus bring the film content and the form to the attention of the audience. Erik Løchen's second feature is the most experimental of the films from the early 1970s, and marks perhaps the end of a short but hectic period of modernist experimentation. *Remonstrance* (*Motforestilling*) (1972) is a meta-film, a film about a crew making a political film, and follows the crew in its work and political discussions. At the same time the film is an 'essay' on filmic representation. Løchen wanted to create a completely different dramaturgy from the one in Hollywood, and explained later that he had written the film so that the reels could be shown in different sequences, thus creating 120 possible versions of the film.

Remonstrance was a more overt political movie than *Exit* or *Love is War*, and at the same time the film marks the end of a short modernist, experimental period in Norwegian cinema, and the beginning of a new sobriety. Political ideas became more important than narrative or character development. This refusal to tell a 'good' story is characteristic of film production in Norway during the 1970s. Feature films not only focused on social problems, but became obsessed with political ideas. Films were used as a vehicle for political propaganda, an instrument in the debates around social and political issues, more than a way to tell stories.

A typical example of this new sobriety is *Strike!* (*Streik!*) (Oddvar Bull Tuhus, 1975). This film chronicles the bitter strike at the Sauda factory – an industrial firm owned by the giant Union Carbide – and re-creates the various stages of the dispute in the spring of 1970. The director examines the tension that builds between the unions at both local and national level, and the division between old and young workers. *Strike!* is social realism at its best; it is a protest film, where political ideas are placed in the forefront. Another example of the new sobriety is Anja Breien's *Rape* (*Voldtekt*) (1971). This film focuses on the suspect rapist rather than on the victim, and explores the legal system. The interest of the film lies in exposing the inadequacies of the legal system, thus overtly criticizing the government's policy. *Rape* is a grim-faced docu-drama, shot in black-and-white, and with long speeches delivered directly to the camera.

Anja Breien is perhaps the most prominent woman director in Norway, and the re-emergence of women directors – after a decade without any women directors in the 1960s – is one of the most important changes in

Norwegian film culture in the 1970s. Directors like Nicole Macé, Anja Breien, Vibeke Løkkeberg and Laila Mikkelsen made important features during the 1970s and early 1980s, and today Eva Isaksen and Unni Straume remain among the most interesting directors. Women characters have become the central players or the central narrative focus in films about strong adult or adolescent women who learn to cope with social injustice, patriarchal abuse and community intolerance. Women directors' criticism of patriarchal forms of discrimination within Norwegian society has become important, and their enunciation of feminist points of view is also important in the development of the new sobriety, and alternative values and forms of expression to those of Hollywood.

The Norwegian cinema of the 1970s and early 1980s was a political cinema; a cinema dealing with social problems and injustice. Most producers and directors seemed to be in agreement that they did not make films solely for the sake of profit, and this attitude was supported by the financing system. Since 1964, the Norwegian government made pre-production loan guarantees covering about 90 per cent of film costs available to those projects approved by a seven-member board, including production representatives, and this new system of support tended to boost production of 'idea films': features focusing on political ideas or social issues rather than on a 'good story'. One of the most important social issues was women's role in society, and many of the new women directors made brilliant films focusing on social outsiders, significant problems of growing up in Norwegian society or community intolerance.

The most outstanding, and most popular, of these films made by a woman director was *Wives* (*Hustruer*) (Anja Breien, 1975). This was a sparkling satire on the role of women in the modern consumer society, and the film not only became a domestic hit, but was popular in other Nordic countries. Inspired by John Cassavetes's *Husbands* (1970), Breien's film tells the story of three women, one of whom is pregnant, who go off on a three-day spree. They are old class-mates, and were once best friends. Over a period of three years, they have allowed themselves to become wholly involved in their respective husbands' lives. They meet at a school reunion party, and in a fit of sardonic humour they agree to ignore the responsibilities of job and children. Thirsty for a few days of independence they tease and harass strange men on the streets of Oslo with sexually suggestive questions, and take the boat to Copenhagen. The film has a slow, contemplative pace, with scenes shot in a cinema vérité-style on the streets of Oslo. The dialogue was improvised by the actresses, who had toured Norway with a play on a related theme, and this gave the film a spontaneous edge. The popularity of *Wives* is obvious, not only through the box-office figures, but also by the fact that Breien was encouraged to produce a sequel entitled *Wives – Ten Years After* (*Hustruer – ti år etter*) (1985). This film picks up the lives of the same characters ten years later, and the three women go on a new binge, regardless of the fact that it is Christmas time. The sequel was also a huge success in Norway. Anja Breien has recently made a third movie about the three women entitled *Wives III – Twenty Years Later* (1996).

Another important, and popular, film made by one of the new women directors was *The Betrayal (Løperjenten)* (Vibeke Løkkeberg, 1981), and the first Norwegian film since Skouen's *Nine Lives* to be commercially distributed in the United States. The setting in this feature is the coastal town of Bergen in 1948. Amidst the post-war turmoil – of rebuilding, trials of war criminals, and the cultural invasion by the USA – Kamilla and Svein grow up. Kamilla is the daughter of a bankrupt factory owner making his living as a shoemaker, and dreaming of a prosperous new life in America. Svein is a working-class child. Together, Kamilla and Svein experience homes breaking up, child abuse, and social and emotional humiliation. In this film, oppression within the family parallels oppression from state welfare institutions, and oppression at the hands of Germans and Americans. *The Betrayal* focuses upon patriarchal social policies and bourgeois family relations. The film adopts the point of view of the young girl, and gives a moving portrait of Kamilla. In recent years, Vibeke Løkkeberg has been the most controversial film-maker in Norway, directing two melodramatic period dramas: the three-hour-long *The Wild One (Hud)* (1986), and the Chekov pastiche *Sea Gulls (Måker)* (1991). Her latest feature *Where Gods are Dead (Der Gudene er døde)* (1993) was a docu-drama set in war-torn former Yugoslavia, a film that met with an extremely negative press in Norway and sparked much controversy.

The new generation of women directors made important contributions to the genre of sobriety in the 1970s, and *Wives* and *The Betrayal* became popular films and box-office hits. Still, attendance seemed to sink even lower during the 1970s, and domestic films ceased to be as popular as before. The films' political and social issues were important, but did not boost attendance figures. Most people now stayed at home when Norwegian films were screened, preferring American movies. Two significant exceptions to this were *The Pinchcliffe Grand Prix (Flåklypa Grand Prix)* (Ivo Caprino, 1975) and the popular film series about the Olsen Gang.

The most popular Norwegian feature ever was also the first, full-length animated film. *The Pinchcliffe Grand Prix* was made by the veteran Ivo Caprino, who had directed a large number of short films in which puppets play the parts of human beings, in narratives taken from Norwegian folktales. Caprino is Norway's answer to Disney, and he built his own studio, and later his own theme park outside of Lillehammer. In 1975, he turned to the artist Kjell Aukrust, and his popular stories about the village of Flåklypa (Pinchcliffe). *The Pinchcliffe Grand Prix* tells the story about a car race, and how local forces win over the international elite. The film uses a highly advanced technique, which has impressed audiences and film critics throughout the world. *The Pinchcliffe Grand Prix* has proved enormously popular in Norway, and quickly became the Norwegian feature film which has attracted the largest audiences. The film has been reissued several times, and proved more popular than ever in 1995.

Another huge success in the 1970s was the film series about the Olsen Gang. In 1968, the Danish film company Nordisk had a big hit with the comedy *The Olsen-Gang* (*Olsen-Banden*) (Erik Balling). The success of this film led to a popular film series resulting in thirteen titles between 1968 and 1981. The first of these films was imported to Norway, but met with virtually no interest. The Norwegian film company Team-Film A/S, which had produced many similar comedies since 1962, saw the potential in the first Olsen Gang film, and produced a Norwegian version of the original Danish screenplay. Norwegian director Knut Bohwim chose popular actors from the Oslo vaudeville, replaced local Danish jokes with Norwegian ones, and adapted the film to Norwegian taste, while at the same time remaining loyal to the plot of the original and providing an almost verbatim translation of dialogue. The result, *The Olsen-Gang* (*Olsen-Banden*) (1969), turned out to be a big success, and led to a series of movies. Just as in Denmark, these films became an institution in film production, and thirteen Norwegian Olsen Gang movies were made between 1969 and 1984.

All Olsen Gang films were profitable, and centre around a main plot which is basically the same in all thirteen movies. The Olsen Gang are a motley crew of petty criminals, and each film starts with gang leader Egon Olsen being released from gaol. He is met by the other gang members outside the prison gates, and each time Egon Olsen has a new and fantastic plan. Through such intricate schemes the Olsen Gang come close to carrying out a successful operation, but due to some small, freakish accident their machinations are always unveiled and Egon returns to prison.

The Norwegian producers blueprinted the first twelve Danish Olsen Gang films, and some Norwegian versions were actually shot mainly in Denmark, on the original Danish sets, thus saving both money and time. Although differences exist between the Danish and Norwegian Olsen Gang movies, as the reception in Norway of the first one suggests, the films are very much alike, both in humour and plot. Some changes were always made, and the chosen Norwegian actors brought their existing comic personae to the series. Interestingly, the reception by the critical establishment was different for each of the two countries. In Denmark the critics often loved the movies, while in Norway they were scorned and hated. They did not fit well with a climate of sobriety and political radicalism. This may conversely partly explain why these films were such enormous box-office hits. Even though they were successful in both countries, it was ten years before the Swedish variant of the series – films about the Jönsson Gang – was produced, and while the production of

Olsen Gang movies stopped in Denmark and Norway in the early 1980s, production is still going on in Sweden. In Norway, the Olsen Gang is currently a big success on video, and by 1993 more than 100,000 video cassettes had been sold.

Despite the successes of *The Pinchcliffe Grand Prix* and the Olsen Gang movies, cinema attendance sank even lower in Norway during the 1970s. At the same time audiences no longer favoured domestic production, and shied away from most Norwegian films. These politically 'heavy' features were often loved by the critics, but were box-office failures. Due to state production support, and a new policy of co-productions between Norsk Film A/S and production companies in other countries, the number of feature films rose to ninety-eight in the 1970s, but Norwegian film production met with a growing crisis in confidence. American movies dominated more than ever, and Norwegian directors and producers met the crisis by copying the American genre films that flooded the Norwegian cinemas.

NORWAY GOES INTERNATIONAL

The year 1985 proved to be one of the most interesting and significant years for Norwegian film culture. Several high-quality productions created international interest, and attitudes among producers and directors seemed to change drastically. The new slogan in the Norwegian film business was: Norway goes international.

An important landmark in the early 1980s was the film *Orion's Belt* (*Orions belte*) (Ola Solum, 1985), which signalled a new international orientation in Norwegian cinema. The production of *Orion's Belt* required more capital than the government, through the State Production Committee, was willing to give, so the producer invited a financial company to draw upon other sources. The solution was found in the shape of a limited partnership, where investors could obtain considerable tax advantages, together with the prospect of a possible profit, if the film earned more than its production costs. The success of *Orion's Belt* resulted in a new Klondike situation in Norwegian film. Foreign companies, like Goldcrest and Buena Vista, as well as Norwegian ones, used the limited partnership for a few years in order to finance projects. This led to a new situation in Norwegian film culture. On the one hand, Norwegian capital was used to partly finance American movies like *Revolution 1776* (Hugh Hudson, 1986) and *Flight of the Navigator* (Randal Kleiser, 1986). On the other hand, Norwegian films were more internationally oriented, striking examples being the black comedy *Blackout* (Erik Gustavson, 1986), set in a studio world complete with its own Chinatown, and *Turnaround* (Ola Solum, 1987), which did not even use the Norwegian language, and thus was denied state support. The social realism of the 1970s had been replaced by action-oriented movies, often intended for an international audience. Norwegian film culture vibrated with excitement, because Norway was going international!

Orion's Belt was one of the first, and the most successful both economically and artistically, of these new action dramas. This political thriller tells the story of three Norwegians on board the freighter *Sandy Hook*, who make their living from dubious assignments on the coast of Spitsbergen. By coincidence, they discover a Soviet listening-post for submarine detection in a cave. Caught red-handed by a Soviet helicopter, two of the Norwegians are killed in battle, but at the same time the helicopter is shot down. The lone survivor reaches Spitsbergen, and the listening-post proves extremely interesting for the Norwegian Secret Service. In the end the discovery has to remain top secret, for diplomatic reasons, and the lone survivor is pursued through the streets of Oslo, no doubt by agents of the Norwegian government who want to obliterate all traces of the unfortunate boat crew.

Orion's Belt was Norway's most expensive production to date, and the film was the greatest box-office hit since *The Pinchcliffe Grand Prix*. The commercial success, and international acclaim, of *Orion's Belt* immediately led to similar projects, winning support from eager investors now willing to invest money in a film culture 'going international'. Action films like *Rubicon* (*Etter Rubicon*) (Leidulv Risan, 1987), *Blücher* (Oddvar Bull Tuhus, 1988) and *The Dive* (*Dykket*) (Tristan de vere Cole, 1989), were classic race-against-time thrillers, either dealing with a NATO neutron bomb explosion in the North of Norway, the hunt for secret papers on a sunken German warship, or a diving accident on an oil rig in the North Sea. Many of these thrillers were well produced, but could have been made in almost any Western country. This new extreme action orientation and international tone, an imitation of classical Hollywood cinema, was also evident in films like *Blackout, Turnaround* or *Karachi* (Oddvar Einarson, 1989), the titles themselves telling something about the international orientation.

The most successful of these action thrillers which was produced in the years after the success of *Orion's Belt* was *Pathfinder* (*Veiviseren*) (Nils Gaup, 1987). This was the first feature film ever to be shot in the Sami language, and the film was an Academy Award nominee in 1988 for Best Foreign Language Film. *Pathfinder* is based on a twelfth-century legend, about a young boy who sees his parents and little sister slaughtered by a raiding party of Tsjudes. The boy is taken prisoner, and forced to act as a pathfinder for the evil raiders. The boy manages to trick his captors and lead them over a cliff to a violent death. This film owes much of its international fame to its close resemblance to the western genre, and is often referred to as a 'cod-western'. The director Nils Gaup has made two more features, both successes: *Shipwrecked* (*Håkon Håkonsen*) (1990) for Disney, and *Head over the Water* (*Hodet over vannet*) (1993). The first film became a huge success on the American video market, and a remake of the latter is currently being planned in the United States. Gaup is currently finishing a large internationally produced movie, *Tashunga,* starring James Caan and Christopher Lambert.

After a few years the excitement in Norwegian film production seemed to wear off, and the Klondike feeling disappeared, but many of the Norwegian films produced today are action ·films closely imitating the Hollywood genre films. Thus there have been radical changes since the cinema of sobriety in the 1970s. Audiences started to return, and once more favoured domestic films. Of course, not only action thrillers were made in the late 1980s, but these thrillers completely dominated Norwegian film culture. Norwegian producers and directors, helped by the state support system, resurrected the Hollywood genres in Norway, and, like Tancred Ibsen in the late 1930s, met with new acclaim when the films looked to Hollywood for inspiration.

Exceptions in this age of thrillers and black comedies were films like *X* (Oddvar Einarson, 1986) and *To a Stranger* (*Til en ukjent*) (Unni Straume, 1990). *X,* which won a Silver Lion award at Venice in 1986, is the story of the relationship between a taciturn art photographer and a 14-year-old homeless girl in Oslo. In a slow rhythm, in long takes, a strange relationship and a social situation is explored. Where Einarson was inspired by Antonioni, woman director Unni Straume was more inspired by Tarkovskij or Wenders. *To a Stranger* is a beautiful cinematic poem about a young woman who is studying in Oslo, but one day decides to hitch-hike back to her childhood home in the west of Norway. She gets a ride with an elderly composer, and during their journey, past experiences become intertwined with those of the present. At the opposite extreme of the spectrum from *Orion's Belt,* these slow, poetic visions continue to use international models in a new way. Norwegian cinema is perhaps more international today than ever before, even though the models are as different as Antonioni or classical Hollywood cinema.

Even if Norwegian film culture and production has been internationalized in recent years, film production is still a national project, and private investors rely on government support. Today, all Norwegian full-length films receive a subsidy from the state, currently equivalent to 55 per cent of the gross box-office takings. This subsidy continues to be paid until the authorized production costs have been recovered by means of film rental income and the subsidy. In the case of films designated as suitable for children under ten years of age, the subsidy is calculated at 100 per cent.

Most Norwegian feature films today are produced with the aid of governmental support, which is granted in one of two ways. First, by the state, in the form of the Norwegian Film Institute's Department of Production and International Relations, after the application has been considered by the film advisory officer (replacing the five-member

National Film Production Committee in 1992). Second, the money can be granted automatically within the framework of Norsk Film A/S, the independent, government-owned production company.

As of the mid-1990s, Norwegian film production consists of between seven and eight feature films per year. Since the mid-1980s, and the revitalization of Norwegian film production due to the internationalization of film output, these features acquire a very respectable share of the box-office. Unlike the 'golden age' of the 1950s, when eighteen of the thirty most popular features shown to Norwegian audiences were domestic films, but most Norwegian films still do very well with home audiences.

The Norwegian peculiarity of the municipal system is the same today as before. Revisions of the 1913 Cinema Theatres' Act were attempted throughout the 1960s and 1970s, but only after Norway suffered a 'video nasties shock' in 1980 were measures undertaken to remedy current legislation. In 1987 the new Film and Video Act was passed in Parliament by a two-thirds majority, and went into effect on 1 January 1988. This Act is a revision of the Act of 1913, and central censorship is maintained for public screenings of film and video. The Act also requires everyone who 'exhibits, rents or sells video tapes commercially to consumers' to acquire a licence from the municipal council. The government has also imposed a tax on video cassettes, and the money from this tax is to be used for cinema purposes.

In these post-television times, the Norwegian municipalities no longer earn so much money from cinemas as before, and they have even been willing to foot the bill for keeping their 200 cinemas operating, for the one important reason that the municipalities once took over the cinemas: community service and cultural benefit. In 1988, 92 per cent of municipal cinemas were operating in the red, with total deficits of approximately NOK 49 million. In recent years this situation has somewhat improved as people seem to visit cinemas more often, but running a cinema is no longer as profitable as it once was in Norway.

Both film production, through state support, and the cinemas, through the municipal system, are today a national project in Norway. Municipalities and central government agree that it is important to support a domestic film culture as a way to ward off the international culture industry. Nationality seems to be under siege, however. Film production is diverse, but many films today look just like American thrillers. Norwegian landscapes continue to be romanticized in many recent films, among them the two Hamsun adaptations *Wanderers* (*Landstrykere*) (Ola Solum, 1989) and *The Telegraphist* (*Telegrafisten*) (Erik Gustavson, 1993), or Liv Ullmann's gigantic adaptation of Undset's novel, *Kristin Lavransdatter* (1995). The most popular retail video cassette is a portrait of the Norwegian King Olav V, who died in 1991. National icons and scenery still play an important role in Norwegian film production.

The situation in the mid-1990s is in many ways similar to the late 1930s, when the horizon of anticipation that Norwegian audiences have created for domestic films is based on previous encounters with Hollywood cinema. Films like *X* or *To a Stranger* point to the diversity of film production, but the American influence is obvious. Today, both thrillers imitating the dominant Hollywood generic modes and modernist film journeys about the tragedy of modern existence are produced in Norway.

Norway no longer goes *only* international, like in the mid-1980s, but continues forward with one eye on the past, to the cinematic roots of the national breakthrough of the 1920s.

APPENDIX

Feature film production in Norway

1906–1919: 16
1920–1929: 26
1930–1939: 26
1940–1949: 37
1950–1959: 75
1960–1969: 63
1970–1979: 98
1980–1989: 94

Feature-length documentaries in Norway, with a nationwide distribution

1920–1929: 9
1930–1939: 13 (including workers' films)
1940–1949: 5
1950–1959: 18
1960–1969: 6
1970–1979: 8
1980–1989: 3

SELECT BIBLIOGRAPHY

The following is a short list of works on Norwegian cinema published in the English language. Only one history of Norwegian cinema exists in the Norwegian language, Sigurd Evensmo's *Det Store Tivoli*, originally published in 1967, and reissued in 1992. Several book-length studies about specific directors have been published in recent years, and specific studies, statistics and general updates are covered by a number of Norwegian film journals: *Film & Kino, Z , Rush-Print* and *Levende Bilder.* In 1995, the Norwegian Film Institute's filmography *Filmen i Norge* was published.

Cowie, Peter, *Scandinavian Cinema*, The Tantivy Press, London 1992.

Gripsrud, Jostein and Skretting, Kathrine (eds), *History of Moving Images: Reports from a Norwegian Project*, Levende Bilder 1/94, The Research Council of Norway, Oslo 1994.

Kindem, Gorham A., 'Norway's new generation of women directors: Anja Breien, Vibeke Løkkeberg, and Laila Mikkelsen', *Journal of Film and Video*, vol. 39, no. 4, Fall 1987.

Myrstad, Anne Marit, 'National romanticism and Norwegian silent cinema', in Richard Dyer and Ginette Vincendeau (eds): *Popular European Cinema*, Routledge, London and New York 1992.

Sørenssen, Bjørn, 'The voice of reconstruction: the Norwegian post-war newsreel as history of a mentality', in Helge Rønning and Knut Lundby (eds): *Media and Communication – Readings in Methodology, History and Culture*, Norwegian University Press, Oslo 1991.

Sørenssen, Bjørn, ' "I have a plan!" The Olsen Gang captures Denmark and Norway: negotiating the popular culture gap', *The Velvet Light Trap*, no. 34, Fall 1994.

Chapter 6

Sweden

Tytti Soila

The new medium of film came to Sweden from the south. The first living pictures were shown at the industrial exhibition in Malmö in the summer of 1896. The following year, during Allmänna konst- och industriutställningen (the General Art and Industrial Exhibition) in Stockholm, cinematographer Lumière filmed King Oscar II opening the exhibition. As the custom at the time prescribed, the film footage was developed instantly and that very night the King saw himself immortalized through living images, which is reported to have amused His Majesty a great deal. It seems that the Royal House's favoured opinion of film would last: one of the reigning King's sons, Prince William, would go on to become a professional documentary film-maker.

That same summer the first 'fiction films' were made; a drunken brawl at Djurgården (*Komische Begegnung im Tiergarten zu Stockholm*) and another *A Brawl in Old Stockholm* (*Slagsmål i Gamla Stockholm*) which as the name suggests depicted a scuffle in the Main Square in Stockholm's Old Town. *Komische Begegnung* was never shown in Sweden – but it is somewhat ironic that brawls and drunkenness were chosen as the first topics to be filmed in this country which would react so fiercely against 'violence entertainment' barely a hundred years later.

During the summer of 1897 regular screenings were organized at several venues in the capital, but it was not until April 1904 that a more permanent cinema was opened in Stockholm, the Blanchs Movie Theatre. By that time Gothenburg had already had the first permanent cinema for two years – Kinematografen in the Gothenburg Arcades (later renamed Alhambra) – and during this period the number of cinemas in Gothenburg had increased to eleven. This large port on the Swedish west coast had good communications and connections to England and thereby gained easy access to new repertory.

The spread of the living image was incidentally handled by a somewhat unexpected party. The very early film debate (which among other things led to the quick establishment of government agency for film censorship) has obscured the historical fact that the early film shows – which functioned through travelling screenings – were associated at the beginning with the popular movements and the Free Church projects. Rune Waldekranz has shown that it was in reality these screenings which to a large extent provided the audience in the countryside with living pictures. He has studied newspaper advertisements during the period 1896 to 1908 and has found that as many as 23.6 per cent of the shows took place in the meeting halls of the Good Templars. It is perhaps surprising that the Free Churches' share of screenings thus amounted to almost 11 per cent, and the workers' associations share amounted to a little over 6 per cent during this period.

The Free Churches had for decades been showing sciopticon images (slides) at their meetings, and it should therefore perhaps not come as a surprise that the new living images were thought to be a natural development of these. A change in attitude took place, however, when the film business tended towards larger industrialization in the early 1900s. Because of this, permanent cinemas were established throughout the country, and to compete with the theatre as an institution, the film shows came to be officially called 'movie theatres' (Biograf-Teater). At this time the doors of the Free Churches were closed – the word 'theatre' referred to the very kind of frivolity no serious Protestant wished to be associated with.

This move took place at approximately the same time as the content of the repertory passed from news and documentary films to more sensation-seeking depictions of crime and erotics in fiction films that were imported from abroad – often from neighbouring Denmark. A heated debate about the detrimental effects of the film shows arose and the need for censorship was voiced at public opinion meetings, in newspaper articles and in parliamentary debates. The responsible circles of society – mainly the members of the Swedish Pedagogical Society – initiated an offensive with the aim of suppressing the corrupting content on offer at the cinemas. The starting point of the debate was concern about the negative influence that the living images were assumed to have on children – and on that section of the viewing public who were regarded as 'insecure' in their tastes. The debate thus came to have a demagogical aspect and to be on the safe side one also frequently employed medical experts to verify one's claims.

According to Jan Olsson, the nucleus of the debate on censorship in Sweden was formed by the dual impression of the medium that one had acquired early on: thus on the one hand you would find a recognition and appreciation of the potential inherent in the documentary ability of the filmic image. It was widely believed that what were called 'nature images' were valuable in the service of the knowledge-seeking of both science and education. These films were labelled 'authentic' as opposed to 'construed images', that is, contrived fiction. Behind the alarmingly avid interest in the latter products were 'man's desire to perceive something' – i.e. base sensation-craving and a wish to be entertained – and it was this characteristic/quality that it was believed should be checked.

As opposed to the American film industry for example, the Swedish cinema business appears to have expedited the establishment of film censorship. When the debate had raged for a few years and *Nordisk Filmtidning* (*Nordic Film Magazine*) – the film business's first publication in the country, founded in 1909 – initiated a petition demanding the founding of a state-run national censorship agency, some discord seems to have prevailed as to the actual location of the censorship agency. The capital was suggested as a possible venue, while Svenska Filmförbundet (the Swedish Film Association) suggested Malmö instead – Malmö was the city in which the currently most productive companies, Svenska Bio and Frans Lundberg, were based.

There was an obvious desire to eradicate the more sensationalist films that had emerged and through this cleansweep gain the interest of new audience groups as an explanation for the business attitude on this issue. At this stage the industry did not have the means to control the content of film through internal censorship as was the case in Hollywood. The majority of cinema owners were as yet not organized (Sveriges Biografägares Förbund (Sweden's Movie Theatre Owner Association) was founded in 1915) and the market had reached saturation point, which in turn forced the competing companies to supply increasingly witty and more spectacular films. Domestic production was small compared to the multitude of imported film, and competition was fierce. To attract new target groups (i.e. a more discerning and wealthy audience) the established cinema owners were keen to make film shows more socially acceptable.

Long before the business began turning the critical trend to its advantage, however, various groups had ranged themselves against the corrupting effects of the 'construed' images. In Gothenburg in 1905, for instance, a meeting had been arranged – a meeting which resulted in demands for tighter supervision of the cinema by the police authorities. This was subsequently realized, and in cities such as Stockholm, a set of rules was issued. The local measures did not satisfy public opinion for very long, however, especially since the edicts were not always followed to the letter of the law. Three years later yet another meeting was held where the initiators demanded a greater adherence to the rules that existed for the censoring of film. Once again the Swedish Pedagogical Society stood up for the censorship advocates and commenced a systematic supervision of the cinema showings in Stockholm – something which, as Jan Olsson points out, latter-day research has benefited from. At the same time connections were formed with 'serious' cinema owners in order to establish an exemplary cinema in the city.

These 'storms of opinion' in themselves have been relatively characteristic of Swedish society and have to do with their specific connection
to the extensive popular movements at the turn of the century: the
revivalist, temperance and labour movements. In 1920 approximately a
quarter of all adult citizens were members of either one of these three
movements, so that most of the population had indirect connections to
them. All the movements worked to radically change society: freedom
of congregation, freedom of speech and social reform were some of the
slogans. The actual ideology behind these watchwords was somewhat
different, however: common to the popular movements in Sweden was an
ambition to rouse, to organize and to remould people and to change their
way of living. Here one can probably find the roots of the deeply set social
reformatory and socially educating politics in Sweden and – among others
– the debate that has continuously flared up over the decades regarding
the content and influence of the media. It is also conceivable that the
aforementioned connection between the popular movements and the film
medium has caused the vigorous and critical opinion that now exists in
Sweden.

As a result of the joint efforts of the industry and public opinion, the
provisions regarding mandatory examination of film came into effect
on 1 December 1911. Sweden thus became one of the first nations in
the world to order a state-operated preliminary examination of all film
intended for public showing. The authority came to be named Statens
Biografbyrå (the National Board of Film Censors), and was located in
Stockholm. Its job was to classify films into three categories: universal,
adults only and prohibited. If a producer disagreed with a category he
could appeal to the government. The first censors to be appointed were
Marie-Louise Gagner, an assistant mistress at a training college (who had
distinguished herself as one of the most active participants in the preceding
debate), Dr Jacob Billström, who in his capacity of psychiatrist had
reported several cases of 'media damaged' children, and Walter Ferell,
Ph.D. and chairman of the Board.

The censors exercised their rights diligently by both cutting the films
and by totally banning them. Here a certain importer of film, N. P. Nilsson
– one of the first and most influential in the industry – seems to have
been a particular victim and adversary of the censors. In the debate, the
Danish films – especially the Danish melodramas produced mainly by
Nordisk Film Kompagni – came to stand as a sort of genre description
of a type of film that was demoralizing and dangerous to watch. N. P.
Nilsson was one of the largest importers of this product. No one appears
to have escaped the watchful eye of the censors and it is interesting to
note that Victor Sjöström, for instance, began his later world-famous
career by having his first film *The Head Gardener* (*Trädgårdsmästaren*)
(1912) totally banned.

THE CONDITIONS OF THE FILM INDUSTRY

When considering the development of the film industry in Sweden at the beginning of the century it is important to realize that at the time the country was very poor and underdeveloped. Up until the First World War, Sweden was – after Finland and Italy – the most agrarian country in Western Europe, and for many decades the population had been bled dry by emigration, mainly to the USA. The emigration wave, which had peaked in the years between 1880 and 1893, did not subside for Sweden until after 1930 with the advent of the worldwide depression. In 1910 an emigration inquiry was set up, since the authorities were anxious to look into the causes behind this emigration. In a report of 1913 the investigator writes that 'Sweden took twenty years too long in ... expanding . .. the railways and thirty years too long in passing universal suffrage.'[1]

Strictly speaking, the wages of the skilled professional industrial workers in Sweden had increased continuously since the 1860s and had actually doubled up to 1907. This was not the case with large segments of the working population in the provinces, however. During the period between 1907 and 1909 the real value of wages began to generally decrease, which naturally enough led to conflicts in the labour market. In June 1909 the Swedish Employers' Association (SAF) initiated an extensive lock-out offensive with a general strike as the consequence. The strike did not have the desired effect, however: the labour organizations were forced to urge their members to return to their jobs – something which caused bitterness among the workers and weakened the unions.

This decline at the end of the 1910s was temporary, however, and the wage situation improved automatically, due to the market upswing. Certain social reforms were discussed, and in Parliament the liberals and social democrats made up a broad political coalition focusing on social reform and suffrage. The State Pension law of 1913, for instance, laid the foundation for a modern pension system. The German labour insurance and labour protection legislation was viewed as an ideal model and as a result of the cooperation the eight-hour working day was introduced in 1919. The demands for universal suffrage were finally forced through in the winter of 1918–19 and gained legal status in 1921 – somewhat later than in many other countries.

In other words, the democratic breakthrough in Sweden did not occur until the end of 1918, in the shadow of the Russian Revolution – and more so still through Germany's defeat in the First World War. The tension between the popular movements' broad influence on the one hand and the ageing centralized state machinery on the other came to stand as the foundation for the particular kind of democracy which was to dominate Sweden in time. Contrary to what has often been claimed, it was not primarily the popular movements that accomplished democracy in Sweden, but the ultimate path-maker for the Swedish democracy was rather the Russian and German revolutions and the armies of the Western powers who overthrew the German empire. In this context many of the leaders of the major companies were able to see the risks involved in the unstable conditions in the country – in other words, the possibility of a revolution – and played an active pro-democratic part in the final stages of the debate.

Simultaneously with the market downswing after the general strike in 1909, the Swedish film industry had also gone through its first economic crisis – but at the time a period of stabilization had also been initiated. Several causes of the crisis have been cited, among others the censorship debate, which had made the possibly detrimental effects of the film medium known to the public, resulting in a certain suspicion of it. In several areas there was also, as mentioned above, an over-abundance of cinemas. One immediate cause of the decline was of course the fact that people had less money to spend on entertainment during the general recession.

Another reason for the decline in the cinema business may have been the very content of the film screenings and their decreasing attraction. The randomly filmed scenes in 'nature images', with scattered and stereotypical themes from countryside and city, no longer attracted an audience to the same extent that it had when the medium was fresh, while the ongoing debate cast suspicion on the 'construed' films. Public interest in the latter was sufficiently great, however, to validate an increase of imported fiction films. Once their apparent success had registered, there was an increasing move to produce them in Sweden.

The city of Malmö, which is situated opposite Copenhagen across the Sound, had seemed on its way to becoming the nation's film capital during the early years, as Jan Olsson points out in his monograph on Frans Lundberg, an enterprising pioneer and film producer based in Malmö. Influences from the opposite side of the Sound played a major role in the fact that a businessman like Lundberg ventured to enact theatrical scenes in front of a movie camera. Lundberg had plenty of connections with Copenhagen and the Danish melodramas came to stand as role models when he initiated his ambitious productions. At this stage these were still made in temporary locations at the summer theatres and used mainly amateur actors. However, the success was significant enough to warrant immediate competition as others sought to establish themselves in the market.

In the city of Kristianstad in southern Sweden the first and – as it turned out – oldest Swedish film company, Svenska Biografteatern, was founded in 1907. Svenska Biografteatern's productions were films with sound, films where famous actors like Rosa Grünberg and Carl Barcklind sang and danced short pieces from operas or operettas. The singing and music were recorded on phonograph cylinders which were synchronized with the moving images. Such short films had been made as early as 1903 through

the agency of a certain engineer, Mortimer Peterson, the son of Numa
Peterson, the Stockholm camera shop proprietor who first held the conces-
sion on Lumière's cinematograph in Sweden, and who managed the first
permanent screenings in Stockholm.

From Kristianstad domestic films were distributed throughout Sweden.
The founders of Svenska Biografteatern – henceforth Svenska Bio –
included two bankers, a lawyer, a pharmacist and the promoter himself,
cinema owner Nils Hansson Nylander. The company established itself
with a capital stock of 150,000 SEK and a chain of nineteen cinemas
nationwide. The founders' concept was thus to supply their own theatres
with films made by the company. For this purpose, photographer Robert
Olsson was employed to travel around making documentary films, and
shortly thereafter the first fiction films were put into production.

In 1909 the Gothenburg citizen Charles Magnusson was hired as a
producer at Svenska Bio and that summer three short features were made:
The People of Värmland (*Värmlänningarna*), *The Wedding at Ulfåsa*
(*Bröllopet på Ulfåsa*) and *Tales of Ensign Ståhl* (*Fänrik Ståhls sägner*).
The first two films were the kind of rural melodramas often performed
by the travelling theatre companies and the amateur theatrical societies,
from which most of the early film actors were recruited: Georg Dalunde
and Ellen Ströbäck played the leading roles in *Värmlänningarna*. *Fänrik
Ståhls sägner* in its turn, was based on the epic story by the Finnish national
poet Johan Ludvig Runeberg and depicts the Swedo-Russian war. The
attempts at lavish scenes which the film displays are embryos of the ambition that would characterize the later work of Svenska Bio.

Charles Magnusson had big plans for his company and began to carry
them out. He soon realized that an important condition for expansion in
the film industry was to move to the capital, which he did in 1911. His
competitor Frans Lundberg employed Danish actors and thus the
tarnished reputation of the Danish films could be used in the competition
by contrasting them with the pure Swedish products. Stockholm was from
a distribution point of view located more centrally – and another consideration must have been the fact that the new censorship agency was
established in the capital. One other factor may have been the importance
of being able to attract the more renowned actors of the capital, even if
many were still prevented from taking part in film productions through
their contracts with the theatres concerned.

After moving to Stockholm, Svenska Bio built Sweden's first real film
studio on Lidingö, one of the islands surrounding the capital. Magnusson
separated production and administration by personally managing the business from his office on Kungsgatan 24, while directors employed for this
purpose – primarily Victor Sjöström and Mauritz Stiller – were put in
charge of production. The third director at Svenska Bio, Georg af
Klercker, was soon to leave the company to engage in a short but brilliant

career working for Gothenburg producer Hasselblad. Since the decision-making process in production and artistically related matters was at least nominally divided among several people within Svenska Bio (Svensk Filmindustri), one avoided the concentration of tastes and power which was the case within Finnish Suomi-Filmi, for instance.

Following the move from Kristianstad, Magnusson immediately directed production towards an international market. That Magnusson did plan for the foreign market from the very start in the 1910s is proven by several stages of his planning. Svenska Bio's feature film production during 1913–17 amounted to over a hundred films, certainly short, but none-theless fiction films. During this period the popularly oriented rural melodramas of the touring theatre companies were set aside and more fashionable topics were filmed from scripts ordered from Denmark. The company also employed international personnel who could contribute new ideas: for example, when Svenska Bio hired its subsequent directors all were foreigners, among them yet another Finn, Konrad Tallroth.

The role model for feature film production was thus the melodramas which took place in upper-class settings that were produced by the Danish companies. These were the very films that had been severely criticized during the censorship debate, but their popularity was indisputable – especially abroad. And, as mentioned above, it was towards this market that Magnusson directed his ambitions. Since Frans Lundberg had left the industry, in part because of the persecution of the censors, Pathé Frères was the only serious competitor for Svenska Bio. Svenska Bio obviously wanted to avoid resource-wasting competition and instead endeavoured to close an agreement of cooperation with the French company, which was also accomplished.

The Swedes with their grand plans knew how to use the large, estab-lished distribution network of Pathé Frères. Through their partners the employees of Svenska Bio also got the opportunity to make study visits to the continental studios where they acquired new knowledge about film production. Stiller, and in particular Sjöström, were experienced theatre men when they were employed by Magnusson, but their knowledge of film production was minimal at this time and improvement was essential. Svenska Bio's interest in the foreign market is also evident in their sending a complete production team (headed by new photographer Julius Jaenzon) to Europe. Their mission was to shoot suitable environments which were later to be edited into films, something which illustrates Magnusson's conscious intention to use this footage to create a sense of identity with audiences in different countries – something that might possibly increase the attraction of Swedish films in the international market.

It may appear cynical to suggest that the outbreak of war in 1914 was convenient for Svenska Bio – but it was. The war created favourable conditions for the company in a country that succeeded in staying out of any military interventions. The war caused a scarcity of film in the countries involved: they not only encountered problems with production personnel and facilities, but they also ran out of raw materials. The Swedes were also favoured politically by the fact that their competitor Denmark's previously popular films were rejected by the Allies: Denmark had close business connections with Germany and this was not approved of by France and Britain. Through the cooperation with Pathé, demands could be met quickly and the increased turnover enabled other film workers besides the directors to practise skills without potential mistakes having fatal consequences for their careers.

Thus the period before and during the First World War was one of continuous growth and copying from Danish sensationalist melodramas – this in spite of having previously criticized the competitor Lundberg for making them. When the market ran into difficulties shortly after the end of the war, the resources and professional know-how of Svenska Bio were such that the step into a new phase was possible. The film industry was quick to disassociate itself from melodrama production and ventured into new thematic territories: copying was no longer of interest, but the ambition was to break new ground not only on a narrative level but – as would become apparent – stylistically as well. A successful formula was to be found in topics that would appear familiar to the domestic audience, but which were conceived as exotic by the international audience. Domestically, recognition was an important part of the experience, while abroad there was an apparent need for confirmation of foreigners' 'otherness'.

This strategy partly involved the filming of a number of known and appreciated literary works written by Nordic authors: among them August Strindberg's popular play *The People of Hemsö* (*Hemsöborna*) (1919), *Sången om den eldröda blomman* (Stiller, 1919) – based on the Finnish sensationalist novel by Johannes Linnankoski – and many others. According to Gösta Werner it was the success of Ibsen's *Terje Vigen* (Sjöström, 1917) that had shown Magnusson and his associates the way to success. This film also established the term 'literary cinema' in Sweden. By connecting the feature film with appreciated works of fiction, it was obviously the intention to raise the low status of the medium. Another link in this project towards better quality and thereby increasing esteem was that the pace of production at Svenska Bio was radically reduced. Instead, larger sums were invested in separate productions and in 1917 – which can be considered as the first year of the new policy – only five films were produced, which was one-fifth of the production numbers of the preceding years.

OTHER PRODUCERS AND PRODUCTIONS

Although Svenska Bio was not the only film company in the country, it really had only one serious domestic competitor by the middle of the decade, namely Hasselblad in Gothenburg. Hasselblad had hired director Georg af Klercker who had left Svenska Bio some years before. For three years he directed a large number of melodramas which, due to their excellent quality may have been one of the contributing factors to the fortunate change of repertory policy at Svenska Bio, but they may quite simply have felt forced to venture into new territories. Klercker's career was short-lived at Hasselblad as well, however. He was hired in the summer of 1915 when he successfully directed four films, this number increasing to fourteen feature films the following summer. The company had by then provided him with more resources and, among other things, built a new studio.

Klercker has recently been rediscovered by film researchers and is now considered to be a visual genius. Leif Furhammar claims that despite Klercker's cooperating with all four of Hasselblad's feature film photographers, it is possible to trace a stylistic similitude in all his films. Nearly all of Klercker's Hasselblad films are preserved intact today and, according to Furhammar, it is possible to witness his ability to transform 'incredible complications of crime and passion into charged dynamic and strangely moving image operas'.[2]

If the summer of 1916 was prolific, it was also intense, and in the winter of 1916–17 Klercker was admitted to a sanatorium. The following summer his career ended when Hasselblad decided – nine completed films notwithstanding – not to renew his contract. The most immediate reason would have been the advantageous merger with a number of other companies that Hasselblad was planning. It has also been suggested that Klercker, who was an out-and-out melodrama director, lacked the ability to follow the new realistic trend which was gaining force in the country through Svenska Bio's productions.

Hasselblad did not intend to withdraw from competition with Svenska Bio, but felt that they could not continue on their own. Because of this the formation of one major company was initiated involving five other competing companies – among them Svenska Bio's former partner Pathé Frères. Thus a new film company, Filmindustri Inc Skandia, was formed in 1918. Skandia was to start out as a major company with millions (SEK) in capital stock, and a chain of some twenty cinemas. Nils Bouveng, former head of Hasselblad, was appointed as head of the new company.

Skandia introduced a number of new directors who were to remain in the industry for many years. One of them, John Brunius, directed the successful film *Synnöve Solbakken* (1919) – which will be discussed in more detail below. Brunius was a trained actor and had made his directorial debut the preceding year with the comedy *Puss in Boots* (*Mästerkatten i stövlar*) (1918) with the – already – unforgettable Gösta Ekman playing the lead role. Yet another actor who was to make his name as a film director was the young Rune Carlsten.

As early as 1915 Lars Björck, one of the founding members of Svenska Bio, had left the company and founded Skandinavisk Filmcentral (Scandinavian Film Central). Björck's two other brothers were also involved in the film industry and supported him against the competitors so that Skandinavisk Filmcentral ventured into film production in 1919. At the end of the 1910s there where thus three fully integrated production companies in the country – apparently too many for economic survival in a small country like Sweden. Only a year after its inception Skandia merged with Svenska Bio in a giant corporation which now had a capital stock of 35 million SEK and two acting presidents, Charles Magnusson and Nils Bouveng. The new company was named AB Svensk Filmindustri (Swedish Film Industry Inc). Besides its massive capital stock the company owned seventy cinemas and other real estate, as well as two production studios: one in Råsunda outside Stockholm and one in Långängen in Gothenburg – and before long it acquired another studio in Denmark.

Skandinavisk Film Central in their turn experienced a series of failures in the serious genre; for example, they began a grand production of Selma Lagerlöf's novel *The Legend of Gösta Berling* (*Gösta Berlings saga*), but failed to complete the project. Through their subsidiary Palladium they also invested in comedies, with, among others, Danish film director Lau Lauritzen. Skandinavisk Film Central sold Palladium to Denmark, however – unfortunately immediately before Lauritzen's comedies, with the popular companions Fyrtornet and Bigvognen, won international success. In December 1921 Skandinavisk Film Central filed its petition for bankruptcy. Not surprisingly, large amounts of its assets went to Svensk Filmindustri.

THE EBB AND FLOW OF CRISES

The years 1919 to 1920 saw the Swedish film industry at its peak. Around that time several artistically appreciated films premièred, among them *Ingmarssönerna* (*Sjöström*), *Herr Arnes pengar* (Stiller), *Synnöve Solbakken* (Brunius), *Dunungen* (Hedquist), *Klostret i Sendomir* (Sjöström), *Prästänkan* (Dreyer), *Erotikon* (Stiller) – and in the New Year of 1921 one of the finest films, with superb photography by Julius Jaenzon, namely *Phantom Carriage* (*Körkarlen*) by Victor Sjöström, premièred at the Röda Kvarn cinema. At the same time, however, severe problems began for the production giant in all areas, problems which Leif Furhammar ascribes to lack of foresight. However, conditions in society as a whole were not especially favourable either.

At the end of the First World War the social conditions and the standard of living for people in Sweden were still lower than in comparable countries in the West. The wages were relatively speaking lower, and the standard of housing and food was considerably reduced. Side by side with the old destitute conditions in the farming communities a new privation had been created through industrial and urban growth. The decade began with a profound depression that sent thousands of workers into unemployment: the dramatic structural transformation which had been embarked upon at this stage in the export industries meant a rationalization and mechanization which to begin with involved nothing but trouble for the individual worker. The eight-hour-day law had been passed in 1919 and initially meant additional cost for production. Agriculture was exposed to serious competition from outside as well and investments in it were reduced. In January 1922 the number of unemployed amounted to 163,000 people – the highest number ever measured in Sweden thus far. The people had narrow means to live by and this had its consequences in the film business as well: in 1920 the Stockholm cinemas had audiences of eight million; three years later this number had decreased by about a quarter.

In the early 1920s, furthermore, radio had come to Sweden. Thousands of families gathered round the machine which offered programmes led by Sven Jerring for the youngest members of the family. The new medium was one of the factors that had negative repercussions for the film industry, although the importance of radio should not be overestimated. To the dismay of the cinema business the entertainment tax that had been introduced as a temporary emergency measure to raise the incomes of the communities during the war remained. It meant that at least 10 per cent of every ticket sold went to the state treasury.

In the mid-1920s 70 per cent of all films shown in Sweden were American and domestic film had only one-third of the market. The increasingly popular American film was marketed in a particularly aggressive manner by the Americans' own distribution agencies. Despite this marketing they succeeded in keeping film rates high, which helped to further drain the cinemas' resources. The trend persisted and as late as the Second World War, when the American share of the market shrank by 15 per cent, the Swedes had to pay the highest rate ever for *Gone with the Wind*. The unrest in the cinema business also created differences of opinion in the owners' ranks which led to the split of Sveriges Biografägares Förbund: in 1924 Svenska Biografernas Förening (The Swedish Movie Theatre Society) was formed.

Towards the end of the 1920s things began to look brighter for the Swedes, however: only now did rationalization in the engineering industry begin to pay off, and an upswing, supported, for example, by such Swedish inventions as the separator and the ball-bearing, led to an expansion that created employment for more people. During the 1920s the expression 'Sweden's Second Period of Greatness' came into use and the national perspective became more optimistic and self-assured. In the papers one could read things like: 'Our matches, ball-bearings, telephones and separators carry the Swedish name on the wings of fame.'[3] Unemployment was considerably reduced and the standard of living increased among the Swedes, with agriculture being the exception as it had not managed to keep up with the increase in prosperity. In 1927 Assar Gabrielsson and Gustaf Larsson delivered the first Volvo and Ivar Kreuger built his financial empire. Through foreign subsidiaries Kreuger and his company – Svenska Tändsticksbolaget (Swedish Match) – came to control major parts of the world's match production. His influence was great everywhere in the Swedish economy – and not least in the Swedish film industry.

Through this general upswing the cinema market stabilized as well and the shrinking number of visitors to the cinemas began to slowly climb. The situation in the major company Svensk Filmindustri deteriorated, however, and at times bankruptcy was considered – or at the very least a shut-down of production activities. In 1925, the management of Svensk Filmindustri had felt forced to reduce the capital stock by as much as 80 per cent.

After this drastic measure, however, Ivar Kreuger was willing to invest another 3 million SEK in the business – something which ultimately gave him a fair amount of control over the company. Three years later shut-down nevertheless seemed inevitable. Reduced audiences and cut price tickets had by the mid-1920s reduced the income sources by more than one-third. The company had invested in the building of large cinemas which were now unprofitable and the three studios that were still owned by Svensk Filmindustri – one of which was in Denmark – stood partly empty, draining resources at a time when production costs were steadily increasing.

At the same time that the market experienced a downswing in Sweden, the demands for Swedish film abroad lessened, as national film production in the countries that had taken part in the war had resumed. The Swedes were forced not only to compete with the up-and-coming European cinema but also with the practically invincible American film. The country faced increasing competition on all sides. A still unsolved riddle is how the president of Svensk Filmindustri Charles Magnusson came to relinquish control – and to lose faith in a company which was largely his own creation. An important factor may have been that the decision-making process in the company had been changed. Not the least thanks to Kreuger's manoeuvres, the bankers had gained great influence and now controlled the company through their demands for profitability and larger gains. Perhaps Magnusson felt that nothing remained of his earlier ambitions for high cultural values. The most renowned of Svensk Filmindustri's directors, Sjöström and Stiller both wanted to leave the company, and Leif Furhammar claims that the constant interference of the bankers in the production decisions was one of the reasons for this. Perhaps Magnusson felt that nothing would be left of his beloved company – and thus he sold his complete stock in 1929.

Plate 6.1 Film reproduces other arts *Synnöve Solbakken* (Brunius, 1919)

Plate 6.2 The spirit of community *Söder om Landsvägen* (Wahlberg, 1936)

Plate 6.3 The rhetorics of freedom and preparedness *Rid i natt!* (Molander, 1942)

Plate 6.4 A rural idyll memorized *Driver dagg faller regn* (Edgren, 1946)

Plate 6.5 Realism and social consciousness *Ungdom i fara* (Holmgren, 1947)

Plate 6.6 Modernity and the inhabitants of the folk home *Åsa-Nisse på semester* (Frisk, 1954)

Plate 6.7 The charm of ordinariness *Sjunde himmelen* (Ekman, 1956)

Plate 6.8 The new generation of the 1960s *Elvira Madigan* (Widerberg, 1967)

Plate 6.9 The feminist scope *Hjälten* (Fagerström-Olsson, 1990)

Plate 6.10 The fathers restored *Jägarna* (Sundvall, 1996)

STYLE AND THE LITERARY CINEMA

The Swedish silent film was characterized during the 'golden age' by realism expressed in films where man was described as an integral part of nature, linked to the environment of his childhood. Changes in weather and seasons, views of mountains and plains, images of roaring rivers and swaying birch groves were actively linked to the description of characters and associated with their fate. Its strength was drama, emphasized by the visual expression in films that derived much of their power from the photographers' know-how. Interesting and paradoxical however is that this visual dramatic force was based on known literary works.

An outstandingly popular author whose works were made into films in the 1910s and 1920s was Selma Lagerlöf. Nobel laureate in literature and herself an early film enthusiast, her name guaranteed the sought-after cultural context for the films. Svenska Bio had acquired the film rights to all of Lagerlöf's novels prior to 1919. From her substantial production of seventy-seven novels and short stories many were filmed in the period before the arrival of the sound film. Her large novel series *Jerusalem* was among the first that Svenska Bio took on. Director Mauritz Stiller went to Dalecarlia to present his script suggestion to her – even though it was eventually Victor Sjöström who directed the two films that the project resulted in: *Ingmarssönerna* and *Karin Ingmarsdotter*, which premièred in 1919 and 1920 respectively.

The relationship between Svenska Bio and Selma Lagerlöf is interesting, because it eventually led to a harsh debate over film ontology and its relation to its original material. Initially, film *aficionado* Lagerlöf was pleased with *Herr Arnes pengar* (Stiller, 1919), for example, obviously because its plot followed the novel word for word. Gösta Werner claims that Stiller later regretted preserving the long-winded intertitles copied from the novel. In his opinion the literary digressions slowed down the film's dramatic process, and he intended to make textual alterations in future productions – something which led to a break between Lagerlöf and Stiller.

Their quarrel began with the film *The Tale of Gunnar Hede* (*Gunnar Hedes saga*) (Stiller, 1923) which was entitled *En Herrgårdssägen* at the script stage after the novel's original title (published in 1899). Lagerlöf, who in the novel gave life to her memories of personal events, could not but feel that Stiller had rendered her work commonplace, and filled it with anachronisms to boot. She complained vehemently at the script stage about Stiller's 'distortions'. The company succeeded in convincing Lagerlöf, however, and managed to prevent her from making her protests public after the première. Several film critics unknowingly pointed out the film's lack of congruence with the original text – this despite the fact that the opening credits made it clear that the story was an independent adaptation with ideas taken from *En Herrgårdssägen*. The reviewer for the newspaper *Svenska Dagbladet* Quelqu'une (Märta Lindqvist) even went so far as to suggest that she saw signs of degeneration in Swedish cinema: she felt that the producers had made too many allowances for 'foreign film tastes'[4] – i.e. Hollywood narrative.

The relationship between Stiller and Lagerlöf became so strained after *Gunnar Hedes saga* that when the venerable lady found out that Stiller was to direct *Gösta Berlings saga* (1924) – one of Lagerlöf's central novels where the events take place in her beloved Värmland – she tried to recover the film rights. When that failed, she demanded to have the director replaced, but Svensk Filmindustri maintained that plans were too far advanced for this to be possible. Stiller was already busy writing the script with Ragnar Hylten-Cavallius.

The novel about an ex-clergyman's adventures in the forests of Värmland is episodic and structured in such a way that the events of each episode represent an individual whole. The various stories are only connected through the recurring central characters, which represented a major difficulty for the script writers and which occasioned major changes in the story. The film production was long and difficult; the interiors were filmed at the studio on Lidingö and the exteriors were shot on location in the Stockholm area. The result was not a success and Lagerlöf bitterly regretted having given permission to use her name in the opening credits. The company had assured her that the script had been followed to the letter and she now felt betrayed. What upset Lagerlöf the most, however, was a fight that took place in a church, a scene that was neither in the novel nor in the script.

Playing the character of the beautiful Elisabeth Dohna was Greta Garbo – she who was to become the Diva, perhaps the most known and celebrated of all the world's film stars. The words of a certain Torsten Tegnér – a reviewer for *Idrottsbladet* (*The Athletic Paper*) – have in several contexts been made to represent a classic example of a critic's misjudgement of an actor's performance: 'A semi-plump and unseasoned piece of bread that neither tickles nor saturates'[5] is what he wrote of Garbo after having seen Part I of *Gösta Berlings saga*. In Tegnér's defence it must be pointed out, however, that he retracts his harsh words after having seen Part II: 'I cannot understand how she was photographed in Part I – or was it I who was not disposed to seeing beautifully?'[6]

The newspaper reviews of *Gösta Berlings saga* were, as mentioned above, rather negative overall. The main argument against the film was that it did not follow the events of the novel. This was not just a general assertion, but an expression of disappointment at the film-makers' having broken with a norm. The dominant conception of film ontology presupposed that the filmic narrative would follow the original material to the letter: its action, dialogue and characters – in other words, films should be illustrated novels.

Cinema was thus not considered to be an independent art form, or as Bo Florin has put it: 'Either . . . the films . . . have been considered the . . . literary . . . text's betrayer or its humble servants.'[7] It appears that this was (and is) the opinion of the public as represented by the reviewers of the newspapers. Among intellectuals, however, other thoughts were expressed which were not entirely uninfluenced by the theoretical ideas put forth in other parts of Europe, for instance, by Krackauer and Benjamin. Author Hjalmar Bergman, for example, held that the path to 'cinema dramatics' led through the pantomime and the mimetical expression. From this point of view, films that followed the literary original too faithfully were only 'a washed out extract'.[8]

According to Hjalmar Bergman, one of Sweden's most important authors, film expression should consist of 'a plastic mimetical representation of the inner action' (of the characters and the relations between them). 'But,' he continued, 'it is necessary that the . . . script . . . writer completely turns away from every thought of verbal means of expression.'[9] Bergman wrote a number of film scripts during the 1920s. His contribution was often noted in reviews, even if there is still uncertainty as to whether his intentions were actually perceived by the reviewers. Tor Burn wrote the following in *Svenska Dagbladet* in 1927 about *A Perfect Gentleman* (*En perfekt gentleman*) (Ekman, Bryde):

> Hjalmar Bergman is our only film writer of any literary significance – literary also in the sense that he prefers to depict a somewhat decadent society, where characters swirl like puppets in a mildly naturalistic action. Elegant, witty and bizarrely original but very little of flesh and blood and living palpable life.[10]

Several people of renown participated in the debate over film ontology – which took place in 1919 to 1920 – among them the famous German director Max Reinhardt who was visiting the Stockholm opera. He held that the cinema needed to have its own poets (i.e. script writers) who 'speak its own language'.[11] He also emphasized that a film which was an adaptation of another art form lacked artistic legitimacy. Both Victor Sjöström, who was to cooperate with Bergman and who also travelled with him to Hollywood, and Gustaf Molander seem to have been impressed and influenced by these ideas, as is maintained by Bengt Forslund.

Interestingly enough it was not only literature that the film industry copied in its endeavours to achieve artistic status, but it was apparently not entirely unusual for films to be largely influenced by famous paintings. Thus Bo Florin cites Brunius's film *Synnöve Solbakken* (1919), for instance, which bears traces of two painters, the Norwegian Adolf Tidemand and Kilian Zoll. The film is based on the novel of the same name by the Norwegian writer Björnstierne Björnson. The narrative centres around a young couple from different backgrounds who fall in love and who meet opposition when they wish to marry – an unoriginal theme. The heroine Synnöve belongs to a strictly religious, pious sect called the Haugians, while her beloved comes from a more down to earth family of farmers. The film's conflict of ideas is condensed in a sequence where there is cross-cutting between a religious revival meeting at Synnöve's home and young people celebrating Midsummer by dancing in a meadow.

The origin of these two scenes cannot be found in the novel, but Bo Florin shows how one of the scenes in the film has been inspired or possibly even been copied by Brunius from a painting by Tidemand called *The Haugians* (*Haugianerna*) (1848). Interestingly the composition of the filmic image is not only exactly like that of the painting, but the scene also begins like a tableau vivant, where the characters keep their immobile poses for an extended period of time. The Midsummer celebration with which the revival meeting is cross-cut, refers in turn to Kilian Zoll's painting called *Midsummer Dancing in Rättvik* (*Midsommardans i Rättvik*) (1852).

THE LIGHT GENRES

From a business point of view what has been described as the golden age of Swedish film was fraught with financial difficulties for the industry as a whole, as has been discussed above. Towards the end of the period production was characterized by demands for profitability from the financiers. This pressure led to a change in repertory policy which certainly contributed to a stabilization of the market, but which according to contemporary critics left much to be desired so far as artistry and quality were concerned. The success concept of the Swedish film at the end of the 1910s and beginning of the 1920s had been literary works remade into movies with the purpose of procuring a higher status for the medium and to raise its reputation above that of fairground entertainment and circus shows. There was of course an ulterior, economic motive behind this ambitious project as well: the industry wished to shed the entertainment tax that accompanied films as a concrete reminder of their shameful labelling as entertainment.

By the mid-1920s production costs for these literary films had escalated. Sjöström and Stiller – who had virtually single-handedly represented 'the artistic' quality in Swedish film – left the country towards the end of the 1920s for Hollywood. Thereafter, production of the 'prestigious' films was reduced, thus leaving the way clear for more popular genres. The bankers, who had gained increasingly tight control over the company in Kreuger's wake, were more interested in profit than in artistic prestige and thus encouraged the more profitable elements in the popularly oriented films that had begun to be distributed in the country, the so-called 'profit films'.

Characteristic of the Swedish theatres was that the major stages in the big cities were closed during the summer. The summer was not however without its theatre, as various amateur societies and travelling companies – of which the royal theatres were also a part – performed plays on the outdoor stages in the big cities and in the amusement parks across the country. The repertory usually consisted of humorous plays and light comedies, which were exceptionally popular everywhere. These theatres and their repertory were often referred to as 'bush theatre' (low-brow travelling comedy theatres), a reflection of their low status. Local vaudeville performers also put on their shows in the parks. These were very popular, and when companies ventured into producing film in the countryside it was frequently with these locals stars in the main roles.

Such popular performers included, for instance, Värmlander Fridolf Rhudin, who, through the films he made, became famous throughout the country and exceptionally successful in the few years prior to his premature death in the early 1930s. In his films Rhudin played the part of an innocent country boy who is harassed by other, more clever types. It is always Rhudin who wins the game, however, through his cheerful manner (and sense of humour). In the same way Edvard Persson, the biggest (literally) and most popular star of the 1930s became known to the nation. With his impressive physique and just the right mixture of local patriotic conservatism and sentimentality, he made two of the most popular films of the 1930s which were seen by over a million people: *Kalle's Inn* (*Kalle på spången*) (1939) and *South of the Highway* (*Söder om landsvägen*) (1936). Incidentally, *Kalle på spången* ran in Copenhagen for eighteen months during the German Occupation; Leif Furhammar concludes that it became a matter of honour for the Copenhagen citizens to keep the film running to prevent it from being replaced by a German film.

As the 1920s went by the number of comedies in repertory increased, and Leif Furhammar distinguishes between several sub-genres, such as, for example, Danish comedies, thriller comedies, sentimental burlesques – and one exceptionally popular genre that Furhammar ties to the extensive debate over the nation's defence which gained momentum in the mid-1920s, namely the military farce. The emergence of this genre, which was perfected and exploited to the full during the 1930s, and its popularity, demands a more thorough discussion.

In the 1920s the issue of the Åland Islands had been at the centre of Swedish debate. National/nationalistic elements were at a peak and when the discussion over defence started up in the mid-1920s, it was at times heated and emotional. Some years later the bourgeois left and the social democrats believed that severe cuts in defence were possible. References were made to the international *détente* and a great deal of trust was placed in the League of Nations, of which Sweden had become a member in 1920. The debate ended in the Defence Order of 1925 which meant a substantial weakening of the effective strength of the country's defence measures. Among other things it meant closing down old and valued units of the army and coast artillery, something which caused heated debate and occasioned nostalgic statements in the press. It is possible that the series of historical dramas and the emergence of the military farce as a genre can be ascribed to these feelings.

Sweden has compulsory military service and, especially before the ideological break in the 1960s, every healthy young Swedish man was expected to fulfil his duty. It was generally believed that the military was the school that turned boys into men and that to be a military reject ('kronvrak'[12]) was shameful. The intrigues of the military farces were often concentrated around the refresher courses that had been a source of fiction and folklore in the country for decades. But, as Leif Furhammar points out, this genre seldom connects the intrigue with the fact that the army trains men for war and killing. One of the few films set in a military environment that referred to this reality where the war was close at hand was *Kadettkamrater*. The film opened in December 1939, and tells the story of a man who voluntarily meets his death in order to warn his comrades of the waters that have been mined by a foreign power.

Kadettkamrater thus deviated from the prevalent military farces which were founded on situation comedy and improvisation. This was characteristic of the acting style of the travelling theatres where the performances of the actors were based on an extended cooperation with the audience, and whence the actors of the genre were brought. The military farce had comparatively fixed characters which included an autocratic sergeant, some sly men, a colonel's beautiful daughter and two non-commissioned officers, one honest and one villainous (who were competing for the young lady's affections). The advent of sound eventually led to many such films containing song and dance routines which were worked into the story.

The director of these films *par excellence* was Weyler Hildebrand, who himself played the part of the choleric Sergeant Karlsson to advantage in film after film entitled *Karlsson* (in Swedish Karl/Carl means a real man or a he-man, and Karlsson could thus be translated as son of a he-man). In the 1930s this genre was developed to perfection by such skilled stars as, for example, Åke Wilhelmsson.

One of the most popular military films was *The Home Guard's Little Lotta* (*Landstormens lilla Lotta*) (1938). It is a story where the events during a refresher course in the Stockholm archipelago are interwoven with a corrupt bank manager's evil intentions of grabbing both the beautiful little WAC Marianne, played by Sickan Carlsson, and her friend's ancestral farm where Marianne helped out. For women had their given places in these films that celebrate male fellowship and its values: she makes coffee while smiling sweetly and admiringly at the uniformed heroes.

The sojourn in the army, and the refresher course in particular, created exceptional conditions under which society's social order could be temporarily turned upside-down: the military hierarchy, it was believed, was built on individual skills, on capability and courage, not – as in the past – on birth and class. Dressed in his lieutenant's uniform, the bank clerk can put his pompous boss in his place, as happens in *Landstormens lilla Lotta*. Under the influence of male fellowship one or two hen-pecked husbands also learn how to become 'real men'. The characters cheerfully join in manoeuvres in the great outdoors. On these occasions Sickan Carlsson's cheerful voice is often heard resounding over it all as she, riding on a loaded hay cart, sings the refrain of the film's title melody.

ACTORS AND ENTERTAINMENT PERFORMERS

Sickan Carlsson was 'discovered' as a young vaudeville performer when she appeared on stage at Södra Teatern (the Southern Theatre) in Stockholm in the early 1930s, her film debut in 1932 marked the beginning of a career that was to last for decades without – as was the case with many other actresses – the natural process of ageing affecting her popularity. Sickan Carlsson came from a poor working-class district in the Södermalm quarter of Stockholm (south of the city centre) and the key to her popularity was her very 'ordinariness': she was her mother and father's good girl, cheerful and fresh. Happy, sensible and enterprising, she portrayed an ideal which had replaced the image of the neurotic, fragile, middle-class woman of the beginning of the century. The new, healthy, modern woman – whom the women's magazines, among others, would increasingly describe as an ideal – was conceived as if for the purpose of contributing to the construction of the Swedish Welfare State. There were numerous films where Sickan Carlsson played the part of an upper- or middle-class girl whose function it was to contrast positively with an idle mother and a spoilt, wayward sister. Time and time again her characters fell in love with an 'average' boy who, in turn through his enterprising nature, cheerful manner and inventive spirit finally became his own man, whether a sports store proprietor, or gas station owner, like Elof Ahrle in the film *Oh, What a Boy!* (*Åh, en så'n grabb!*) (1939).

During the 1910s most of the actors at the Stockholm theatres had been prevented through their contracts from participating in film productions. The actors at the Gothenburg theatres were thus able to perform all the more diligently in front of the camera. Dagmar Ebbesen, one of the most popular actresses in the history of Swedish cinema, began her film career with Hasselblad, a career that was to last well into the 1950s. Like so many of the actors in the travelling theatre companies who had their set roles in repertory, Dagmar Ebbesen was to shine in quite a number of films through her accurate portrayal of cooks, housekeepers and working-class wives. Another popular Hasselblad film star, namely Adolf Jahr, was to achieve great success as a uniformed charmer in numerous military films.

Actors who were recruited from the provinces had a more popularly oriented image and their style of acting deviated from the style that was characteristic of those actors recruited from the Royal Dramatic Theatre (Kungliga Dramatiska Teatern). The older generation of RDT actors are easy to identify thanks to their inflated and stylized acting and above all – after the introduction of sound film – by their unnatural manner of delivering lines. Actors like, for instance, Lars Hanson and Inga Tidblad never succeeded in liberating themselves from this formal style of acting. It is important to note that this was not a fact that troubled the audience: what purported to be realism and 'naturalness' to the contemporary audience was created through these grand styles.

In the long run it became impossible for the major theatres to prevent their employees from entering film, and thus the film actors of the 1930s were divided into two sections: the stars of the big theatres excelled at the more 'serious' genres like literary melodrama, while their colleagues from the provinces brightened up the comedies. The latter's acting style was based on small gestures and improvisation, which appears more realistic to a modern viewer, but which was equated with popular low-brow culture by the contemporary arbiters of taste. These popular artists frequently spoke in dialect, something which by itself placed them in the lightweight categories – as was the case with Fridolf Rhudin and Edvard Persson, for example.

An actor's popularity was not dependent on his or her training and genre, however, but on personality and charisma. A bright and genial star who stood outside all categories in the 1920s and 1930s was Gösta Ekman, forefather to several generations of theatre people in Sweden. He ran the popular private Folkan theatre and mesmerized his audience with his extraordinary charismatic presence. As early as the 1920s he was making memorable roles in films like *Who Judges* (*Vem dömer*) (Sjöström, 1922) and *Karl XII* (Brunius, 1925). In 1927 *En perfekt gentleman* opened, a film written especially for Ekman by Hjalmar Bergman. In the 1930s Ekman made other films from Bergman stories, such as *Swedenhielms* (1935).

One of Ekman's unforgettable performances was in the film *Intermezzo* (Molander, 1936) where he plays a violinist who falls in love with his daughter's piano teacher, played by the young Ingrid Bergman. In the long acting sequences the photography of Åke Dahlqvist envelops the androgynous figure of Gösta Ekman in a secretive, shimmering light and invites the viewer to linger over the softly rounded eyelids, the involuntary, appealing movements of the lips and the shadow of eyelashes against the cheek. Gösta Ekman died in January 1938 and a devastated Ingrid Bergman wrote in her diary: 'I cannot find words for my grief.

Dear God, give him peace and help us poor creatures who have to live without him.'[13]

The talent of Ekman knew no boundaries. He mastered all the genres, from heavy drama to vaudeville shows. The vaudeville tradition has always been popular in Sweden, and many exceptional stars were recruited from these theatres. One of them was Tutta Rolf, the young Norwegian wife whom the famous vaudeville king Ernst Rolf brought back with him from one of his tours. In films like *We Who Use the Servant's Entrance* (*Vi som går köksvägen*) (Molander, 1932) and *Sara lär sig folkvett* (Molander, 1937) she stood up to everyone. The dashing young-girl roles that she came to portray broke with the period's stereotypical portrayal of women and made her a transgressor of boundaries. Tutta Rolf made nine successful films in the 1930s, most of which functioned as vehicles for her stage persona. She also tried her fortune in Hollywood, but with poor results.

Film actors in the 1930s still followed the conventional pattern of the theatre and played the same roles throughout their careers: Ruth Stevens always played the degenerate girl, Margit Manstad was the vamp and Ruth Holm was the perpetually weeping, silly maid. The extremely popular Bullen Berglund played jovial middle-class uncles, while Edvin Adolphson excelled in several roles as first lover. It was not until the second generation of film actors began appearing on the screen towards the end of the decade that a more homogenous acting style came to the fore. Young actors like Ingrid Bergman, Signe Hasso and Sture Lagerwall – who all got their careers underway in the mid-1930s – had the ability to adapt their acting style to the character of the medium. Thus the combined efforts of Signe Hasso and Sture Lagerwall led to unforgettable performances in films like *Career* (*Karriär*) (Bauman, 1938) and *We Two* (*Vi två*) (Bauman, 1939). *Karriär* tells the story of the successful career of a young actress and her ultimate decision to leave her profession to get married – a story that seems absurd and in the light of later days also reactionary. The film distinguishes itself above all, however, through its excellent character direction and the acting style that by this time had become characteristic of the silver screen: low key and realistic. In *Karriär*, not only Signe Hasso and Sture Lagerwall but also Tollie Zellman – a comedienne cast in a tragic role of a drunken actress past her prime – portray their characters with a feeling and sensitivity that lack counterparts in contemporary repertory.

Signe Hasso later moved to Hollywood, as did Ingrid Bergman. The latter's singular talent led to her international breakthrough in the film *Intermezzo – A Love Story*, a film whose script had been purchased by David Selznick, and which followed the original Swedish version to the letter.

VEHICLES FOR IDEOLOGIES/A SOCIETY UNDERGOING REFORM

One knew nothing of all this at the beginning of the 1930s however, when the destiny of the Swedish film industry seemed uncertain at best – not least because of something that to begin with seemed destined to be the final death-knell of the industry, but which turned out to be the very opposite: sound. This novelty portended large – even impossible – expenses and would entail all sorts of conceivable and inconceivable transitional difficulties, from the mass redundancies of cinema musicians to apprehensions about the end of cinema as an art form. The first sound film, *Säg det i toner* premièred at the end of 1929. It was a musical containing no dialogue and was received with no more than moderate enthusiasm.

The period of transition to sound was protracted and marked by substantial insecurity, both as far as the technical apparatus and the films themselves were concerned. The patent war over sound systems dragged on well into the decade. For some years Svensk Filmindustri used the German system Tobis, for example, but they were worried about the cost: rental for the recording apparatus is reported to have amounted to 5,000 SEK per day (including technicians) in a period when incomes were limited to 1 SEK per ticket sold. The Swedish system Aga-Baltic in combination with Danish Petersen & Poulsen was eventually established as the dominant sound recording and reproduction system in the country.

As far as film production is concerned, there were several attempts at keeping the ambitions for international success alive through production of various language versions, among others, on the initiative of the American film company Paramount. These attempts met with no success, however; neither the critics nor the audiences liked them. The films were made in France, and remained both anonymous and stereotypical. In the same way the poor audience ratings for Josef von Sternberg's *An American Tragedy* made it clear that dubbing was not a phenomenon the Swedish people wanted to listen to. From then on subtitles were to be the solution when showing foreign films.

Language was thus the final obstacle for all the dreams of international success that possibly still lingered in people's minds. But the provincial character that the domestic film was now reduced to turned out to guarantee its survival. The Swedish people seemed to never tire of hearing their language spoken on the silver screen by their beloved actors. By and large, the films of the 1930s lacked the international outlook of many of the productions of the 1920s. The cinema became a popular mass medium directed towards the average person and familiarity was one of its distinctive features. This was expressed in the films' frequent reflections on everyday life and its ordinary events. The focus of repertory was on popular entertainment in familiar settings: middle-class country homes, in particular their kitchen quarters, offices, shops and farms, where most Swedes still originated.

The 1930s in Sweden began with everyone's eyes fixed on the future as the Stockholm exhibition opened in 1930 and introduced the most recent developments of modern society. That same year Sweden, which was directly dependent on the foreign market, was affected by the world crisis and the resulting unemployment. In May 1931 there were food riots at Ådalen – a sawmill district where unemployment was exceptionally high. People had gathered to demonstrate against the scabs at the sawmill, when the army, which had been engaged to act as guardians of law and order, opened fire on the demonstrators. In the tumult some people lost their lives, among them a bystander. This led to considerable agitation in domestic policy in a country that was still on the verge of a communist revolution.

One year later, in 1932, Sweden was in turmoil over the Kreuger crash, the Swedish version of Wall Street. In order to acquire monopoly rights to the various match markets in the world, Ivar Kreuger had given sizeable guaranteed credits to several countries, and in March 1932 he committed suicide in Paris. The consequences were devastating. There was panic on the stock market, many people lost their entire fortunes and the Swedish krona (SEK) was devalued. The Swedish economy was, generally speaking, largely unaffected however, including the film industry which had become sufficiently stable to manage on its own without the Kreuger millions. The country also profited from its initially more developed neighbours' situation. The demand on the world market for the very goods that Sweden could provide was bigger than it had been for a long time, while competition was virtually non-existent: the export of oats to Britain, for example, lacked competition due to the collapse of Russia, and the Norwegian forests could not meet the demands for wood from the British construction industry. In 1934 trade conditions thus improved in the country and unemployment decreased – production had set the ball rolling. An augmented capacity for competition had been achieved through the structural rationalizations of the 1920s and through the devaluation two years before.

The parliamentary election of 1932 is considered as epoch-making in Sweden because the social democrats won the ballot together with the communists and the farmers' league. When Per Albin Hansson became Prime Minister in the spring of 1933 the social democrats were given a free hand to enforce their unemployment policy. The most important goal of the new government was, as Minister of Finance Ernst Wigforss wrote in the Keynesian spirit: 'to institute jobs, ordinary useful jobs with average wages on the open market'.[14] In order to initiate this programme it was necessary to raise the income tax, the inheritance tax and the tax on spirits, which was also carried through as a result of the 'horse-trading' between the social democrats and the farmers' league. A complex political and social process that would eventually take the shape of a historic compromise between labour and capital was set in motion and was to lay the foundations for the exceptionally peaceful conditions on the labour market and the unique social and political development in the country.

In Hansson's government it was the Minister of Health and Social Affairs Gustaf Möller who handled the labour market policy and it was also he who set up the guidelines for the housing policy. The state had supported the own-your-own-home movement for some time and it now began to support the construction of sound, spacious homes. An unemployment insurance had been instituted in 1934 and in the following year the people's pension arrangements were improved. In 1936 the Swedish Employers' Confederation (SAF) and the Swedish Confederation of Trade Unions (LO) decided jointly to call on the government with a declaration stating that they wanted no state interference in labour market issues. In the light of this action the main agreement of 1938 was entered into. This set out a rationalization of the negotiation system, rules for the dismissal of workers, retirement plans and third-party rights. Statutory vacation terms for all wage earners were also realized in 1938 and thereby created a guaranteed break for the working population. The agreement was closed outside Stockholm in the small resort of Saltsjöbaden, which lent its name to the 'spirit' that was to dominate the Swedish labour market policy for the next fifty years: the spirit of Saltsjöbaden, the spirit of consensus, which reaped its first fruits during the Second World War.

In effect, however, the reforms instigated by the social democrats did not prove fruitful until much later; the economic recovery had begun 'on its own' as it were. But as the situation stood, the positive development on the economic market appeared to be the result of the efforts of the social democrats and conveyed to the party the trust it was to enjoy for decades. The important force behind Swedish politics at this time was that the Welfare State would be shaped by being both a goal and a means. Besides promoting a higher and more evenly distributed standard of living, the welfare policy was also intended to create increased economic growth and efficiency. It is this pragmatic and ideological merger that is the foundation of 'the Swedish model', with its marked traits of collectivism and order that the social democratic party upheld.

During the 1920s the social democrats had been largely perceived as a party without an ideology. In the early 1930s it developed from being a class party to a broader 'ordinary' people's party, a change of image that was strengthened by the agreement between the farmers' league and the social democrats in 1933. It was also at this time that the ideology that was to last into the twentieth century was formed. Its principal metaphor was *folkhemmet* or the people's home (as the Welfare State is known in Sweden), a home for everyone, where every individual has his or her given place. Per Albin Hansson's description of this home, whose foundation is community and affinity, was a cogent symbol of the new cooperative endeavours between ordinary people, farmers and employers.

The ideal of the folkhem was a society that would eliminate social want: 'In the good home there is equality, concern, cooperation, helpfulness.'[15] Interestingly enough this was not an idea that appealed solely to workers and other ordinary people; young academics also supported the new policy. One of the most difficult problems that the social democrats had to deal with was the alarming decrease in the nativity statistics (i.e. the number of babies born in this period) during the first half of the 1930s. A solution to this problem was suggested in the book *Kris i befolknings-frågan*[16] (1934) written by Gunnar and Alva Myrdal, who were to become two prominent figures of the theory of social democracy. The book contained a mixture of well-meaning suggestions for reforms and a patriarchal view of planning that was to characterize the attitude of the 'social engineers' who now took over responsibility for the social structure. The actually existing social policy was fused with liberal and conservative ideas about self-help and moral rearmament which had been in circulation since the turn of the century. At the centre of these ideas stood an educated mother, trained for her task, who tended her home and her children, supported in her duty by society's agencies of pre-natal and child care, children's recreation and a well-planned school system.

The film medium which in the name of pure survival addressed broad segments of the population, reflected these ideas sensitively. It is of interest to note that although the productions of the 1930s were largely comedies and lighter entertainment, it was nevertheless not uncommon to find demagogical elements amidst the jokes. Films that reflected the new social spirit became ever more explicit towards the end of the 1930s. A general kind of down-to-earth realism was not uncommon in Swedish cinema and films that were considered to reflect society had always been highly prestigious. As early as 1913 Victor Sjöström's film *Ingeborg Holm* occasioned a heated debate over the nation's institutionalized care, which led to a change in the law regulating the custody of children.

The decreasing population numbers, for example, were reflected directly in the intrigues of several films: *Walpurgis Night* (*Valborgsmässoafton*) (Edgren, 1935), starring Ingrid Bergman and Lars Hanson, celebrates the affectionate young woman who wishes nothing more than to become a good wife and mother, while the independent, pleasure-seeking woman, who has an abortion, perishes. Other films, like *What do Men Know* (*Vad veta väl männen*) (Adolphson, 1933) and *One Single Night* (*En enda natt*) (Molander, 1939), depict children born out of wedlock as the fruit of genuine love, without any appendant moral lecturing directed at the mother. No doubt reality differed from this picture and the concept of an 'illegitimate child' lived long in popular speech despite its official abolition in the 1930s.

Quite soon in the early 1930s when the social democratic government had only just introduced its social policy programme, this was reflected in films such as *Karl Fredrik Reigns* (*Karl Fredrik regerar*) (Edgren, 1934). In this film popular actor Sigurd Wallén plays the role of a poor farm labourer, Karl Fredrik, who is appointed Minister of Agriculture through his political commitment. Through his programme for financing the modernization of agriculture, he saves the farm from which he was once banished. The film ends with the opposing parties having a reconciliatory meal that is characteristic of the period. The scope for social mobility and reconciliation between the classes is created when Karl Fredrik's daughter falls in love with the son of the manor.

The 1930s thus meant many major upheavals in Swedish society, not least as far as its ideology and structure were concerned. In the early 1930s a never before witnessed growth also began in the film industry. As mentioned above, it soon became apparent that the Swedes loved hearing their own language spoken on the screen and seeing their popular actors in key roles. In the space of only a few years film production became a profitable business. Svensk Filmindustri strengthened its position as the leading company in the industry, and new companies were formed. Audience figures shot up and the number of cinemas multiplied and exceeded 2,000 by the end of the decade. It has been estimated that at this time people living in the capital visited the cinema at least once every other week, and virtually all domestic feature film produced was profitable. The Swedish film constituted approximately 10 per cent of all films shown, but it contributed a total of 30 per cent of the film rentals. The interest in film stars grew, new film magazines were established and some publications ran contests for would-be stars. The upswing in the industry did not always reflect what critics had perceived and defined as quality, however, and the 1930s are more often than not referred to as a decadent period. It was the small companies that were apparently responsible for the dubious quality of film, according to the arbiters of taste. The new films were constantly compared to the productions of the 1920s – and for the most part the comparison favoured the latter.

If the 1920s are known as the golden age in Swedish film history and are characterized by concepts like quality and artistic development, then the 1930s became known as the Klondike period because the numerous 'golddiggers' and fortune hunters in the business were reported to be fortunate enough to be able to make a great deal of money. The industry grew explosively – or so the myth of the movie industry in Sweden in the 1930s would have it. Per Olov Qvist has pointed out that the seven major companies – each producing at least ten films per year – were responsible for 78 per cent of the total amount of films available. The two biggest companies Svensk Filmindustri and Europa Film were accountable for almost half, or 44 per cent of the repertory, and of the seventy-something production companies that put feature films on the market during the decade, some thirty companies produced only one or two films.

The industry was also smaller than it appeared, as one person could be involved in several companies or productions at the same time. The system with temporary producers had to do with the system of cinema bills that came into use during this decade. The system resulted from the great demand for domestic film and the fact that many cinema owners were lacking this coveted merchandise when the major producers showed their films in their own cinemas. The system worked as follows: the independent cinema owner advanced the anticipated film rental through a bill made out to the producer, who in turn cashed the bill and put the money into the production. This entailed certain risks for the owner of the cinema: the rental could in some unfortunate cases amount to 100 per cent of the ticket sales. Certain laboratories also contributed to this system by investing their costs for developing into the production, but overall it was a phenomenon of temporary productions.

Several companies merged in this period, many of which were to survive for decades. Two of these, Europa Film – which was founded in 1930 – and Sandrews – which began its eventually quite substantial film production as late as 1939 – turned out to be the most important besides Svensk Filmindustri. Europa Film had been founded by a certain Gustaf Scheutz together with Schamyl Bauman. Scheutz headed the company for many years, while Bauman, who was initially active as a film distributor, was to direct lighter genres. A fact that is often forgotten is that he was also an excellent personal instructor and a sensitive director of a number of intimate, down-to-earth films. Among the other relatively diligent film companies at this time, it is worth mentioning Nordisk Tonefilm, Publikfilm, Svensk Talfilm, Irefilm and Wivefilm.

The well-being of Europa Film in the following decades was largely founded on the success of its absolute star, Edvard Persson. In the same way a small company by the name of Svensk Talfilm would become interesting through its long survival which was entirely dependent on one character, Åsa-Nisse. While Edvard Persson stole the audience through his personal charisma as a performer, Åsa-Nisse, on the other hand, was a fictitious character in a long line of films based on the popularity of a comic character, not on the personality of the actor.

Sandrews and Europa Film cooperated for the better part of the 1930s in that Europa Film productions were shown regularly at the Sandrews cinemas. When Europa Film eventually began to acquire their own cinemas, the head of Sandrews felt the time had come for them to venture into film production themselves. Anders Sandrew, who gave the company his name, was its absolute ruler, but he also knew how to tie competent associates to his company. Thus, in the early 1940s he hired Bengt Idestam-Almquist – the legendary film critic 'Robin Hood' – for the job of the company's first literary director, and later Rune Waldekranz, the critic who wrote under the pseudonym 'Roderick' in *Svenska Dagbladet*, who was to remain at Sandrews until the mid-1960s.

'DISGRACE TO OUR CULTURE'

The popular genres that were introduced at the end of the 1920s were widely developed so that they could oust the ambitious literary films which carried the sophisticated filmic expression of the silent era. The attitude of the arbiters of taste was quite severe and the relatively large numbers of serious melodramas and well-directed drawing-room comedies that were actually produced could not survive in this discourse that was directed against the medium. The protests from concerned representatives of the public were extensive and the decade itself was opened and closed by two public meetings where rabid attacks were made as to the quality and state of the domestic film.

In this context the young author Arthur Lundkvist, who became one of the country's most assiduous and respected film critics, was to play an important role. The status of film criticism had, moreover, begun to be raised, something that manifested itself, among other things, in more and more film reviews being signed, frequently with a pseudonym however. Renowned critics like the aforementioned Robin Hood (Bengt Idestam-Almquist) and Roderick (Rune Waldekranz), also included Pavane (Gerd Osten), Jerome, and Elsa-Britta Hansson (later Marcussen), daughter of the then Prime Minister. Many of them were active in the profession for many years. Robin Hood was the leading theoretician and film historian, and although he has been much criticized in latter days for his inadequate use of sources, it is none the less almost impossible to mistake his enthusiasm, sensitivity or love of the film medium when one reads his reviews.

Besides the intellectuals there was one other group which was indefatigably critical of the domestic film: the popular movements. If the intellectuals criticized the cinema for its lack of artistry, then the representatives of the people's movements noted the films' potential moral deficiencies. A recurrent object of criticism was the frequent occurrences of beer and other alcoholic beverages in a series of films with a popularly oriented image. The label 'Pilsner film' – taken from the light beer known as pilsner – that has remained with the films of the 1930s up to the present day was launched in connection with the film debate in Klara folkets hus (the People's Palace at Klara in Stockholm) in February 1931, where the necessity of 'liberating the film art from the commercial strait-jacket it had been placed in towards the end of the 1920s'[17] was discussed.

The second and better known debate took place at the Concert Hall in Stockholm in February 1937 on the initiative of Svensk Författareförening (the Swedish Authors' Association). Per Olov Qvist states that the direct cause of this public meeting was the première of *A Boarding House Named Paradise* (*Pensionat Paradiset*) (Hildebrand, 1937) starring the popular actor Thor Modéen. The film is a popular comedy of errors that provoked outrage because, among other things, Modéen appears in one scene with a pair of ladies' knickers on his head. As a result, Swedish cinema was called a 'disgrace to our culture'[18] in the subsequent article 'Svensk film – kultur eller kulturfara'[19] by critic Carl Björkman. A positive outcome of this storm of opinion was possibly the appointment in 1941 of a state inquiry, whose task it was to formulate a proposal for a system that would support the production of culturally valuable film.

Such a storm of opinion did not subside without its consequences, one being that the film industry did its best to raise the unique prestige of film by means of the old formula of the 1920s: the literary film. The impending war also affected the general mood and it was apparently felt that a more serious image was necessary. Concrete measures were taken, for example, to employ university graduates as heads of departments in the companies, among them Carl Anders Dymling – formerly a radio manager – appointed head of Svensk Filmindustri, or the above-mentioned Idestam-Almquist and Waldekranz as literary directors at Sandrews. When Olof Andersson left his office as president of Svensk Filmindustri, Karin Swanström, the actress who had ruled as the company's artistic head during the 1930s, also had to make room for Victor Sjöström. Swanström's husband Stellan, the company's studio manager, was also replaced, by Harald Molander, Gustaf's son.

The discrepancy between those who advocated on behalf of the people and its education and the people themselves could not have been greater than in the 1930s – as well as later: *Pensionat Paradiset* was, and still is, one of the best loved films of Swedish popular culture. The demand for film was great and thereby also the demand for scripts – a fact that led to an increasing number of films being made from original scripts, besides stage plays that had proved successful. It was only natural that Gustaf Molander, who had started as Stiller's script writer, would begin writing his own scripts in an ever increasing capacity, sometimes in collaboration with Gösta Stevens – who incidentally was one of the most prolific script writers at the time, together with Sölve Cederstrand and Torsten Lundqvist.

The basis for the much abused repertory was still the popular plays, however, that were now being filmed – the plays from the 'bush theatres' that had the popular audience in mind. One of the most popular films of this genre was *The Southsiders* (*Söderkåkar*) (Hildebrand). The film premièred in 1932 and starred three well-loved actors: Sigurd Wallén, Edvard Persson and Dagmar Ebbesen. *Söderkåkar* is a straightforward story about the working-class district in the part of Stockholm known as Södermalm. It has an obvious moral which shows that wealth is not always a precondition of happiness, but that hard work, honesty and contentedness are. One of the highlights of the film is a scene showing a married couple surrounding by summer foliage; the coffee stands on the table, the wife sews and the man plays his guitar and sings a ballad to please his wife. The film depicts an idyll in the city and reflects a sense of contentment that was to be the guiding light of the Welfare State ideology. As a portrayal of the people *Söderkåkar* is unsurpassable and was remade for television in the 1970s.

Current novels and books on topical issues also gave rise to films, if not for any other reason than for lack of other subjects: one example of this phenomenon is a film from the early 1930s, *Vi som går köksvägen* (Molander, 1932), which was based on a documentary novel in which a reporter writes in a humorous way about her experiences as a maid. The film was a success in several Scandinavian countries. Molander directed a number of the period's most interesting melodramas, but also many of its sophisticated comedies, like *Dollar* (1938). Gustaf Molander's style of production is unique in Sweden, where he made a total of sixty-three films – not including the films he merely scripted. As the son of a renowned theatre theoretician and director, Harald Molander, sen., Gustaf had the theatre in his blood as it were. He was for a time married to one of the silent era's most popular stars, Karin Molander, and his brother Olof, who was head of the Royal Dramatic Theatre, was also to direct a number of films in the 1940s.

Gustaf Molander excelled in all genres, but he was the greatest director of melodrama in the country, with a profound and insightful understanding of the expressive possibilities inherent in the filmic image. Some of his best-known films of the 1930s were *Intermezzo* and *En kvinnas ansikte* (1938) – both starring Ingrid Bergman and both remade in Hollywood, the latter having been substantially rewritten and starring Joan Crawford (*A Woman's Face*, 1941). Particularly in the melodramas, Molander used the composition of the image with the purpose of showing something essential about the existential situation of the characters. The pictures are 'tight' and on the verge of being claustrophobic, as props and other details of the set fill the frame, competing for room with the characters. The lighting is generally dark and full of contrasts. In, for example, *Intermezzo* an outward picture is created of the ideal family, living in a home that is beautiful, comfortable and well run. The tones in which the characters address one another are mild and subdued, the choice of words is careful and the characters are considerate towards one another. However, a contrasting mood becomes noticeable and threatens the apparent harmony, so that the security tends to become oppressive and the cozy setting claustrophobic. Thus, for instance, when the main character Holger Brandt practises his violin, he does so before a large window taking up an entire wall which allows the light to surround the artist and show the world outside. Simultaneously, however, the bars at the windows cast shadows on the walls and the upper part of the image is framed in heavy dark beams, which together give a closed-in and sinister character to this *mise-en-scène*.   •

THE WORLD BEYOND THE IMAGINARY UNIVERSE OF THE CINEMA

Because the Swedish film of the 1930s – independently of genre – mainly depicted intimate relations between people, it was exposed to severe criticism. Behind the criticism it is possible to discern a normative demand for the feature film to somehow also reflect the political events that took place in- and outside of the country's borders – in other words, a demand for concrete, contemporaneous realism. The commitment to foreign policy among the Swedes was in fact much greater than their interest in entertainment films reveals. In 1935 Italy attacked Abyssinia without declaring war. There were hardly any events during the period between the world wars that caused such outrage in Sweden as this war. Sweden had maintained good relations with Abyssinia ever since the early 1900s when two rival groups established missions there offering medical care and education services. When the message was received that the ambulance equipped by Sweden had been bombed by the Italian Air Force – despite its Red Cross symbol – the anti-Italian mood escalated. The following year saw the start of the Spanish Civil War and money was collected for the legal left government. Swedish volunteers joined up in order to fight for the government forces in Spain and in the same way Sweden was also committed to Finland's cause, particularly during the Winter War and thereafter.

Immediately following the outbreak of the Second World War Sweden issued its declaration of neutrality. The government and parliament believed their primary task was to keep the country out of the war, and Sweden's wartime policy was focused on balancing the various demands from the respective sympathies for the warring nations. In autumn 1939 the government issued a number of export prohibitions in order to protect domestic supply. The large iron ore export (approximately 10 million tons per year) continued uninterrupted, however, as it was imperative to ensure the supply of coal and coke to the country. The Swedes were also compelled to make a number of concessions to the Germans, among which they allowed transportations of supplies by boat to Narvik to pass through Swedish territory. This decision evoked violent protests from the British government and the Norwegian exile government. Subsequently in 1941, Germany demanded a transit conveyance permit for transporting 18,000 men from Norway to Finland; permission was granted after a schism between the government and parliament that involved the old King Gustaf V.

After the USA had entered the war the allied criticism of the Swedish concessions to the German demands escalated, but the transit conveyances of arms and personnel on leave did not cease until 1943, after Stalingrad and the German setbacks in North Africa. That same year the Swedes also reduced their iron ore export to 7.5 million tons per year and suppressed all credits to the Germans. Sweden also opened its borders to refugees, large numbers of whom entered the country from both Denmark and Norway towards the end of the war. People from northern Finland also fled to the Swedish side of the border with the evacuation of German troops in the winter of 1944.

After the collapse of Germany it seemed inevitable that there should be a political orientation towards the West, where the Swedish film industry had always had its best relations. It is of interest to note that at the beginning of the war, however, the Swedes made many concessions to Germany as regards film censorship. During the war years the Swedish film censors worked closely with what was in effect the nation's ministry of propaganda, called Informationsstyrelsen (the Board of Information), whose task was to 'prevent the formation of un-Swedish opinion and to promote national thinking'.[20] The censors – i.e. the National Board of Film Censors – did not have much to say about domestic films, whose makers were aware of what was considered appropriate and right in terms of what this authority would tolerate. It was deemed necessary to prohibit a number of foreign feature films, however. In 1942, nine feature films were banned (three German, four American, one English and one Finnish), in 1943, a total of ten feature films were banned, while 1944 saw the prohibition of thirty-eight fiction films, all of which had been produced in the Allied countries. In 1945 only one or two films were banned. The Board was particularly strict with regard to all newsreels, which were closely scrutinized and cut extensively as well as being totally banned. Interestingly, there was one category that was consistently allowed through and that was the Finnish, frequently avidly anti-Russian films that were imported into the country.

The war years brought crowds of people to the cinemas. The influx of foreign films decreased, as it had during the First World War, to 18 per cent in all. French films disappeared almost completely while the German imports increased, not least because their most popular film star during the war was the Swedish singer Zarah Leander. English films maintained their share of the market during the war, while the share of American films dropped by 15 per cent. However, the income from American films increased, in spite of the smaller number of films being imported. Because of this general decline the demand for domestic film naturally escalated further, and in fact Swedish cinema was at its most productive in the 1940s. The export of films also increased, mainly to countries allied with Germany thanks to the connections and agreements that the industry agency Sveriges Biograf- och filmkammare (Sweden's Chamber of Movie Theatres and Film) had through their membership of the International Film Chamber[21] – of which incidentally the Swede Olof Andersson was vice-president for several years.

The International Film Chamber was run by the Germans who used the trade in raw film as a device for extortion: the Germans wanted to bring about a boycott of Allied, and in particular American, films and those members who did not want to take part in the boycott were prevented from buying raw film. The largest Swedish film producers barely managed to keep their own cinemas going, while the independent cinema owners suffered badly from the lack of foreign films which were their primary source of income. The need to import film from the Allied countries was thus a question of survival for them. At the same time it was crucial to keep in with the Germans. The Swedes cashed in on an unclear formulation as regards their membership status, and succeeded, through various subterfuges, manoeuvres and some horse-trading to, on the one hand purchase German raw film – and moreover to sell their films in the membership countries – and on the other hand to avoid participating in the film boycott. They even went so far as to found a new industry agency, Föreningen Svenska Filmproducenter (the Association of Swedish Film Producers), to replace Sveriges Biograf-och filmkammare, a member of the International Film Chamber. In 1942 when Sweden was finally subjected to a German raw film boycott, Kodak relieved the resulting shortage as a gesture of thanks for the solidarity shown with the Allies.

The upswing the film industry experienced during the war was therefore not without its problems, especially for those companies which lacked one of the links in the chain of production–distribution–screening. One financial problem was that the entertainment tax was made permanent in 1940, and two years later a price control for tickets was instigated, together with the introduction of a general price and wage control. At the same time as the state implemented the entertainment tax, however, it heeded the complaints from the film industry and in 1941 it set up an inquiry into state support for film production. However, the inquiry concluded that the film industry was doing very well without the help of the state. The idea had been planted, however, and was to surface from time to time.

The circumstances of the Second World War led to Sweden's film production increasing by one-third, from twenty-seven films to some forty films per year. Leif Furhammar identifies three factors which primarily contributed to the expansion experienced by the Swedish film industry during the war and which led to the consolidation of the three major integrated companies: Svensk Filmindustri, Europa Film and Sandrews (by order of size). New companies were also established, such as Film AB Lux (1941), which was owned by a group of cinema owners, and Filmo, owned by the Popular Movement. The three factors were, first, the large increase in cinema audiences, second, the upgrading of 'Swedishness' to which the political situation gave rise, and finally the diminished amount of imported film.

The threat of war that had affected the nation at the end of the 1930s left few if any traces in domestic film production. When the Second World War had just broken out it might happen that Edvard Persson called out 'Say Hello to Hitler', as if on second thoughts, when someone was to go abroad. And in films like *Med folket för fosterlandet* (1938, Wallèn) *With the People for the Fatherland*, the father could – in the after-dinner speech so typical of the Swedish cinema – refer to the dark clouds gathering on the horizon. Naturally, the war itself came to affect the film repertory in many ways and first and foremost the increasing cinema audiences led to intensified film production.

The sizeable repertory makes it difficult to determine clear thematic lines in the wartime production of films, because virtually all genres, ideas and patterns were tested. Certain tendencies emerge more clearly than others, however. Thus, among the genres it is possible to discern the so-called *beredskapsfilmerna* (the 'state of alert' films) which were specific to wartime, the so-called *literary film* which the industry produced to protect itself against severe criticism – and in whose wake the *problem film* was developed in the post-war era – and finally the augmented *rural romance*, whose roots were grounded in the people moving from the country into the cities. The 'state of alert' films were a genre characteristic of the war, while the latter three would be developed further to become permanent features in Swedish film production.

The industry's willingness to develop the medium artistically in the early 1940s also enabled a handful of directors to make themselves known through their desire to use film as a personal expression of private artistic visions. It was a change of generations of sorts for the film industry which had previously been dominated by directors who saw themselves as members of a skilled craft tradition. Hasse Ekman, the son of Gösta Ekman, became a film director in this period, and Per Lindberg, Alf Sjöberg and later Hampe Faustman and Ingmar Bergman were directors whose ambition and self-confidence were sufficient for the production of films that strove to give visual expression to inner ideas.

THE WARTIME REPERTORY

The films evolved in two different directions, so to speak: those that depicted the Swedish military machine directly and those that in one disguise or another reflected the German occupation of Denmark and, in particular, Norway. The films which reflected Swedish military life were to begin as an extension of the popular military farces but, in contrast to those of the 1930s, these films contained more serious undertones with integrated lines about duty and responsibility in accordance with the principal watchwords of the 'spiritual state of alert': 'a spirit of community, watchfulness, silence',[22] as can be seen in *The Crown's Brave Lads* (*Kronans käcka gossar*) (1940), or *Kadettkamrater*, discussed above (p. 165).

In the wake of the military farce there were also films where events took place among representatives of various service branches, but which had a more dramatic appeal and which glorified professional officers as heroes. Such a film was *The First Division* (*Första Divisionen*) (1941), directed by Hasse Ekman, who was to begin his long career as a skilled and energetic director of virtually all genres. 'A strict and to the point Swedish and male film without any phony beating of the drum and attempts at affected heroism,'[23] is what the reviewer in *Svenska Dagbladet* wrote about *Första Divisionen*. Hasse Ekman played one of the lead roles himself, that of young second lieutenant Bråde who perishes in flight training towards the end of the film. Because a new young second lieutenant takes his place in the wing at the end of the film, it is made clear that there is always a man standing by to take over when another's strength gives out.

When the European large-scale war approached, Per Albin Hansson had assured the nation that 'Our alert is good'.[24] The early alert films seemed to confirm the truth of this particular statement. The country was in a state of partial mobilization, and conscripts were stationed in various parts of Sweden: from April to October 1940 400,000 men were posted throughout the nation. Worries about loved ones 'somewhere in Sweden' were ever present. At the same time food rationing had been instigated, so that in effect everyone experienced the crisis in a tangible way. The families of the conscripts did not always have an easy time: a young wife might write to her husband saying, 'I'm sorry I haven't written to you in a long time but I haven't been able to afford the postage stamp.'[25]

The themes of the other category of alert films were freedom, the fight for liberty and the moral responsibility of the individual. Due to political considerations, the Swedish film industry was very careful about stating when and where the stories took place. The only exception were the films that dealt with the Finnish Winter War, for example, *A Day Will Dawn* (*En dag skall gry*) (Ekman, 1944). Generally speaking, the events were either placed in the historical past, as in *Snapphanar* (Ohberg, 1942) and *Partisan's Ride Tonight* (*Rid i natt*, 1942), or as the war neared its end – when the outcome appeared certain – the films were contemporary depictions set in unnamed countries, for example, *My People Are Not Yours* (*Mitt Folk är inte ditt*) and *There's a Fire Burning* (*Det brinner en eld*) (Molander, 1943).

Snapphanar starred the ever popular Edvard Persson, an arrangement which in itself indicates that the film did not belong to one of the serious genres. Historically, the film deals with the war between Sweden and Denmark (the Scanian War of 1675–79), where the 'snapphanar' were free marksmen recruited by the Danes to act as guerrillas in Scania (the southern end of Sweden). The film received positive reviews, which indicates that its many references to the contemporary situation hardly escaped anyone. *Rid i natt*, in turn, was based on the renowned author Vilhelm Moberg's novel by the same name and was directed by Gustaf Molander. It appears to be the only Swedish film that, prior to Stalingrad, took a clear stand against Germany, its historical guise notwithstanding. Leif Furhammar wrote in retrospect that 'There was a rage and political clarity in the film that broke right through the oppressive facade and the affected theatrical tone of the settings.'[26] The film is also set in the mid-1600s when a farmers' rising took place in Värend in Småland (southern Sweden). Moberg wrote the novel, and later the script for the film together with the director after he had himself been conscripted during the state of alert in 1940.

The narrative begins with a meeting where the villagers decide to oppose the new sheriff's – on one occasion he is referred to as being German – demands for day-work. The conflict refers to the historical fact that Swedish farmers have always been free taxed farmers (i.e. they paid their taxes directly to the Crown and were represented in Parliament) and thus they refuse to comply. When the sheriff shows up with his armed men, however, the determination of the men is quickly broken as Stånge, the village leader and elder, gives in to the sheriff. The elder holds that he stands by his wish to defend the right of the farmers, but that he feels it should be done cautiously by avoiding open conflict: 'I want to settle everything so that the village is happy and tread gently doing it.' The elder wants both peace and his rights without realizing that in the existing situation a choice has to be made.

Stånge's solution is not accepted by everyone in the village and the conflict between the collaborator and the resistance man is expressed through the antagonism between Stånge and his future brother-in-law, Ragnar Svedje, who refuses to give in. When the count's men storm into his house, he wounds one of them and is forced to seek refuge in the woods and to live there until the queen is able to grant him a new trial. Despite the priest pleading on his behalf, he is declared an outlaw. He is hunted by the count's men and is at one time looked after by a highwayman who suggests they join forces. Svedje refuses because the man is a thief. The highwayman brings the issue of crime to its head, however: 'but who is a thief and who is not a thief? I steal a lamb and a lord steals ten thousand', he says, and points out that Svedje is now considered a criminal as well.

Eventually the pursuers catch up with Svedje, and bury him alive in the forest. Before this happens, his beloved Botilla (Eva Dahlbäck), who has been accused of witchcraft, drowns herself in a spring. The outcome of the rebellion is never revealed, but the film's message is in the farmer's dying words: 'I concede my life but justice stays on earth.' Throughout the narrative we hear the voice of the young farmer's mother, who tells us of the fiery cross the farmers have sent to each other since the beginning of time to defend themselves against intruders:

But the time comes when there goes a fiery cross over the Värend land. It passes through night and day. From village to village, from hand to hand – a fire, somewhere secretly lit, runs wide about. No one knows where it originally started, but perhaps it was sent by farmers just come home from their day-work. Now their way has become too hard, now they want to set themselves free. . . . Fiery cross comes, fiery cross goes! Ride tonight[27] or set a man in your place! So it passes through night and day bringing its urgent message: Ride tonight! Tonight!

The voice is accompanied by the clip-clop of horse's hooves, and the woman's aged face is cross-cut in a suggestive montage where the silhouettes of the riders are outlined against the night sky and the fiery cross is passed from one man to another in the light of a flickering torch.

The alert films were a sign that the industry had acknowledged the vehement criticism directed against it during the last years of the 1930s, as has been discussed above. The major companies like Svensk Filmindustri and Sandrews invested in a series of films that were regarded as 'serious,' and such concepts as 'culturally valuable film' and 'literary cinema' were once again common in the industry. The new head of Svensk Filmindustri, Carl Anders Dymling, wrote brief editorials regularly in the company magazine *Filmnyheter*, airing his opinions about quality film and, in connection therewith, the question of finding an audience for it. The following quote is from 1950 but represents the nucleus of the ideological programme he advocated on his appointment ten years earlier, which had the education of the audience as its basis:

A prerequisite for an artistic cinema that keeps a high cultural standard is an advanced audience, which is sufficiently large for this sort of film production to be financially sound: in other words the audience ought to be mature and have left the less complex entertainment forms behind them, and be prepared to appreciate artistic film. The overriding issue above all is thus the question of the spiritual maturity of the audience and its active demand for culture.[28]

The critics of the film industry certainly believed that it was the job of the producers to guide the audience through a thoroughly considered repertory of edifying films, while the industry in its turn was only partially prepared to accept this difficult task – as it had proved to be less profitable.

Thus during wartime a number of literary classics were filmed, some of which were disappointments, such as the remakes of the works by Selma Lagerlöf. One of the most successful productions was the film made from Hjamar Söderberg's well-loved novel *Doktor Glas* in 1942, directed by Rune Carlsten – the film was moreover produced by Svensk Talfilm, which was known for its production of popular comedies.

Doktor Glas is played by Georg Rydeberg, one of the great stars of the 1940s, who with his mysterious and lugubrious appearance splendidly portrays the itinerant loner Glas, who takes his endless walks in the summer heat of Stockholm. Doktor Glas is the main character in a story where he, the doctor, falls in love from a distance with a clergyman's young wife. The woman, who is having an affair with another man, visits the doctor since she suffers terribly from her husband's revolting intimacies; she asks the doctor to tell her husband that she suffers from a condition which does not allow sexual intercourse. Glas develops a crush on her, and poisons the clergyman at an opportune moment. No one suspects the doctor, who testifies to the effect that the clergyman has suffered from a heart condition for years. Glas in turn is condemned to living, to continue as before, by watching other people's lives from the outside.

During one of his walks in the old town of Stockholm, Glas happens to see a watch with no hands in a shop window. The watch fascinates him and he enters the shop where the proprietor comments on it: 'There is something peaceful about a watch with no hands – like the face of a dead man.' A little more than ten years later this scene would appear like a palimpsest in Ingmar Bergman's *Wild Strawberries* (*Smultronstället*) (1957). The film opens with a dream sequence in which the aged doctor Isak Borg wanders the summer-hot streets of the old town. All the clocks he sees have no hands, and shortly after having checked his pocket watch – which resembles the one Glas saw in the shop window – he encounters the face of a dead man.

The post-war period in the history of Swedish cinema is considered to be the period when the social and sexual revolutions took place, as a time when many of the norms that were characteristic of earlier society were abandoned. During the period of the alert many marriages were put under strain because of the enforced absence of husbands, and the insecurity of the crisis was reflected in an increased number of broken and temporary relationships. A number of psychologizing marital portrayals appeared in the repertory. One of the first was *Take Care of Ulla* (*Ta hand om Ulla*) (1942) which, in its capacity as a contemporaneous film with realistic and serious undertones was to be the model for many others.

It was also at this time that film critic and theatre director Per Lindberg began to experiment with films like *Talk of the Town* (*Det sägs på stan*) (1941) where he gives film photographer Åke Dahlqvist free rein. One of the most sought-after photographers at Svensk Filmindustri, Dahqvist's skilful touch is characteristic of many films. When Molander directed he restrained himself with a subdued but none the less expressive play of shadows; while in Lindberg's company he used the whole range of visual expressions and paint in light and shadow.

Films like *Steel* (*Stål*) (1940) and *A Crime* (*Ett Brott*) (1940) were among those films which, during wartime, reflected the reorientation that had taken place. It was partly a question of a change in the social climate: people were demanding new ideas; but they were also part and parcel of the general facelift that the film industry had instigated. Working-class portrayals had been absent from the repertory until now, with the exception of the idyllic comedies of *The Southsiders* (*Söderkåkar*) type, while films like *Stål* and *Ett Brott* put the representatives of the working class in a societal context.

In the 1930s a group of so-called proletarian writers – 'The Five' – had attracted much attention and appreciation in Sweden's literary circles. The name 'The Five' stood for a group of young autodidacts who had left behind their poor adolescent background in the country and written a series of popular novels about their childhood experiences on the big farms where the agricultural labourers, who were paid in kind, lived. These working-class novels now became the subject of films. The author Ivar Lo-Johansson was one of the most exploited in this context, and was himself interested in participating in scriptwriting.

One of the most widely read of Lo-Johansson's novels, *Only a Mother* (*Bara en mor*) (1949) was directed by Alf Sjöberg and is today a typical example of his directorial style. *Bara en mor* is, together with *Miss Julie* (*Fröken Julie*) a typical example of Sjöberg's films where he uses the *mise-en-scène* effectively to create a conflict between the individual and the collective, and where time and space are woven in and out of each other. The film begins with a long, sweeping shot of the faces of the workers who have lined up in the yard for a group photo. In this shot each individual face blends with the others to become so many anonymous ovals; at the same time the camera stops, as if by accident, at the film's main character Rya-Rya. Similarly, the bodies of the workers merge into the field, from where they are bringing in the hay in the midst of the summer heat.

The actual narrative begins when the general establishing of the environment of the camera is transferred to registering Rya-Rya's breaking of the norm: a young woman runs screaming across the field and everyone abandons their noon-day rest to follow her to the lakeside. Rya-Rya attracts the negative attentions of the entire workers' collective as she has decided to take a swim, and the people now gather on the rocks by the lake, where their bodies form an imposing monolith that towers like a mountain over the young woman as she, naked and defenceless, seeks shelter in the reeds.

At the end of the 1940s Rya-Rya's nude swim did not cause any sensation among the audience, if it ever would. In the consciousness of international film audiences however, it was scenes like this that were to lay the foundation of what was eventually to be called 'the Swedish sin'. In Sweden the context was somewhat different, however. In the Scandinavian world, nature is namely perceived as a fundamentally positive phenomenon – something that provides strength and competence for survival and which is a source of renewal and re-creation. The naked human body is perceived as part of nature, and is assigned the same values as nature itself. In addition to this – and despite the hostile views of many nonconformist movements – sexuality is considered as natural and thereby principally positive. The popular sports movement that developed early in the century, and which quickly spread to all layers of society, also contributed to this conception.

It is in this context that one should view the more cherished stereotypes of Scandinavian cinema: the loving couple who take a nude swim together surrounded by summer greenery. At a ritual level the swim proves they are suited to each other and seals the bond between them. At the beginning of the 1930s the swim happened within a framework of necessity, as, for instance, in *The Song of the Scarlet Flower* (*Sången om den eldröda blomman*) (Branner, 1932), where Olof and Kyllikki's raft is destroyed and the couple have to swim across the river to make it home in time. In *She Danced Only One Summer* (*Hon dansade en sommar*) (Mattson, 1952) the swim begins as childish and innocent play, only to quickly shift to a serious exchange of looks and ultimately to sexual intercourse, while the swim in *Summer with Monika* (*Sommaren med Monika*) (Bergman, 1953) demonstrates elaborate erotics on the rocks in the Stockholm archipelago.

However, it is to a very large extent the context that dictates the interpretation: nakedness in the green of summer is read in quite a different manner from undressing within four walls. The Swedish film censors let their reins run loose in a determined way in this context as well, even if the 1960s saw the final squabbles over the matter. Besides the realistic portrayals of married life, there appeared a genre in the post-war era known as the 'problem film'. In these films sexuality is made out to be a destructive force and the victim is frequently a young girl who comes from the country to the city, as in Hampe Faustman's *The Girl and the Devil* (*Flickan och djävulen*) (1944) and *Anna Lans* (1943). The small company Luxfilm had the young and beautiful actress Viveca Lindfors under contract – one of the many who would presently disappear to the USA. In *Anna Lans* she plays the title character, a fallen girl from the country who eventually turns her life around and becomes a Salvationist.

In the fictive universe of the 1940s in Sweden, the city represented the evil, corrupt nucleus of disillusioned people and to live there was perceived to be fraught with peril. Similarly, moving back into the country could occasionally restore a broken spirit. The rationalization of agriculture, the growth of industrialization and the shortage of labour caused a large-scale move from the country into the cities, and in its wake the resultant structural changes were reflected in a wave of nostalgia on the screen. One of the most popular films of the 1940s – and Svensk Filmindustri's biggest box-office hit thus far – was the film *Rain follows the Dew* (*Driver dagg faller regn*) directed by Gustaf Edgren with Mai Zetterling and Alf Kjellin in the leading roles. These two were perhaps the lovers *par excellence* besides Georg Rydeberg and Viveca Lindfors.

Driver dagg faller regn (1946) was based on Margit Söderholm's novel by that name, which was published in 1943 after having won an award in a writing competition. When Svensk Filmindustri's Gustaf Edgren, who had been one of the judges, wanted to make a film of the story, Dymling, the company president, received the proposal very coldly. In his opinion it was an unoriginal story in the worst ladies' magazine tradition, and did nothing but confirm the prejudices he already had about Edgren as an inferior director. Dymling's ambitious venture into an 'artistic' and highly prestigious series of films in the early 1940s had flopped, however, and certain people at Svensk Filmindustri made sure that Edgren, who had by now approached another company, was reinstated. This was fortunate for Svensk Filmindustri, because the film became its biggest hit of the sound film era and made more than a million SEK.

The reviewers were somewhat more restrained than the audience and *Driver dagg faller regn* was perceived as a well-made but unoriginal film, and in one sense this was true. But the film is also an archetypical fairy-tale that unites many mythical elements within its framework which appealed to contemporary audiences. It tells the story of a well-to-do farmer's daughter who falls in love with a young fiddler of dubious origins. Her blonde hair and his black curls create a contrast between the familiar and the strange that is given expression at many levels throughout the film. *Driver dagg faller regn* contains magnificent views of nature where the young man plays his violin by the stream, a scene that exploits ancient concepts of the water god Näcken who lures people to their doom through his playing, and it gives voice to nonconformist concepts of the music as sinful and the belief in love as a saving grace.

The new era was also portrayed through popular film, and the musicals starring the vaudeville actors of the 1930s were replaced by jazz films. The early 1940s introduced a young singing star who was to become very important to Swedish jazz: Alice Babs (Nilsson). In the main role in the film *Swing it Teacher!* (*Swing it Magistern*) (1940), Alice Babs – who some thirty years later was to become court singer – was considered by its self-appointed guardians to be a danger to the morals of young people. The young people themselves and the older audience loved the dashing young girl. She was quite soon to devote herself to her singing career and left the cinema after taking roles in only a few such films.

One might have assumed that as the war ended the films about military life would have ceased as well, but this was not the case. The military farce genre created new variations. A cartoon, *Private Karlsson (91:an Karlsson)* was launched as a series of films which became popular, above all as matinees.

THE ROAD TO ORDER

After the end of the Second World War Sweden's foreign policy was characterized by caution which emphasized the country's policy of non-alignment. It was generally considered, however, that this non-alignment called for strong defence and, among other measures, the length of compulsory military service was extended. When Norway and Denmark joined NATO the Swedes decided to stay out of political blocks. It would have appeared that the country promoted an inward-looking and reformist social structure without any substantial interest in the rest of the world, had the Swedes not at the same time actively worked for a Nordic cooperation. This was to result in the Nordic Council which was founded in 1952 on Danish initiative. Several agreements were closed that facilitated trade and labour mobility between the Nordic countries – something which led to a considerable immigration from Finland, that had been devastated by the war, to the Swedish industrial centres in the 1950s. At the same time, a large number of Italian immigrants also came to Sweden, which needed workers for its growing industries.

The Swedes' – in all other respects – neutral foreign policy was characterized by a certain compliance towards the Soviet Union which had integrated the Baltic States into its territory after the Second World War. As a result, there was a relatively large number of Estonians and other Baltic refugees in the country. A traumatic post-war event, the so-called Baltic extradition, took place in 1946. At the end of the war a group of 167 Balts had come to Sweden. These had participated in the fighting against the Soviet Union and now that the Baltic States were occupied, the Russians demanded that the 167 refugees be extradited. The Swedish government complied with this demand, despite widespread protest.

Sweden's position as a neutral country found expression when it joined the UN in 1946, whereupon it adopted an active stance and participated in peace-keeping missions in various parts of the world. Several Swedes worked as mediators in conflicts, among them Folke Bernadotte who was murdered in Jerusalem in 1948. The Swede Dag Hammarskiöld was elected as Secretary-general of the UN in 1953. Swedish women also participated in the international peace work: for example, Alva Myrdal was elected chairwoman of the UN's Department for Social Issues. In 1960 there was a lively debate over the so-called tactical atomic weapons. Through the suggestion of a certain Östen Unden in 1961, a proposal was put forward in the UN for the founding of a nuclear-free zone.

After the pause in reform caused by the Second World War, the social democrats had presented their programme of 'the twenty-seven points' which, among other things, included proposals concerning industrial democracy, active employment policies and increased state influence over trade and industry. An expression of the general radicalization of Swedish society had been the major strike in 1945 when 120,000 engineering industry workers went on strike in their demand for reforms. In the winter of that year several inquiries were set up to investigate the possibility of several branches of Swedish heavy industry becoming state-owned. The Swedish export industry was ready and waiting for war-torn Europe to begin reconstruction work. Products from the steel and engineering industries as well as the sizeable export of lumber answered the demands in Europe, and it was intended that the resulting income should finance the country's rising living standards.

The Parliament of 1946 ruled on increasing the state pension in order to guarantee a moderate income for older citizens. Two years later the general child allowance was introduced: every family with children under the age of 16 received a sum of money (which was gradually increased in subsequent years) that was to subsidize the augmented expenses involved in supporting a family. Despite continued building there was a need for more housing, and the state stimulated building by granting subsidized loans and housing discounts. The vacation law of 1951 stipulated that the two weeks' leave be extended to three weeks – and was eventually to be increased to five weeks.

The labour market parties closed the agreement of instituting works councils for information and counselling in trade and industry. The export industry grew, and when the Swedish krona (SEK) was devalued successively in order to check inflation – the devaluation of 1949 was particularly great – this further increased the profits of the export industry. At the same time, cautious economies were made: the rationing of foodstuffs was kept until 1949, after which the price controls were maintained to further avoid inflation. The real wages began to climb steadily at the beginning of the 1950s, however (and were to do so for almost a quarter of century to come), which benefited the entire population. This affluence naturally led to an increase in private and public consumption. The Swedes could among other things increase their purchases of so-called endurable consumer goods: vacuum cleaners, refrigerators and cars – which in turn favoured the domestic industries.

In the 1950s the Swedish population thus began to harvest the results of the economic policy that had been introduced in the latter half of the 1930s, and which was the foundation of the social structure that the social engineers attached to the social democratic party represented. The three main goals of the programme were growth, full employment and price stability. At the beginning of the 1950s there was considerable faith in the ability of the industry to create growth, and there was a unanimous conviction that it was the job of society to divide the resulting income in as equal a way as possible. There was thus consensus as to these goals: increased growth and affluence for all, and the means to accomplish this development were also accepted, i.e. increased rationalization, greater efficiency and the closure of unprofitable industries. Maximal growth could only be achieved by increasing efficiency and by structural rationalizations. This also presumed an expanded mobility of the labour force – a circumstance which meant that the individual worker had to move with his or her family to where the profitable jobs were. As a consequence the countryside began to be depopulated.

In the 1950s people still accepted these structural rationalizations – criticism was not to surface until the late 1960s – but somewhere in the hearts of the people there lingered a nostalgia that, according to film historians like Leif Furhammar and Per Olov Qvist, among other places found its expression in many films that were set in the country, films which were either explicitly nostalgic or which romanticized the countryside. 'It would appear that the Swedish rural films contributed with some sort of fiction therapy to the psychological working through of this collective trauma ... which the popular move from the country into the cities meant',[29] wrote Furhammar, who distinguished three dominating film typologies that succeeded each other on the screen in the early 1950s. First, he says, there was the historical peasant film. *Driver dag faller regn* was a typical example of a film that upheld the values and traditions of the farmer communities in a national romantic form. Second, there appeared a series of farcical films which at once ridiculed and celebrated the rural way of life that was now on the verge of disappearing. A classical representative was the series of films entitled *Åsa-Nisse* (1949–68), about a Småland farmer whose pastoral adventures people never tired of watching. The critics in their turn tore their hair: the ever conciliatory Robin Hood pointed out that surveys had found that a not inconsiderable proportion of the audience had an intellect of a 10–12-year-old and 'why not indulge these backward elements in innocent amusement in the cinema as well?'[30] Åsa-Nisse – who was based on Stig Cederholm's cartoon – turned out to be exceedingly long-lived and a total of twenty films had been made by the end of the 1960s.

In the third category of rural films which P. O. Qvist has called 'contemporary dramatizations',[31] are the films that considered life in the country with a nostalgic melancholy and which in their most genuine form expressed such a sensitivity as to warrant speaking of mourning proper. These films – writes Furhammar – portrayed life in the country as wholesome and humane as opposed to the corrupting existence in the city. The dichotomy of country–city has always been a feature of Swedish film, but this new, nostalgic dimension came about through an awareness of the obsolescence of rural life. *Hon dansade en sommar* (1951) was one such film and was to be its producer Nordisk Tonefilm's biggest box-office hit ever.

Such an upheaval as the virtual evacuation of the Swedish countryside would not have been accepted had not affluence steadily increased during the 1950s and 1960s. The working week was reduced to 40 hours and Saturdays off were introduced. In 1955 compulsory health insurance was instigated and in 1957 the old poor relief law was substituted by the law of social assistance. A complex system of housing subsidies was developed and the country continued along the general welfare line by accepting a system of supplementary pensions (ATP), where part of every employee's salary was deducted for state pension funds and the money administered and paid as service pensions, a form of supplement to people's pensions. Through such an arrangement people were able to maintain their incomes virtually intact upon retiring. The weakness of this system was if it were to collapse due to a rise in inflation and if pension expenses were to exceed incomes – in effect contemporary pensions were financed largely through current incomes. Faith in the never ceasing growth of the Welfare State was unwavering, however, and the vehement political fight that the introduction of this system caused was about something else, namely the relationship between private initiative and government control. The conservative parties spoke warmly on behalf of a voluntary pension saving system, but the Swedes chose differently. The faith in justice and in the care of the state system's principles was strong.

What was to be called the Swedish model was thus both cause and consequence of the rapid economic growth. As of the 1950s the wage policy that showed solidarity with low-paid workers was the most important corner-stone of this model. The wages were negotiated centrally between the organizations which represented the various parties of the labour market. In order for industries to expand, the principle demanded that wage earners did not enforce such raises as they could have so that the companies could invest their profits in further expansion instead. On the other hand, this meant that companies who could not pay wages similar to the ones that the major industries could afford were at risk of being forced out of business. However, this had been anticipated by the social planners. To counterbalance this effect, society invested in various measures to facilitate mobility within the labour market: for instance, retraining and relocation grants for those workers who might be affected. In order to accomplish this, massive public funds were allotted to the expansion of the Swedish Labour Market Board (AMS): in 1950 only 1 per cent of the state's expenses went to this agency, while the corresponding figure twenty years later was 7.4 per cent.

The public sector's insurance systems, medical services and health care, child care and the schools were expanded in the 1950s and in particular in the 1960s. To be able to finance the expansion of the public sector the tax burden was increased for both individuals and companies, a policy which led to severe fights in domestic politics. In 1947 a new taxation system had been introduced, which brought some relief for low wage earners, but which involved increased taxation pressure for high earners, a feature that has been characteristic of the Swedish model ever since. As early as 1945 a practice had been introduced where tax was deducted at source.

The result of these reforms was that the state income multiplied over a short space of time. The number of public posts increased, many of which were filled by women. In 1950 only 15 per cent of married women had entered the labour market while the corresponding figure in 1980 was 64 per cent, the major part of these working in low-paid service occupations and part-time employment, however. In 1959 the comprehensive school was introduced and it is interesting to note that it was only then that one started from the old ordinance according to which the parish clergyman was to be a natural member on the board of a school. Twelve years later nine years of compulsory schooling was established. Because Scandinavian children do not start school until they are seven years old, they were to live at home at least until they were sixteen years or so, sometimes later. The entry of young people into the labour market was thus postponed by a few years. This was to have its consequences for family life, the consumer patterns of families and contributed to the spread of youth culture.

This sense of order extended right into people's homes, and an interesting document from this time is the so-called 'housewife films' which were shown for free in cinemas throughout the country on behalf of, among others, the Cooperative Wholesale Society (KF). The housewife films were exceptionally popular and the last ones were made as late as the mid-1970s. As a historical document they portray the dominant ideology in society by their focus on the home and its dependence on the Welfare State, the folkhem rhetoric. The explicit goal of these films was to educate housewives and foster them towards the ideal that had been established in the 1930s: at the centre of the folkhem is the housewife who is well trained for her task and who directs the chores and duties of the home.

The housewife films did not solely address the woman of the home, however, but also other members of the family. They did not only portray the home and its appearance but touched on its inhabitants as well. The whole family was encouraged to help around the house in order to facilitate the work of the mother who, through her ministrations, was able to make the home comfortable and cozy for everybody: 'Help your mama, change your pajamas!'[32] Through images and narrative the family was described as a chain that – in order to maintain its strength – required that none of the links (i.e. the mother) be exposed to undue strain. The home in its turn was to be a source of rest and recreation for its members. It was important to tend to both the corporeal and the spiritual health of the family members, but it is clear that material well-being was perceived as the foundation of spiritual health.

Almost all the housewife films advertised various types of products: thus a scene about sleep and its beneficial effects would promote the planned, controlled and thoroughly tested beds and bedroom furniture of KF, and an information film about coffee would promote a certain brand as being the best and most modern kind. The word *modern* is one of the most frequently used in the housewife films, as is the word *practical* and, self-evidently, *planning*. If the family is to fit a new kitchen, advice is asked of experts – who know best because they have conducted studies as to how the housewife works in the kitchen. Planning is long term and one saves money for part of the financing and borrows the rest. Characteristic of the rhetoric in these films is a note of caution against all kinds of wastefulness and excess: 'On the contrary it is possible to create a beautiful frame for the meal with small means!'[33]

The housewife films represent an ideal world where the order creates an overall pattern for people's lives. They were not as humourlessly wholesome as one might easily imagine, however. Very early on these short sketches showed a filmic self-awareness that was also characteristic of the feature films produced by the industry. Thus, for instance, the characters could suddenly break the illusion of reality, and address the audience in self-ironic terms, as did the expert guide in a fruit beverage film when he introduced himself as 'one of the men in these films wearing white coats, who knows anything and everything'.[34]

THE FILM INDUSTRY IN THE WELFARE STATE

As the expenses of the state increased, so did the tax burden for both wage earners and industries. The film industry did not quite belong in the favoured and lucrative export category, and many of the measures that were taken to facilitate profitability for the latter – such as devaluation, price control and the general wage policy – dealt the film industry a particularly hard blow. The devaluations raised the price of raw film and made the import of foreign film more expensive, the collectively agreed raises in wages also affected production costs and price control prevented the industry from retrieving its losses through the income from ticket sales. The head of Svensk Filmindustri, Carl Anders Dymling, pointed out in a debate article in the early 1950s that production costs had increased since the end of the war by 20 per cent, while incomes had decreased by 10 per cent.

The period immediately following the end of the war heralded a decline for the cinema business as it was exposed to competition from other amusements that had been in limited supply during the war years. To a certain extent people were also beginning to save their surplus money in order to buy capital goods, not the least of which was a car. The income of the industry soon rose again, however – a case which gave the state, led by the Minister of Finance Wigforss, direct occasion to act. What was felt as a staggering blow to the film industry was the increase at the end of the 1940s of indirect taxes – among other things on wine, spirits and tobacco. This group included the entertainment tax, which was raised in 1948 from 24 per cent to 39 per cent of the income from ticket sales.

The film industry subsequently began an offensive and initiated the 'film stop' in the spring of 1951. No films were produced during the stop period, with the exception of *Hon dansade en sommar* directed by Arne Mattsson, which was concluded by dispensation. The remarkable and famous Bris films directed by Ingmar Bergman, for want of anything else, also date from this time: they were commercials for Bris soap and each included a subtle reference to the theatre and its conventions.

The film stop quickly achieved practical results that same spring; a state inquiry (set up by the new Minister of Finance Per Edvin Sköld) put forward a proposal that was passed by Parliament within days: 20 per cent of the state entertainment tax was to be returned in order to support Swedish film production. This was not a very large sum considering that the state share of the entertainment tax consisted of 75 per cent, while the rest went to the communities. The film industry had suggested 30 per cent, but accepted what was offered. In 1957 – one year after the introduction of television – a film inquiry was set up and it presented its report two years later. On its advice, Parliament decided to lower the entertainment tax to 25 per cent and to allow the entire state share – which was half of this tax – to be returned to the movie industry, with the provision that 20 per cent of this sum was to be allotted as quality premiums for individual films. In 1959 there were further tax reductions which resulted in a refund of 30 per cent of the state tax revenues on black-and-white films and 45 per cent on colour films.

Despite these financial difficulties during the first half of the 1950s, it still appeared as if the crowds attending the cinemas would continue. In 1956 the attendance figures were measured at 80 million. The same year the film business invested in a large number of cinemas, namely in the cities' – for example, Stockholm's – suburbs, in the newly built dormitory towns that had been completed and enthusiastically inaugurated in this period. Little did one know that the massive audiences were to be reduced by half in the following seven years, and that by 1972 the cinema audiences would be down to 22.5 million people.

In 1956 Sveriges Television (Sweden's Television) began broadcasting regularly in the country and in less than ten years the number of television licences was to exceed two million. Rune Waldekranz recounts in the 1950s section of *Svensk Filmografi* (*Swedish Filmography*) that Anders Sandrew – the head of the Sandrews group – who was one of the first to get a television set of his own, had gloomily predicted that every family would within a short space of time acquire their own television sets. Because of this he believed that the film industry faced a very uncertain future. Sandrew knew his audience and was proved right, even if television was not the only reason for the downturn in the fortunes of the movie industry. The more important reason was the diversification of the audience.

In a small country like Sweden the audience had been particularly homogeneous in the past. People shared a common frame of reference as well as similar values and laughed at the same things. A characteristic of

Swedish cinema had always been its lack of different genres which was at least partly due to the domestic audience being so small that films, in order to be profitable, had to be directed to as many people as possible. The genres that did exist – the military farce and slapstick – originated in the theatre and were considered appropriate as a source of income, but there was no interest in developing these or other genres. To the extent that a development did take place – for instance in Ingmar Bergman's productions of the 1940s and in Arne Mattsson's films of the 1950s – it met with disapproval from the critics.

Genre films were by definition considered as entertainment and, in the producer ranks as well, there was a predominant ambition to achieve artistic or 'culturally valuable' film. This often resembled what was known as 'literary cinema' and was, as discussed above, based on well-known literary works and staged in accordance with the structure and visual images of theatre melodrama. In a way it can be said that the domestic cinema was one huge genre by itself – not least because its content and modes of expression had become fairly predictable through a sort of understanding between the producers and the audience. The film director was a craftsman who carried out the plans according to the script, and in the 1930s it had not been at all uncommon to credit the script writer rather than the director in advertisements.

In the 1940s the ambitions of the professional directors began to largely change. The generation of directors who had begun their careers at the beginning of the decade wanted to express their own ideas more so than had the older generation of more craft-oriented narrators. Per Lindberg in his films of the early 1940s had experimented with expressionistic shadow play. Alf Sjöberg favoured long takes and deep focus in his literary interpretations and Ingmar Bergman had begun to explore the expressive possibilities of the cinema, to begin with as script writer, and not least, Hampe Faustman expressed his socialist stance in films such as *Foreign Port* (*Främmande hamn*) (1948). Faustman had been much influenced by the early Soviet cinema, for instance, directors Pudovkin and Eisenstein – and in his attitude towards the importance and function of the medium he heralded the 1960s generation.

The independent ambitions of the directors led to an increased mobility as regards the production companies: if the idea one had was not cleared 'at home', one approached another company. This was particularly characteristic of, for instance, Ingmar Bergman, who had the script for *The Night of the Jesters* (*Gycklarnas afton*) refused at SF, but approved at Sandrews. When the management at Sandrews began to have doubts, Bergman always found support from Lorens Marmstedt at Terrafilm, or from Nordisk Tonefilm owned by the popular movements.

Added to this mobility there were also changes in the tastes and preferences of the audience, which were no longer so predictable. The audience was divided into at least three large groups, of which no one group alone would be quite sufficient to fill the cinemas: the general audience, the teenagers and the connoisseurs. The first group comprised the old-fashioned ordinary cinema audience, the people who were now growing older and were saving to purchase a car or a summer cottage. They preferred staying at home on a Saturday night in front of their newly acquired television sets watching *Hylands hörna*[35] – one of Sweden's most popular programmes ever, which went on air for the first time in 1962. The programme was presented by Lennart Hyland, who had become a famous radio personality in the 1950s.

Comedies were still popular and thus profitable, even if the old slapstick, with the exception of *Åsa-Nisse*, had disappeared from the silver screen. The 1950s comedies took place in a middle-class setting or an artistic sphere. They were often fantasies featuring song and dance routines. Towards the end of the decade it was not uncommon for the film industry – particularly in the comedies – to comment on and parody the other (competing) media. Hasse Ekman – who with his light touch had succeeded Schamyl Bauman as the director of Sickan Carlsson – directed, starred in and scripted the film *Seventh Heaven (Sjunde himlen)* (1956). In this film he presents a good-humoured parody of Hyland in the character of the radio charmer Willie Lorens in a way that had one reviewer exclaiming: 'an unusually charming chap, pleasant, friendly and in a charming way in love with his own artistic world'.[36] Willie Lorens ends up in hospital where he meets a young doctor with principles, Lovisa, played by Sickan Carlsson. He becomes interested in her and perhaps she in him, but she has promised to marry the major, a man of principles like herself, Ernst C:sson (i.e. Carlsson) Kruse (Gunnar Björnstrand), and to travel to Italy for the wedding. Willie joins the travel party and after many complications on the journey, he finally wins Lovisa. The film exploits a second contemporary phenomenon as well, namely the tourist travels that were becoming accessible for increasing numbers of Swedes. Thus with the scenic photography of Åke Dahlqvist the bus travels through the most beautiful of southern European landscapes.

Travel was once again a theme in the sequel to this film, *Heaven and Pancake (Himmel och pannkaka)* (1959), where Willie Lorens hosts a television show and takes a trip to Guatemala by banana boat. This time Lovisa, who is now his wife, has misinterpreted the relationship between Willie and his programme hostess. She accepts an invitation to go on a trip from Kruse, her ex-fiancé, now the chief supervisor of the banana boat. Needless to say, at the end Willie runs away with Lovisa and Kruse proposes to the television hostess. Robin Hood wrote: 'It is an excellent commercial for banana companies and banana eating, and like all excellent films it is entertaining.'[37] The film had a postscript in that several parties protested against the commercial promotive qualities of the film; for instance the Advertising

Agencies' Association wrote to the Movie Theatre Association claiming that they had the exclusive right to produce commercial films.

The topic of the film *Little Fridolf and I* (*Lille Fridolf och jag*) (Anderberg, 1956) was also taken from the radio. The series, about the diminutive office manager Fridolf Olsson and his tyrannical wife Selma, had begun to be broadcast on the radio in autumn 1955 and had become very popular. The film version, with the author Rune Moberg's own script, was a formidable success and made almost three million SEK. The film had three quick sequels which did not live up to the first success, however. In 1959 Douglas Håge, who had played Fridolf so superbly, died, but the character lived on as a cartoon. A similar first-time success was the debut film of Lars Magnus Lindgren, *There are no Angels* (*Änglar, finns dom . . .*) (1961) starring the young Christina Schollin and Jarl Kulle. Lindgren had previously only made short films and now he had the opportunity to demonstrate his ability with a comedy which in its basic formula was very conventional: young man enters workplace, meets a girl who is already engaged, shows his competence, is promoted and wins the girl. The film was considered unconventional however, through its immediate acting style, and its way of interweaving a serious love story with the more comic complications at the bank. *Änglar, finns dom . . .* was seen by 2.8 million people and was thus the biggest box-office hit of the Swedish film industry after *Hon dansade en sommar*. What the two films had in common were the aesthetic love scenes in the Swedish summer archipelago and the views of the countryside as a source of strength and recreation. The difference between them lay in *Änglar, finns dom . . .* having an optimistic outlook on city life in combination with the rural idyll.

The second group comprising the Swedish cinema audience was the still growing teenage audience of the cities. They were difficult to please and their preferences were increasingly for foreign film. The industry rather clumsily tried to appeal to this group by producing a number of films that have been characterized as 'young people going astray'.[38] The role models for these films were the American rebel films starring James Dean, but in reality these films had their predecessors in the Swedish social problem films of the 1940s. One such early film was *Youth in Danger* (*Ungdom i fara*) (Holmgren, 1947) where Svensk Filmindustri's future head, Kenne Fant, starred in the main role. *The Dance Hall* (*Danssalongen*) (Larsson, 1955) is another example. The film was a youth thriller shot at Nalen (short for National), Stockholm's most popular jazz palace. Lars Ekborg played the young gangster Daggen who, after a period in prison, tries to re-establish his 'business' and win back his fiancée, the young singer Sonja. The film's soundtrack features the music of some of the most renowned jazz musicians of the time, among them Gunnar Siljablo Nilsson singing his famous bebop song 'Sil-ja-bloo-ba-du-ba . . .'.

The film *Rockers* (*Raggare!*) (Hellbom, 1959) was Olle Hellbom's second main feature film (see below) and received an enthusiastic reception. The film was labelled 'neorealistic' and contained apparent references to such films as *Rebel Without a Cause* (Ray, 1955). Raggare referred to the young men who drove their big American cars up and down Stockholm's main street Kungsgatan at night. The film is an episodic portrayal of young people with tough façades, who took drugs; it is about high speed and sudden, suspicious death. Many reviewers were enthusiastic about the realistic nature of the film, but it also caused some people to take a moral stand: many believed that *Raggare!* encouraged young people to adopt the lifestyle it depicted.

As well as the teenage audience, children made up another group and would, in time, become an important target and source of income for domestic film. As early as the 1930s, films had been produced with a child audience in mind, among others *Andersson's Kalle* (*Anderssonskans Kalle*), *Two Years in Each Grade* (*Två år i varje klass*), and a number of other rascal films. However, it was only now that the film producers began to address the youngest members of their audience. Above all, the works of children's book author Astrid Lindgren became a lucrative source of income, even if filming of her works was not to reach its peak until during and after the 1960s. A remarkable phenomenon occurred after the mid-1970s when the elderly, socially committed author became all but canonized by the inhabitants of the Welfare State (the folkhem), who had almost all grown up with her books.

The first films made from Astrid Lindgren's books were her children's detective novels: *The Master Detective Blomkvist* (*Mästerdetektiven Blomkvist*) (Husberg, 1947) which became an immediate hit, as did its sequel *The Master Detective and Rasmus* (*Mästerdetektiven och Rasmus*). Ten years later Olle Hellbom made his debut as a feature film director with *The Master Detective Lives Dangerously* (*Mästerdetektiven lever farligt*) (1957). Margareta Norlin explains the rise and success of the detective films by maintaining that they represent dramatic conflict which most other films of the time seemed to lack. She holds that, particularly during the war, the social dramas, for example, focused on conflict between different classes and social groups, but that these disappeared towards the end of the decade, in particular films that were aimed at younger children. The detective films presented a distinct conflict and dramatic construction that caught the audience's attention.

In *Mästerdetektiven lever farligt*, the master detective's 13-year-old friend Eva-Lotta happens to witness a murder when she is searching for a stone that a rival gang has hidden in a ruin. The shocked Eva-Lotta cannot remember much of the events, but the newspapers make the most of the story and the murderer believes himself unsafe as long as the girl is alive. He sends Eva-Lotta some poisoned chocolate which she happens to give to a neighbour, whose dog dies when it is fed the chocolate. This appears highly suspicious to Kalle Blomkvist and he begins to enquire into the affair on his own initiative. The story has a happy ending as Eva-Lotta manages to convey a message to him, singing in the gang's secret language that the man she is talking to is the murderer: 'Mom-u-ror-dod-e-ror-e-ror.'

Despite the fact that *Mästerdetektiven lever farligt* is a film aimed at children, it contains several elements that are characteristic of other detective films of the period. The events take place in a small, sleepy town where the sun shines and the lilacs perfume the summer breeze that sweeps over the tidy houses. With their well-tended lawns and gardens they form a reassuring unlikely contrast to such powerful passions that lead to nasty murders. Thus, for example, the events of Maria Lang's – the pseudonym for the girls' school principal Dagmar Lange's – murder stories take place in a sleepy little town she calls Skoga (in reality, Lange's hometown of Nora). In 1961 Arne Mattsson directed a film based on Lang's detective novel *Kung Liljekonvale av dungen*, whose title refers to a poem by the Värmlander poet Gustav Fröding. The film was entitled *Lovely is the Summer Night* (*Ljuvlig är sommarnatten*), which is a somewhat less sophisticated – but decidedly better known – reference to a line from the popular waltz which, arranged in the minor key, accompanies the story.

A young bride, Annelie Hammar disappears on her wedding day and is later found murdered with a bouquet of lilies of the valley clasped in her hand. *Ljuvlig är sommarnatten* is an ordinary whodunit which is animated by carefully conceived camera work. In pace with the advancement of the story, it also retreats into the past, which takes shape on the screen in a dreamy fashion, with no other sound than the minor chords of the waltz. The time transfers often happen through sideways camera movements; thus for example, in a scene where the main character, detective superintendent Christer Wijk, makes a phone call from the cabin to where he has followed Annelie's tracks. He holds the receiver in his hand in the foreground of the frame, his face is in shadow and his voice faded out. The camera moves slowly to the left to take in the view through the window to a meadow, where Annelie walks slowly while the light plays in her blonde hair. After thus having confirmed Christer's suspicions the camera moves back to his face, and back to the present.

Mattson also directed a series of the so-called Hillman detective stories – Hillman himself was played by the male idol of the 1950s Karl-Arne Holmsten – in which Mattson applied the various codes of film narrative in a sophisticated manner, conscious of form and style. One example is *The Lady in Black* (*Damen i svart*), a mystery story where Hillman's wife Kajsa's friend feels that her life is threatened at the mansion where she is living. The couple are invited to stay one weekend to try to solve the mystery. Although events certainly take place in the country which is normally given a positive image, the film evokes a claustrophobic atmosphere by being principally staged indoors. *Damen i svart* applies an elaborate American film noir style with deep focus and low-key lighting where the characters are trapped in the dark or are observed through various frames in order to underline their precarious situation.

The sophisticated camera work of the Mattsson films did not elude the contemporary critics, who were careful to praise photographer Tony Forsberg's work on *Ljuvlig är sommarnatten*, for example. The fact was, however, that the critics believed that such elaborate modes of expression should not be wasted on a common detective story, but ought to be used to create 'art'. When some directors neither wanted, had the ability nor were allowed to do this, they were attacked all the more fiercely. Nils Beyer wrote in *Stockholmstidiningen*:

> Certainly *Ljuvlig är sommarnatten* has been directed by a considerable image artist and there are deceptive devices in the very narrative technique with slides in time and space, of dream and reality. The fatal part is only – and here we come to Arne Mattson's besetting sin as a director – that this exquisite form has not been inspired by the subject at hand. He mounts a common little detective story as if he were creating a monster of beauty and marvel.[39]

An elaborate narrative style was to be cast aside for heavy, serious or 'marvellous' subjects.

It obviously became difficult to work in such an atmosphere. Towards the end of the 1950s many directors, among them Hasse Ekman, retired because of it. The exception among the critics was the veteran Robin Hood, who was capable of seeing nuances in the film narrative as an asset for any film. He could read the meta-signals behind a certain film's transparent realism which told of an awareness of the difference between reality and fiction. Such a case was Gustaf Molander's *Sången om den eldröda blomman* (1956), for instance, which was one of the films that Molander had scripted in his youth and which he could now return to in the venture into remakes that SF had decided on. The film was described by the critics as pretentious trash, with the exception of Robin Hood, who in the opening titles of the film, in their exuberant display of colours and acting style, saw the excess which clearly signalled that this was a tribute to a genre, the farmer melodrama, whose time was without a doubt at an end.

Besides the old-fashioned, now falling audience and the teenagers discussed above, the third group consisted of discriminating and critical film enthusiasts who ever since its birth had cavilled Swedish cinema for its provincialism and lack of artistic ambition. This group was the most influential, in that its members had access to the printed word and a security which gave them precedence in matters of interpreting what was good or bad. The younger generation, headed by Mauritz Edström, Harry Schein, Jurgen Schildt and Hanserik Hjertén, gathered to form a broad critical offensive, which was to pay dividends at the beginning of the 1960s in the form of an altered production ideology and state film policy. At the same time certain forces in the industry had since the late 1940s showed a desire to invest once again in a more prestigious production.

Thus, for example, Rune Waldekranz believed that Sandrews, while he was head of production, should in a time of rising production costs invest more in such films as would be internationally marketable. According to Waldekranz, it was the only way that the domestic producers would be able to count on having their investments returned. At the same time Sweden would be able to assert itself as a country with a national, artistically superior film production. In order to guarantee international success the production, in his opinion, needed to offer something novel, unexpected – even exotic – to the international market.

The Sandrews film company had expanded extensively in the late 1940s by acquiring their own studios. On top of that, the company joined Europa Film as a partner in buying a laboratory company which made them independent of outside laboratory techniques. Sandrews was thereby in a position to rent out its services to others as well. By beginning to import film it was also able to supply its extensive chain of cinemas. Production was increased in the 1950s so that some ten films were completed every year and thereby SF's position as the leading production company in the country was threatened. The cautious Sandrew pursued a more popular line of production and when this paid off he felt ready for a more adventurous series of prestigious productions. Waldekranz was also cleared for his line, where the first production was to be August Strindberg's *Fröken Julie* (1951) directed by Alf Sjöberg.

In the filming of this destructive drama of passions, where the parties take turns in humiliating one another, it is also possible to follow a theme of the voyeuristic gaze. Focusing on the look of a woman that expresses her desire is relatively rare in the world of film melodrama and always ends in disaster. At the very beginning of the film, where Julie is compared to a canary locked in a cage, her piercing gaze follows the servants' celebration of Midsummer from a distance. The object of her desire is her possibility of knowing and the consequences of knowledge: more than sexual satisfaction and love, the drama is about acquiring sexual experience and knowledge about sex.

Fröken Julie won the Grand Prix at the Cannes Film Festival, sharing first place with Vittorio de Sica's *Miracle in Milan* (1951). Encouraged by this success, Waldekranz was to carry through several ambitious projects, among them the production of *Gycklarnas afton* (Bergman, 1953). After reading the script the advisory staff at Sandrews discouraged him from producing it, and the film was a box-office failure in Sweden – in spite of being seen by 320,000 people. However, it won the directorial award at the film festival in Sao Paolo in 1954 and was sold to a number of countries. Today the film, with its theme of humiliation, is thought to be one of Bergman's most important works. When yet another ambitious and expensive investment in a literary theme, the movie *Barabbas* (Sjöberg, 1953) was a huge financial and critical failure, Waldekranz's ambitious programme for quality film ended.

An interesting venture that Sandrews undertook in the early years of the 1950s was the production of the film *The Great Adventure (Det stora äventyret)*, with Arne Sucksdorff directing. Sucksdorff achieved fame for his lyrical and sensitive documentary films about animal life and had won an Oscar in 1947 for his short film *City People (Människor i stad)*. When he suggested his idea of a feature film about animal life in the forest, loosely connected to the story of two boys who were to take care of an otter, the management at SF expressed doubts. Sucksdorff then approached Sandrews who were willing to invest in the idea. *Det stora äventyret* was the biggest Swedish box-office hit in the winter of 1953–54, quite a unique achievement for a film considered to be a documentary. The film contains extraordinarily beautiful and lyrical scenes of nature shot in black and white and founded the school for the style that stretches the definition of a documentary film to its absolute limits. It is held together by a continuous narrative where the images illustrate the voice's narration, and creates a closed world that is built on assumptions about the state of things rather than their reality.

On the prestigious side, Svensk Filmindustri invested in grand colour remakes of classics like *Herr Arnes penningar* and *Sången om den eldröda blomman*, all of which ended in disappointment. SF's backing of Ingmar Bergman in the mid-1950s was more successful, however, and the company's faith in him was now so great that his film *The Seventh Seal (Sjunde inseglet)* was chosen as the company's jubilee film when it celebrated its fifty years in the industry. The success at Cannes (the directorial award in 1956) with the light sophisticated comedy *Smiles of a Summer Night (Sommarnattens leende)* definitely established him as one of the great film directors in the world. Scores of texts would be written about him and his films – he was to be controversial, celebrated and criticized. His films were to influence the image of the Swedes abroad and the Swedes' image of themselves. But the money that his films made and which were to make him his own producer was to come from abroad. He was forever to be the director of the initiated, the enthusiasts; a magician and a wizard to people who perhaps recognize their own personal problems in his films. Birgitta Steene has found that his domestic audience appears to be fans from different classes who continuously return to the cinema where in the 1990s his films have run continuously. Possible exceptions were his last film, *Fanny och Alexander* and the opera film *Magic Flute (Trollflöjten)* (which was made for television) and – interestingly enough – in both films he takes a step back towards melodrama and its aesthetics of illusion.

Ingmar Bergman has had and, in retrospect, been given a place apart in the history of Swedish cinema when viewed from several angles: there has been no one to equal his genius. Or rather: no one has achieved even half of his international success. Bergman is in no way representative of Swedish film production of the 1950s and 1960s. All this is of course true – but it is important to understand that Bergman has always been a vigorous and faithful follower of the tradition of melodrama which has its roots in the bourgeois Swedish theatre and its style; the intimate chamber play (*Kammerspiel*) and the art of drama as they were developed at the turn of the century by, for example, August Strindberg and Harald Molander. Many of the films that Bergman made in the 1950s – *Sommarnattens leende*, *Gycklarnas afton, Ansiktet, Sjunde inseglet, Smultronstället* – bear unmistakable signs of influence from the productions of Sjöström, Stiller, and not least af Klercker – the melodrama director *par excellence*. Like them, Bergman, and later Olof and Gustaf Molander, Per Lindberg and Alf Sjöberg had received their training and scenic experience on the stage, not in the cinema.

Bergman has from the beginning been very well read in domestic literature and drama, and he began his film career as a script writer as did so many others in the industry. He is a conservative theatre director and a supporter of literary theatre and when one sees his stage productions – and for that matter, his films – it is as if Artaud, Craig, Reinhardt or Brecht never existed. There is a straight line that runs from Swedish theatre at the turn of the century – the melodrama and its effects: a well thought-out *mise-en-scène*, the play of light and shadow, extravagance in one form or other and the Strindbergian employment of dialogue (monologue) – to the films of Ingmar Bergman. It is also important to realize that it was as the representative of the earlier craftsman tradition, as a creator of an aesthetics of illusion that he was attacked in the 1960s.

It is therefore interesting that Maaret Koskinen has discovered that under this surface of an aesthetics of illusion there is a strong undercurrent which counteracts this aesthetics and creates cracks in the transparent surface. She has shown that this dichotomy is concentrated in two recurring nodal points in Bergman's production: the mirror and the play-within-the-play, through which the relationship between the performance and its audience is constantly under scrutiny.

THE GREAT CHANGE

Anders Sandrew died in 1957, as did Edvard Persson, the most popular actor in Swedish cinema and for three decades the golden goose of Europa Film. Four years later Carl Anders Dymling, the head of SF, and Karl Kilbom, the initiative force behind the foundation of Nordisk Tonefilm, also both died. Alf Sjöberg returned to the theatre after several failures in film. Hasse Ekman and Arne Mattsson, deeply hurt by the criticism that had been directed at them, moved abroad at the beginning of the 1960s: both had, with Hampe Faustman, continuously and unfairly been compared with Ingmar Bergman who always 'won' by comparison. Faustman's career had crashed in the mid-1950s and he died in 1961. Gustaf Molander had quit the directorial profession after making *Sången om den eldröda blomman* and was only to reappear in 1967 with an episodic film, *Jewel* (*Smycket*), where Ingrid Bergman plays the second lead. Gösta Stevens, who had written and co-written a large number of the scripts for Swedish cinema, retired after *Himmel och pannkaka*, and many others in the profession followed suit.

This meant that there was not only a void at the top during a period of transition, but also that a good deal of knowledge and decisive power was lost – which, however, was not to have direct consequences until the 1970s. The post-war generation who now took over had not only grown up in accumulating affluence, but had also been the first of the new teenage culture which was by definition dismissive of the adult world. This was a generation who had joined the film clubs that had been established after the war and where audiences had had access to films banned by the censors. In a filmic sense they had the wherewithal to appreciate the European films that had washed over the country in the late 1940s – for instance, the productions of Italian neorealism did not reach Sweden until the 1950s.

It was this generation of critics who, towards the end of the 1950s, so relentlessly cavilled the domestic cinema. They had maintained their high standards through their experiences before the collective selection of moving and innovative films. The young academics knew of and were influenced by the ongoing discussion in the French critical publication *Cahiers du Cinéma*, for example. The directors' fixation for the auteur-criticism suited the Swedish discussion on quality cinema exceptionally well, particularly as several films had indeed won international recognition in the early 1950s.

The 1960s in the history of Swedish cinema thus opened with a wide generation gap. The old craftsmen were retiring, leaving behind such veterans as Ingmar Bergman, who had by now been appointed artistic leader of SF. Kenne Fant, who had only ten years previously played the young rebel in *Ungdom i fara*, was appointed President of the company. On the opposing side stood the young well-educated intellectuals, who in actual age were not much younger than the generation they were attacking – Bo Widerberg was only thirteen years Bergman's junior – but the two sides' attitude and relationship to the medium were completely different.

That transition in the early 1960s in the history of Swedish film was greater than the transition to sound thirty years before. It is important to discuss at this point one of its figure-heads, Bo Widerberg, who, in the articles he wrote, shaped the ideological and aesthetical programme which was applied virtually unchanged for twenty years or more. When in 1962 Widerberg directed his general attack at the film industry in his book *Visionen i svensk film*,[40] he had been active as a film critic for many years and had in that capacity travelled to many film festivals and had had the opportunity of seeing the advance of the French new wave at Cannes in 1959. This had obviously left a lasting impression on Widerberg. He wrote: 'One drinks water from a puddle until one has the opportunity to taste it from a well, and after one has done that one would rather go thirsty than return to the puddle.'[41]

Parts of *Visionen i svensk film* had been published as debate articles in the newspaper *Expressen* and were of a particularly polemic nature. Widerberg seldom attacked individuals, however (with the exception of Ingmar Bergman and Arne Sucksdorff), since he felt that the poverty of Swedish film repertory was not due to the ignorance or inability of individual directors, but that the depressing results on the silver screen were the consequences of the restrictions that the film companies imposed on the directors. Widerberg demanded that the companies should 'assume their responsibility'[42] and make it possible for film directors to express their opinions about important issues in contemporary society. He thus called for a new contemporary committed content of films, a content that was to bring with it a new filmic style: 'a more expressive style which was to be better suited to describe the living conditions that . . . the films' characters . . . were living.'[43]

Widerberg was convinced that the portrayal of 'ordinary people' and their actual conditions would make the films more interesting to the contemporary audience and thus lure it back to the cinemas. He also believed that the neorealistic style – which he was recommending – where films were shot on location would be far less expensive than contemporary studio productions. This could solve some of the financial difficulties that the film industry had to wrestle with.

Thematically, Widerberg's starting point or point of view was clear and admirable. He felt that everyday life in Sweden was sufficiently unique and interesting to constitute the theme for a number of films. He believed that film workers should be commited to issues that were central to the lives of 'ordinary people'; issues like unemployment – conflicts in the labour market in whatever form or shape – or, as he put it: 'questions of people's dignity and responsibility as they occur and are discussed in their own environment.'[44]

As discussed above, Widerberg considered the directors in the industry to be victims more or less of the commercially dictated speculations of the producers. He attacked Bergman, however, in the latter's influential capacity as artistic adviser to the nation's largest film company. In such a position one had the possibility to create a style and act as a mentor for new film directors. Another reason why Widerberg attacked Bergman, and Arne Sucksdorff as well, was that both of them were, according to him, in a position where they had the opportunity to shape their films independently of the production companies and their profit concerns. Despite this they failed to use their talents – Widerberg never questioned their artistry – towards discussing current problems in society.

According to Widerberg, Bergman refused to assume his responsibility as an artist by repeating in film after film his own personal problematics, which Widerberg felt were stuffy. He believed that Bergman should instead 'dare to take risks in new and innovative projects'.[45] Widerberg's view was thus highly normative and in this respect he did not differ from the earlier generations of critics. The only difference was that he now narrowed the limits even further and wanted to dictate the content of the films as well, not just their form.

Widerberg was also concerned about the kind of image Bergman's films would possibly project abroad about the Swedes: 'What Bergman exports abroad consists of mystic light and undisguised exotism – not suggestions for alternative modes of action or of moral possibilities. Bergman reinforces the most trivial myths about Sweden and the Swedes,' Widerberg writes. He continues:

> The question that Bergman poses in film after film – most likely voiced by Max von Sydow against the backdrop of dark pine woods – is whether there is a God, whether there is supreme justice. Virtually always he either directs his question upward, or – in jest – downward but less often sideways, to people. He makes vertical movies in a situation where we more than ever need a horizontal cinema, a sideways art.[46]

If this 'private nostalgia'[47] was to be allowed to found a school, it would be fatal to a rising generation of Swedish films.

Ingmar Bergman was not to found a school, however. His aesthetics of illusion was dependent on the craftsmanship that had been lost in the great transition. The imitators of Bergman can be found only towards the end of the 1980s and early 1990s; for example, his own son Daniel's unfortunate attempt at filming his father's script of the film *Sunday Child* (*Söndagsbarn*) (1992) and Bille August's more successful *Best of Intentions* (*Den goda viljan*) (1992). Significantly enough, both films are based on scripts by Bergman himself. Bo Widerberg on the other hand was to belong to or perhaps even create a new wave in Sweden – and a thematic school with the young radical film workers.

When it was announced that Widerberg – who had never directed a film before and who had no proper training for this task – was to make a film, there were perhaps a few who wished for the end result to be a failure. *Raven's End* (*Kvarteret Korpen*) (1963), like the earlier short story film *The Pram* (*Barnvagnen*) (1963) which he had made with Jan Troell, was unanimously applauded as a masterpiece. 'Kvarteret Korpen' (the Korpen (Raven) district) is a working-class district in Malmö. The story takes place at the end of the 1930s, shortly before the outbreak of the Second World War, but also in the dawn of the Swedish Welfare State. Some of the actors are professionals, others are amateurs. Among them, Widerberg's own little daughter Nina contributed to a couple of charmingly improvised scenes with Thommy Berggren, who plays the main character Anders. The fact that the actors were a group of relatively unknown players from the Malmö stadsteater (the City Theatre of Malmö), such as Keve Hjelm who played Anders' father with Emy Storm as the mother, contributed to the freshness of the film.

The film employs wide-angle, deep focus and long takes according to André Bazin's concept of realism; expressive modes that allow the characters to emerge from their daily environment and at the same time give the viewer the opportunity to linger over the scene and to focus on what appears to be of momentary interest. In *Kvarteret Korpen* the director takes a clear personal stand with regard to his characters and, often as an invisible commentator, expresses his values, frequently with the aid of music, camera angles and props. At the beginning of the film for example, when Anders returns to the district, he does so accompanied by a resonant brass band (Concerto in D-major for Trumpet and Orchestra by Torelli). It is 'regal music' of sorts, triumphant and ostentatious, somewhat ironically heralding the arrival of the king, or at the very least the prince, the young man who dreams of a career as an author and of fame.

Yet another example of a personal commentary is the funeral scene at the beginning of the latter half of the film. A young boy in the district has died of appendicitis because his parents could not afford to get him to the doctor in time. The rain falls heavily on the coffin in the graveyard. As the clergyman reads the benediction and scatters earth on the coffin, the rain reduces it to mud which forms into lumps as it falls into the grave. In this scene there is no atonement: not even earth is allowed to fall smoothly on to the coffins of the poor.

If Bo Widerberg had the power to create constraints, standards and limits in the new era, then Harry Schein was its pragmatician and organizer. In his civilian profession as an engineer he had made himself a fortune through an invention that made the chlorination of water possible, and he now devoted himself to film criticism in the distinguished publication *BLM*, and to playing tennis with the future Prime Minister Olof Palme. In 1962, Schein published a book entitled *Har vi råd med kultur*[48] in which he put forward a proposal for administering the state subsidy to domestic film productions. The subsidy, which had been distributed in the 1950s in the form of a refund from the entertainment tax, was considered unsatisfactory in several circles. To begin with it only benefited the production companies, while the remainder of the film industry was effectually left without – and towards the end of the 1950s it had become apparent that it was the cinema owners who were to end up in difficulties first. Severe criticism was also directed at the refund system itself, which was distributed in proportion to a film's box-office receipts, without taking into consideration its potential quality.

Harry Schein's proposal for film reform was passed through the relevant departments and a decision was made in Parliament by acclamation and after a minimum of discussion. A national Film Institute was to be founded in order to administer the film subsidy and other film cultural measures. The political left expressed their apprehensions about a proposal that gave a relatively substantial amount of influence to the commercial film industry. The conservatives in their turn foresaw a risk of underhand socialization.

The establishing of the foundation the Swedish Film Institute (SFI – Svenska Filminstitutet) was preceded by negotiations between the representatives of the film industry and the Swedish state, negotiations that resulted in a twenty-year agreement. The agreement took effect halfway through 1963, and prescribed that 10 per cent of the gross receipts from cinemas that gave more than five shows a week were to go to the Film Institute. The entertainment tax was abolished. Harry Schein was predictably appointed as head of this newly established organization.

On its establishment the Film Institute took over Filmhistoriska samlingarna (the Film Historical Collections), and initiated the distribution and screenings of 'culturally valuable film'. It also assumed the publication of the very active film magazine *Chaplin*, which had been started by Bengt Forslund – who was later to be appointed artistic head of the Institute. Eventually the film clubs were also to be centrally organized from SFI. The first professional school for film workers Filmskolan (the Film School) was founded and run by the Institute and the initiative to institute a Chair to enable a faculty for cinema history and theory to be established at Stockholm University was taken. Furthermore, a large studio and office building at Gärdet in Stockholm was planned: Filmhuset (the Film House), which was opened in the spring of 1971. The building looks like a perforated shoe box cast in concrete and was designed by Peter Celsing, who was also responsible for a number of other 1960s bunkers in Stockholm, including Kulturhuset (the Culture House) at Sergels Torg.

The capital that the Film Institute received ended up in various funds from which the subsidy was distributed in accordance with stipulated principles: approximately one-third of the capital was distributed as a general grant, one-third as a quality grant and one-third went to various measures that were to promote film culture in the country, part of which was the work of the Film Institute itself. Harry Schein's central idea had been to have society recognize the cinema's status as an art form with the help of this reform. An immediate consequence of this was that the film subsidy primarily went to what was called quality film or culturally valuable film.

In negotiations between the state and the representatives of the film industry the latter had desired a general subsidy, while the state had preferred a selective one that was to be based on criteria of quality. It was prepared to invest in the 'culturally valuable', but not in 'entertainment'. There were several alternatives however: were one to decide on a general subsidy this could be distributed either in terms of the ticket revenues or as guarantees for losses, for example. The selective subsidy could be distributed as an advance in the form of production guarantees or as deferred payment in the form of quality premiums. The result was a compromise and in the years to follow SFI was to distribute all the types of production subsidies discussed above. In addition, the Swedish Film Institute would in a little over ten years after its foundation be itself accountable for the production of half of the Swedish feature films.

Initially, the quality subsidies were distributed by an appointed jury consisting of 'film experts'. The jury awarded points to the films that had premièred during the year. The criteria of the quality that the jury had to evaluate were to be found in one of the supplements to the film agreement: crucial were factors that dealt with the following:

> renewal of the cinema's expressive modes and stylistic language, the degree of urgency in the film's message, the intensity or freshness of its conception of reality or criticism of society, the level of psychological insight and the spiritual plane, playful imagination or visionary strength, epic, dramatic or lyrical values, the technical accomplishment of the script, direction and acting, as well as the other artistic elements of a film.[49]

The criteria are all sufficiently bombastic and nebulous to encompass everything. In time, a policy was shaped where the jurors of the different foundations refrained from motivating their decisions and any minutes have not been made public. Harry Schein writes in the Preface to the 1960s part of *Svensk Filmografi* (*Swedish Filmography*) that the jury responsible for the quality evaluations was, as a rule, despite its heterogeneous constitution, more consistent and conformist than contemporary criticism has given reason to suspect.

The quality points were put to the vote by the jury. In the eighteen-year period that this system was in operation, Ingmar Bergman's film *Whispers and Cries* (*Viskningar och rop*) (1973) received the highest score ever given: 4.05 points. Second place is held by *A Simple-minded Murderer* (*Den enfaldige mördaren*) (1982) directed by the serious comedian Hasse Alfredsson, with 3.55 points. *The Emigrants* (*Utvandrarna*) (1971) by Jan Troell received the lowest score – 1.4 points – but still merited a grant. Financially, however, these points were not fair, since there was a rule blocking any one film from receiving more than 20 per cent of the yearly allotted means, partly because the amount of the subsidy varied from one year to the next depending on how much money the Film Institute had at its disposal. Thus, for example, *Viskningar och rop* received 317,000 SEK, while *A Respectable Life* (*Ett anständigt liv*) (Jarl, 1979) with its 3.45 points received 721,000 SEK.

At the same time that a film received a quality grant it could also be eligible for a subsidy covering losses. Thus *Persona* (Bergman, 1967), for instance, collected a total of 1,020,000 SEK in subsidies covering both quality and losses. It is not surprising that the films which attracted the largest audiences to the cinemas were not those which received quality grants: out of eighteen films that had more than a million viewers in the period between 1963 and 1982, only four were eligible for quality grants: *The Silence* (*Tystnaden*) (Bergman, 1964), *The Emigrants* (*Utvandrarna*) (Troell, 1971), *The Apple War* (*Äppelkriget*) (Danielsson, 1971) and *The Adventures of Picasso* (*Picassos äventyr*) (Danielsson, 1978).

The immediate effect of the film reform of 1963 however was to stimulate film production: in the years 1959 to 1963, when the recession had had time to strike severely, only seventeen films per year were produced. In the budget year of 1964 to 1965 a total of twenty-five films were produced. The overall effect was shortlived, however, as film production declined again: in the 1960s only 177 feature films were produced, only about half the number produced in the 1950s (315 films). In the Preface to the section on the 1960s in *Svensk Filmografi*, Harry Schein moreover claims that the indirect effect of the founding of the Film Institute was the opportunity for a large number of new directors to enter film production – more than one-third of the directors were new to the profession. The fact remains, however, that there was plenty of scope for new talent, as virtually everyone of the old guard had left the scene.

There was as yet no professional school for film workers. There was also a different kind of change in the background of the directors: previous generations had, as discussed, largely been men of the theatre. Now new professional groups laid claim to the job of director: authors, teachers, actors and painters. One of these, Vilgot Sjöman, was to be regarded as the *enfant terrible* of Swedish cinema for many years because of his first film *491* (1964). As with *Hon dansade en sommar*, sun, summer, glittering seas and lovers had been considered as more or less standard features of Swedish cinema. In the 1960s, however, the attitude towards sexual intercourse in films changed in an unprecedented manner: to some it was offensive, to others liberating. It was said that the 1960s broke through the sex barrier, an expression coined when *491* was reviewed.

491 was a film without illusions, where violence and sex were mixed in such a way as to awaken the attentions of the slumbering censorship agency. The film was at first totally banned; one scene in particular which depicted sexual intercourse with an animal caused widespread offence. After this film the censors often felt compelled to consult their superior agency Filmgranskningsrådet (the Board of Film Examiners). The Board of Film Censors believed *491* had 'a brutalizing effect and caused injurious excitement'[50] by its 'presentation of what was offensive to discipline and public decency'.[51]The government recommended releasing the film after a number of cuts had been made, however, a practice that was to become the norm during the 1960s.

What had happened was that the demand for realism from the filmgoing public had extended to include depictions of sexual intercourse, which were now longer, more detailed and – of course – realistic. Realism in this respect however came dangerously close to pornography and was therefore offensive to many. It was also the ever more frequently occurring combination of sex and violence which both the censors and parts of the audience reacted to. The film *The Virgin Spring (Jungfrukällan)* (Bergman, 1960) gave rise to a heated debate the very day after its première, and *Tystnaden* (Bergman, 1963) *before* its première. The negative consequences of this were that the censorship authorities remained in power, even though there had been plans to abolish the system. In 1964 a state inquiry was set up which presented a report four-and-a-half years later with a proposal to abolish adult censorship. The loud campaigns for morality that had been launched around the country in the mid-1960s resulted in the withdrawal of the proposal, however.

The later productions by Vilgot Sjöman, the *Curious* films – *I Am Curious – Yellow (Jag är nyfiken – gul)* (1967) and *I Am Curious – Blue (Jag är nyfiken – blå)* (1968) – followed the same semi-documentary line as *491*. Sjöman obtained the money to make the first film solely on the story outline he had prepared. Most of its content was improvised and put together with the help of those who participated in the film. *Jag är nyfiken – blå* premièred one year later and received considerably less attention. *Jag är nyfiken – gul* was banned by the US customs and the court of appeal only released it after having considered the matter for over a year. When it was finally released, it became the biggest Swedish box-office hit thus far in the United States, in spite of the fact that eighteen states had banned it. In just a few years it made an amazing 50 million SEK. It is doubtful whether the audience saw the film for its political message however.

Curious is a metafilm where the different planes of reality flow in and out of each other. The director Vilgot Sjöman and the drama student Lena Nyman (who act themselves) decided to make an investigative and provocative documentary film about Sweden. Lena travelled around the country interviewing people and arranging happenings, had her erotic adventures and recorded everything, keeping an impressive register of such events in her room.

They Call us Misfits (*Dom kallar oss mods*) (Jarl and Lindqvist, 1968) began as a student project at the newly established Filmskolan where Stefan Jarl and Jan Lindqvist were studying. The two of them had submitted an outline of the film to several producers, but no one was willing to back it. The school finally allotted the amount of 50,000 SEK and SFI came up with the remaining one-third of the finance needed to make the film a reality. The entire production costs amounted to 88,000 SEK, an exceptionally modest amount. In this film as well there was a scene containing sexual intercourse which the Board of Film Censors wanted to remove, but which Filmgranskningsrådet did not hold to be offensive to public decency. *Dom kallar oss mods* gave rise to a heated debate on the issue of society's responsibility towards young people who had gone astray, however. The politically correct criticism was enthusiastic and used expressions that were to be repeated *ad nauseam* towards the end of the period: 'sarcastic and pushingly vigorous', 'an active political action in the very here and now', 'biting and harsh language', and so on.[52] The film was later developed into a trilogy with the addition of Part two, the sensational *Ett anständigt liv* (Jarl, 1979), during which one of the main characters of the film, Stoffe, dies from an overdose of heroin. The third and concluding part, *Det sociala arvet* (1993) tells the story of the children of the mods and is shaped like a personal coming to terms with his view of society for Stefan Jarl.

The students at Filmskolan (later Dramatiska Institutet – the College of Film, Television, Radio and the Theatre – with which it was incorporated in 1969) were the makers of several debated documentaries, of which the best known is *Den vita sporten* (1968). *Den vita sporten* was an interview and documentary film made about the demonstrations held before the Davis Cup tournament at Båstad from 3–5 May 1968. The tournament was to be played between Sweden and Rhodesia (now Zimbabwe), but Rhodesia was at this time the object of UN recommended sanctions. The white minority government under the leadership of Ian Smith practised apartheid and repressed the black population. The demonstrators who came to Båstad for the tournament demanded that the match be stopped, which was achieved after an altercation between the demonstrators and the police.

The film was a collective work made by thirteen students and one teacher (Bo Widerberg). It premièred in September, but during editing some conflicts arose that were energetically debated and commented on in the press. Among other things the question of who was to be considered the director of the film led to a schism between SFI and the students at Filmskolan. The students accused Bo Widerberg of having represented himself as the actual director of the film and Widerberg in his turn blamed the Film Institute. Virtually every film made occasioned debate: either they were felt to be offensive to morality, or, as in this case, there was controversy over the origin of the film. Or it was directed by Ingmar Bergman. Or one tripped over the question of quality.

The young radical film workers, not least those who finished their education in the late 1960s (as well as the students of the newly established cinema history and theory courses) saw SFI as a representative of the establishment and therefore considered it to be their opponent. Because of its 'mixed economy', the Institute was felt to be an extension of the profit-hungry film industry. The concept 'alternative film' was developed as opposed to fictive feature film and it was felt that it ought to have been the duty of the Film Institute to support this type of film. In this context one disregarded the fact that SFI *had* in fact granted money for the production of several such films. The radical, 'free' film-makers set up a new 'alternative' distribution company which was called FilmCentrum, and which comprised the main opponents of the Film Institute when the debate was at its peak.

Harry Schein, the autocratic ruler of the Film Institute, was also its mouthpiece. His standard argument in the debates about the film subsidy was that the films produced by independent film-makers rarely exhibited such qualities as to warrant a reward. This was expressed, for example, during the so-called 'catalogue feud': the representatives of FilmCentrum applied for funds to enable the publication of a catalogue of its repertoire of films. Harry Schein thought that if SFI granted the money for a catalogue, they should be party to the decisions regarding the selection of films to go into the catalogue. FilmCentrum in its turn believed that in the name of democracy all the members of Centrum should be allowed to include all their films in the catalogue.

Schein's sarcastic and disdainful way of voicing his opinions about certain film-makers and the quality of certain films caused the debate to be quite heated at times, occasionally even spectacular. This happened, for example, when famous public debater and author Jan Myrdal took part. In 1966 Myrdal contributed to the making of a television-film called *Myglaren* (Myrdal and Hassner, 1966), about the employee of a company which is owned by the popular movements who eventually wangles his way into an influential position in society. After being shown on television, the movie was enlarged to 35 mm format and screened once in a cinema in order for it to qualify for the quality subsidy. The management at the Film Institute initially did not want to acknowledge *Myglaren* since it was a film financed by Sveriges Television and produced for television. The board of directors subsequently changed their minds, but the film did not accrue sufficient quality points. Many, with Myrdal at their head, felt that the result had been agreed before the vote was taken, and labelled Schein a 'cultural wangler'.[53] When the film was eventually shown in the cinemas in the regular manner, it was seen by 297 people in all. In 1977, Harry Schein concluded: 'The attendance for *Myglaren* ... is still the total and hopefully unbreakable all-time low of Swedish cinema.'[54]

The attacks on the Swedish Film Institute had the parodoxical effect of the critics appearing to seek the power of the very agency whose power they were criticizing. The generally rebellious and provocative atmosphere that had evolved among the increasingly radical culture workers was set against a deserving and idealistic background however. In retrospect, Carl Johan Malmberg has aptly written:

> In the 1960s there emerged . . . a view of film which briefly can be characterized as wanting a cinema that made the reality in which people lived distinct and tangible, which penetrated beneath the surface of events and took a stand by letting reality speak for itself, realistic and unembellished. The film-makers began to regard themselves as a small but very important part of a context that far exceeded the narrow reality of the cinema and art. As film-makers of special professional abilities one had the expressed goal of rendering one's services to people and groups who had difficulty claiming their rights.[55]

Apart from the rebelliousness and reality that was gripping films, a genre that had its own life prospered while creating its own intimate world, devoid of any discord: children's films. Children's film production of the 1960s is fairly comprehensive and was principally based on the books of Astrid Lindgren and directed by Olle Hellbom. During the 1950s children's films had been produced that were exciting and occasionally even threatening. The 1960s films were straightforward and clear, based on binary oppositions of good and evil, but lacked tension since the idea behind the stories was moralizing: if you are good and kind the world is good and kind in return. It is interesting to note that in this period when there was a continuous call for struggle and conflict, these features are completely absent from children's films. The demand for realism did not include the children's film.

The Saltkråkan films[56] of which five were made in the 1960s, paints the picture of an idyll in the Stockholm archipelago, involving excursions on sun-warmed rocks, picnics and pleasant adventures with or without the well-meaning and sometimes slightly crazy adults. The story about Pippi Longstocking, *Pippi on the Seven Seas* (*Pippi på de sju haven*) (Hellbom, 1970), instead of dealing with the anarchistic individual's rebellion against the conventions of society, contains adventure and rebellion inside certain carefully defined and safe boundaries. Such rebellion is only there to acknowledge the individual spirit in order for it to be of use to society at a later stage. The story of the rascal Emil is only too familiar – *Emil i Lönneberga* (Hellbom, 1970) – who subsequently becomes chairman of the community board.

A loss of identity characterized the film industry in the period following the stormy years of the 1960s. It was only now that the loss of the craftsmen's knowledge became evident. It was not so much a question of how to force a production through, but of industry know-how and a feeling for narrative devices. A widespread disdain for 'commercial film' – and any and all older domestic film – quite simply made a whole generation of film workers so choosy in their visits to the cinemas that they never learned how it was done properly. They lacked the history, background and knowledge of the standard devices and conventions – and consequently had only a blurred understanding of the violation of these and what that meant.

A stylistic and thematic search was part of the period. By the end of the 1960s two of the figure-heads of the Swedish new generation, Bo Widerberg and Jan Troell, left behind the subdued, black-and-white and documentary-style films to direct in cinemascope and colour: *Elvira Madigan* (Widerberg, 1967) and *Utvandrarna* (Troell, 1971). Both directors made a name for themselves internationally with these films which received awards at festivals around the world.

Ingmar Bergman returned to the illusory world of classical narrative and had his biggest hit so far with *Viskningar och rop* in the early 1970s. Towards the end of the decade he was accused of tax evasion, brought in for questioning by the police and left the country. When he subsequently returned, he concluded his career with the excessive four-hour long *Fanny och Alexander* (1982), a tribute to the mother genre: the melodrama.

The early 1970s films of Jan Troell's *The Emigrants* (*Utvandrarna*) and *The Settlers* (*Nybyggarna*) (1972) follow the old Swedish tradition of the literary film through a cooperation between author and film director. The problem with these films (as with all epic stories) was the long timespan the story covers. Troell succeeded in solving this problem and was in Sweden celebrated as the director who had the ability to transcribe prose into images and be faithful to the original text while using the filmic medium as an independent expressive form. It could thus be said that in his work was a synthesis of the debate conducted several decades before, in the silent era.

Utvandrarna was the first of the films based on Wilhelm Moberg's emigration trilogy and was soon followed by *Nybyggarna*. Moberg's series of novels is in some quarters of Sweden considered to be the Swedish national epic (interestingly enough it recounts the story of people who left the country to go and live in America). The film starred the most renowned actors at the country in the beginning of the 1970s, Max von Sydow as Karl-Oskar and Liv Ullman as Kristina, at that time a well-known couple from many of the Bergman films. The role of Kristina's closest friend is played by the famous jazz singer and vaudeville artist Monica Zetterlund and Allan Edwall plays the priest. The film is designed as a tribute to hard-working people, to the men who through sheer force of will carry out what seem impossible tasks, and who do so despite the high price.

The emigration films may justly be called auteur films, even if Moberg was still alive and contributed his opinions to the script, and even if Troell had Bengt Forslund as his adviser. Troell not only directed these films; he scripted, photographed and cut them. It is remarkable, however, how Troell's touch has changed the focus of the book without any objections from Moberg. What is characteristic of the novels is that although they are written by a man, the events are largely seen from a woman's point of view. Both *Nybyggarna* and *Utvandrarna* instead express the misogyny that permeates all Troell's film productions and which always focus on the struggle of one solitary man with an impossible task: nature, destiny, and so on. In a way Troell was also wrestling with an impossible task when he took on Moberg's epic.

Troell portrays poor people through simple and archaic language, and he mixes long takes with intense close-ups. Moberg's novel is largely written in monologues that describe the inner life of the characters, concepts which they are unable to express in their daily lives in which dialogue consists of abrupt lines. Troell has avoided the obvious trap and refrained from an officious voice-over which would have been the easiest solution for expressing these inner thoughts. Instead he has chosen to rely on the narrative force of the image. The rhythmic interplay between long takes and extreme close-ups is an impressive way of representing the lives and emotions of these simple people. The camera focuses on working hands: hands kneading the dough on the table, hands wielding the hammer and plough, hands weaving. And finally as people come to the end of their lives, the camera focuses on everyday objects, small details that tell of daily life put aside, like a needle pinned to a curtain, glasses left on a window-sill, saucepans on the top of a stove.

The genre films that had previously been employed on a trial basis in the search for an audience in the 1950s turned out to be one of the real hits of the 1970s. The challenge was to make a specific Swedish variant of these without imitating Hollywood action too closely. When this goal was realized, even the norm-setters found these films acceptable. Bo Widerberg directed several films based on the popular detective stories that were critical of society and written by the author collective Sjöwall and Wahlöö. *The Man on the Roof* (*Mannen på taket*) (Widerberg, 1976) was his first film in this genre and was produced by the Swedish Film Institute. The film with its troubled hero was a success and paved the way for several imitators in the action genre. Thus, for example, Jan Guillou's popular novels about the count Carl Gustaf Hamilton's adventures as a Swedish secret agent were soon made into films.

IN SEARCH OF WOMEN

The Swedish film industry had all through its existence resembled a medieval guild system where a master took on an apprentice who eventually learned the profession. This system was most patriarchal and there were few women who had been able to establish themselves in the industry. Anna Hoffman Uddgren was the thrifty manager of a vaudeville theatre when she directed several films in the silent era, among them Strindberg's *The Father (Fadren)* (1912) – but in the following decades the female directors can be counted on the fingers of one hand. Pauline Brunius, who was head of the Royal Dramatic Theatre for a time, directed one film in the 1930s.

In the 1950s two films were directed by a woman. Barbro Boman had worked as a production assistant in the 1940s after which she wrote scripts herself and was also head of Svensk Filmindustri's script department for a period. She directed two films, of which *It's Never Too Late (Det är aldrig för sent)* (1956) was her first. It tells the story of a couple who are planning to divorce. The film is based on flashbacks that recount three generations of women: the main character Görel, her mother and grand-mother, and their methods of solving their problems. As a new director, Boman was treated well and the reviewers wished her the best for the future. Only a few days after the première of *Det är aldrig för sent*, the actress Mimi Pollack brought out her first film *The Right to Love (Rätten att älska)* (1956). The film was regarded as a contribution to the debate on and an educational film about sexual issues and was to be Pollack's only directorial assignment. Bohman's second film, *Swedish Girls in Paris (Svenska flickor i Paris)* (1962), on the other hand, was condemned as a failure – it was felt among other things that the film gave a negative image of Swedish girls abroad. It also led to a controversy with Peter Weiss, the experimental film-maker and author who had contributed to its inception.

In the mid-1960s a sensational debut took place: Mai Zetterling, a popular and esteemed actress – the sweet and blonde one – premièred with a film called *Loving Couples (Älskande par)* (1964). *Loving Couples* is based on the scandalous series of novels *Fröknarna von Pahlen* from the 1930s, written by Agnes von Krusenstierna. The events take place at the turn of the century and initially the film resembles the classical melo-drama: the extravagant scenery, props and costumes suggestive of the 1950s melodramas – perhaps above all *Fröken Julie* and *Smultronstället*. Furthermore, the film makes several visual references to the latter. Not entirely unimportant in this context is the fact that the film was produced by Rune Waldekranz at Sandrews.

However, even if the visual elements as to the internal relationships of the characters point towards the classical melodrama, it was only thus far that Mai Zetterling was interested in developing the genre. Instead she used the remainder of the film's modes of expression for breaking down the structure of a classical play. The story takes place at a delivery ward and is about three women, Angela, Agda and Adèle who all have some form of relationship with one another. Angela and Agda will each give birth to a baby while Adèle goes through a miscarriage. In the film's present (the events at the clinic) the narrative is curtailed; it begins when the women arrive at the clinic and ends when the babies are delivered. Within this frame however, the action follows several parallel stories that examine memory, experience and time while revealing the background and personality of each woman. The memories of each woman are triggered by Proustian sensory perceptions. Thus, for example, Adèle panics on realizing that she is going to have to deliver her dead foetus, and runs out of the ward. Running reminds her of another time when she ran, not away but *towards* her lover out in the open air. The fleeing Adèle in her nightgown and bare feet is stopped by the nurses whose hard and unrelenting arms are cross-cut with the embrace of her lover. She is both literally and metaphorically trapped in her sexuality and its consequences, trapped in her woman's body.

Mai Zetterling's first film was received very positively. At this time it was unusual for reviewers to note a film's associates, with the exception of the actors' performances. It is thus remarkable that this time there were comments from different sources on how Zetterling had received much help and support from her (male) associates, among others Sven Nykvist who photographed the film and Ingmar Bergman who had given her much encouragement. It was as if the critics had a hard time accepting that a woman directing her first film had achieved this extraordinary success.

Zetterling directed another three films in quick succession – the last one backed by Danish and American money – where she consistently followed up on the study of the expression of time and the filmic modes of interpretation. *Night Games* (*Nattlek*) (1966) was perceived as controversial because of its portrayal of incest and other features. The film was the cause of much controversy during the Biennial at Venice in 1966 where the public screening was banned and the film could only be shown to the jury. *The Girls* (*Flickorna*) (1968) is based on Aristophanes' play *Lysistrata* and is a feminist attack on the cultural elite in Stockholm. It was considered to be a failure and scored no quality points.

Doktor Glas (1969) received devastating criticism, as it was felt that Zetterling's adaptation of Söderberg's novel was clumsy and that the film was blurred and confusing. Thereafter Mai Zetterling's career as a director was over in Sweden. She moved to England, where she played the part of dumb blondes in a number of films while simultaneously directing several interesting documentaries, among them *Scrubbers* (1982), a film about a women's prison. She was to direct a feature film in Sweden one last time, namely *Amorosa* (1986) – a film about the author Agnes von Krusenstjerna. The film, where Zetterling returns to her earlier problematics and iconography, had mixed reviews and she never had the opportunity of realizing her other film ideas.

When Filmskolan (later DI) was set up in 1964, the patriarchal guild system was destroyed and it became much easier for women to train in the industry as photographers, editors and directors. Traditionally, professions like script girl and to a certain extent also script writers and editors had been available before to women. But it took a government institution to make the profession of director more widely accessible. Maj Wechselmann, Ingela Romare and Lena Ewert were some of the first students at Filmskolan who were later to direct a considerable number of documentaries.

In the last two decades a growing number of women have had the opportunity to go into film direction, particularly documentaries. Several important feature film directors have also come through, among them Suzanne Osten, Marie-Louise Ekman and Agneta Fagerström-Olsson. *Hjälten* (1990) was Fagerström-Olsson's first feature film. It is an inverted replica of Verdi's opera *Rigoletto*. The film emphasizes the daughter instead of focusing on the father, who loves his daughter so much that he perishes when he loses her. The (symbolic) death of the father in the film becomes meaningful through the daughter's coming of age. The film is obviously based on an opera (and uses sound and music in an exciting way), but its narrative mode is modernistic and it constantly refers to its own expressive means.

What is interesting about Swedish cinema following the mid-1980s is that the dividing line between genre film – made in accordance with the patterns of classical narrative – and 'artistic film' – which since the 1960s has been identified with modernism – is today sex typed. It would appear that the men have resurrected their slaughtered fathers and taken on action and detective films, while the women deal with problematizing the cinema's expressive modes in stories that are personal in content and open in form.

TO THE BOTTOM?

On considering the history of Swedish cinema one gains the impression that there has always been a crisis of some sort somewhere, at one time financial in nature, at another artistically related. The artistic crisis has often been accredited to a lack of good scripts. In the 1970s this explanation or accusation, depending on who voiced it – was to become permanent. The biting, fresh and urgent 'look-no-further' films became conformist relatively quickly and stopped being interesting. It was claimed that the film directors had nothing important to say and that they had no idea how to tell a story. In some quarters there were attempts to remedy the situation by arranging classes in script writing and inviting expensive American professors of film to come and share their know-how. It seemed a waste of time: the artistic successes did not happen.

There were about thirty production companies in existence in the mid-1960s but only four of these produced more than four films in a five-year period. These companies were SF, Sandrews, Europa Film and a company called Minerva. When Anders Sandrew died, Sandrews had a new artistic leader in Göran Lindgren, who sold off some company studios, cut down production and in 1969 became president of the company. Under his management, production was reduced further, only to eventually cease entirely. Instead, Sandrews concentrated on film distribution and its cinemas. Roy Andersson's strange film *Giliap* (1975) was the last film produced by Sandrews – after about a ten-year gap, the company was to resume production again however.

In the late 1950s Europa Film had undergone an interesting metamorphosis as regards their production policy: it had turned from popular entertainment to more serious repertory – for instance, *Kvarteret Korpen* and other Widerberg films were produced by Europa Film. Gustaf Scheutz, one of its founders, still headed the company in the 1960s, but he died in 1967 and his office was taken over by a certain Ejnar Gunnerholm. Under Gunnerholm's management Europa Film stopped film production and the company decided to invest in the development of its recording studio. The company experienced a brief upswing in the 1980s when it produced a number of successful comedies. For a while it even appeared as if Europa Film would take over SF, but the opposite was eventually the case. Among other things the losses over one extravagant production – *Kalabaliken i Bender* (Åberg, 1983) – contributed to the fall of Europa Film.

The film giant Svensk Filmindustri had run into trouble in the 1970s when its owner, a large real estate company, sold SF to *Dagens Nyheter*, the country's biggest newspaper. *Dagens Nyheter* in its turn sold SF to the gargantuan publishing company Bonniers. Relying on the financial stability of Bonniers, SF launched an offensive and took over their old competitor Europa Film. But even better times were in the making for SF: as of the expansion of the video market the company was to begin a new financial era. Svensk Filmindustri was to produce the period's most popular comedies, action films and above all the Astrid Lindgren films, which was to be some of the most sought-after merchandise on the video market.

Despite the difficulties of the major companies, the number of production companies in the Swedish film industry increased by fifteen up to 1972. This was perhaps to do with the stimulating effect that the work of the Swedish Film Institute occasioned, but it might also have been the result of many of the so-called 'free' film-makers forming companies and remaining their own producers. In the mid-1970s it was also discovered that owning a company was a superb way of evading taxes and resulted in an increase in the number of small one-man companies. At the end of the 1970s some fifty film companies were registered in the country, among which the most active companies were Ingmar Bergman's Cinematograph, MovieMakers and Drakfilm. Swedish Filmproductions and Omega were the most prosperous companies producing pornographic movies. The porn film industry had at the end of the 1960s turned out to be a lucrative export business for Sweden. Because the pornographic prohibition laws were abolished in 1972, the genre prospered. About one-fifth of the feature films produced in the country in the 1970s were pornographic. In the 1970s some twenty such films a year were produced on average.

The domestic cinema was also relatively popular during this period: the Swedish films stood their ground and were seen by some 20 per cent of the audience, a fairly satisfactory result since Swedish cinema's share of the total market in the 1970s was only a little more than 6 per cent (with the exception of 1976 to 1977 when domestic cinema laid claim to approximately 7.5 per cent of the total repertory). In comparison, Swedish cinema had twenty-five years previously (in 1951) occupied 9 per cent of the market, while after the introduction of television eight years later, it was 4.7 per cent; however, it did account for 25 per cent of the total income at that time as well.

When viewing these figures another fact is clarified, however, namely that it was primarily foreign film which was to largely finance Swedish (quality) film – the Swedish Film Institute's revenues came solely from ticket sales. In the 1970s, the to some people embarrassing fact that what contributed to the making of quality films was first and foremost pornography and so-called 'trivial films' became obvious. It was these films that attracted a large audience. Only a few domestic films were seen by a million people – usually audiences were significantly smaller than that. The most popular film of the 1960s was *The Sound of Music* (Wise, 1965) and in the 1970s it was *The Jungle Book* (Reitherman, 1967), which were both seen by 3.5 million people. The James Bond films *Goldfinger* (Hamilton, 1964) and *Thunderball* (Young, 1965) were seen by 2.3 and 1.8 million people respectively, and *Doctor Zhivago* (Lean, 1965) had 1.8 million viewers. *Foul Play* (Higgins, 1978), starring Goldie Hawn, reached 1.7 million viewers. In more recent years the attendance of foreign movies has significantly decreased as well: *Dances with Wolves* (Costner, 1990) was only to have an audience of 1.3 million.

PRESTIGE AND LOSS

The feud between the left-oriented film workers and Harry Schein entered its second decade and the controversy grew more intense because Schein did not want to listen to any potentially good advice, but rather strove to increase his power in the film industry in various ways. FilmCentrum's publication *Film & TV* contributed to the pungent criticism, as did the film department at Teaterförbundet (The Theatre Federation). Primarily because of this criticism a reorganization of SFI was undertaken in the mid-1970s where the power was, at least in appearance, divided between Schein, who continued as acting chairman of the board, and Bo Jonsson, who was appointed president. Jonsson had been the producer of a one-man company called Viking Film. Bo Jonsson resigned after only two years however, and when Schein fired Stig Björkman, the editor in chief of the magazine *Chaplin*, who had been criticizing the management of SFI, albeit for good reason, the demands for Schein's resignation became ever more frequent. When the three major companies later agreed to form a consortium called Treklövern (The Three-leaved Clover), through which they committed to contribute half of the financing of all of SFI's film productions, others besides the left faction felt that Schein had gone too far.

In 1976 the Swedes elected a non-socialist government and thereby a change of direction at the Film Institute. The new Minister of Culture received a letter of protest signed by forty-two film directors, which enabled the ministry to act. Schein was offered a one-year contract instead of the customary three years. He declined and resigned, whereupon Liberal party member Per Ahlmark was made the new chairman of the board and Jörn Donner appointed president. Donner had been responsible for the culture section at the Film Institute since 1972, and he was an author and the *enfant terrible* of Finnish cinema through his preference for playing gynaecologists in the spectacular films he directed in the late 1960s. He turned out to be an imaginative but financially irresponsible president. He invested large amounts in, among other things, international productions that were never made. The cooperation between Ahlmark and Donner was unfortunate. Furhammar writes in a commentary: 'The management couple . . . turned out to be . . . a rather unsuccessful constellation. Donner eventually publicized his commentary on the failure of the cooperation. It was marked by perfidious eloquence. Ahlmark's comments have yet to be made public.'[57]

Klas Olofsson became president of the Film Institute through political appointment after the resignation of Donner. Although Olofsson lacked experience in the film industry he was an able cultural administrator who was willing to learn. Under his management in the 1980s the finances of SFI were stabilized – video rentals also contributed to this effect. In 1989 he was offered the post of president at Sandrews, which was once again planning to venture into film production. Ingrid Edström, formerly the head of Riksteatern (the National Touring Theatre), was left in charge at SFI to face the effects of the recession when it hit.

The industry's knowledge and feeling for timing and rhythm that was so urgently called for in the debate in the 1970s, naturally existed then as well. But it was to be found primarily in the entertainment business, for example, among the makers of musicals. As usual, however, these did not count. The company Svenska Ord (Swedish Words) occupied a sort of middle ground, however, because their productions contained a sufficient amount of 'political correctness' to be acceptable. Svenska Ord was not a film company but had been established in the early 1960s through the cooperation of two young students who worked with satire at Lund University: Hasse Alfredsson and Tage Danielsson.

Alfredsson and Danielsson went on to produce entertainment programmes for radio and television and subsequently some very popular musicals. In the mid-1960s Svenska Ord began producing films under the wing of SF. *Docking the Boat* (*Att angöra en brygga*) (Danielsson, 1965), one of the most intelligent comedies of Swedish cinema, is based on a simple formula: three couples plan to celebrate the opening of the crawfish season (August). Half of the participants are on an island in the archipelago with the food – the crawfish – and half of the guests are on board a boat with the alcohol. The film portrays the difficulties that arise as these two groups try to get together. More such comedies were produced in the 1970s, principally directed by Tage Danielsson: *The Apple War* (*Äppelkriget*) (1971), *Let the Prisoners Free – It's Spring* (*Släpp fångarne loss – det är vår*) (1975) and *Picassos äventyr* (1978). Towards the end of the decade Hasse Alfredsson took on a different kind of problematics in the much praised *Den enfaldige mördaren* (1982), and Danielsson directed a huge success: Astrid Lindgren's *Ronja Rövardotter* (1982). *Ronja* was Danielsson's final film, as he died of cancer shortly after the première.

Hasse o Tage, as they were called, were popular in their choice of subject for film, but also politically correct in their lighthearted portrayal of the social democratic establishment and its government. Their ideological message was closely aligned to that of Astrid Lindgren's 'use your common sense and be nice to everyone, and everyone will be nice to you' – which most people could subscribe to. Characteristic of Svenska Ord was that it favoured working with the same popular artists, and who contributed to the company's successes: for example, the jazz singer Monica Zetterlund, Lena Nyman who had become familiar to the Swedish people in the *Curious* films, Gösta Ekman (junior, the son of Hasse).

Gösta Ekman developed his comic talent in the 1980s and created his classical character Herr Papphammar in short television sketches among other things. After his collaboration with Svenska Ord ceased at Danielsson's death, Ekman continued his career in films whose success appeared to be largely the result of his cheerful presence in such varying films as *Morrhår och ärtor* (Ekman, 1986) and *Jönssonligan dyker upp igen* (Mikael Ekman, 1986). Both films were seen by close to a million people in the same year. The Jönssonligan films were considered to be family films, with their lovable villains of which Gösta Ekman plays the gang leader Sickan. The idea was originally Danish and the first film was called *Jönssonligan* (Cornell, 1980).

Lasse Åberg was originally a television entertainer, a graphic artist by training with few aspirations towards being a film director. His popular breakthrough took place in the 1970s in a well-loved children's programme on television, where he played 'Trazan' ('the rag'): a parody of the character Tarzan. Åberg's formula for film followed the success of Svenska Ord and tied the simple stories of the films to phenomena that were thoroughly recognizable to all Swedish people, and preferably something that everyone had experience of or knowledge about. The mechanisms of recognition are important to Åberg's dramaturgy and the comic points of a situation are based on identification. He plays the leads himself, a nice, rather clumsy guy who is bullied by his mother, but who still wins the beautiful girl in the end. Military refresher courses (*Repmånad* (1979)), vacational trips to the Mediterranean (*Sällskapsresan* (1980)), ski trips to the Alps (*Sällskapsresan II* (1985)), and dabbling in trendy sports: (*Den ofrivillige golfaren* (1991)) were all experiences that most Swedes had had. All the films were seen by more than a million people, *Sällskapsresan* by two million.

When the Swedish Film Institute embarked on film production, it soon dominated other companies in the industry, as discussed above, and was to produce many prestigious films. Andrej Tarkovskij's last film *Offret* was made in Sweden in the summer of 1985 and was one such production. Kjell Grede's *Hip Hip Hurra!* (1987) was one of the most successful 'prestigious films' that the Film Institute ever produced. The film is about Danish painter Søren Krøyer and the artists at Skagen who founded a school at the turn of the century. Using lighting and photography, *Hip Hip Hurra!* re-creates the works of art painted at Skagen. It aestheticizes its subject but also deals with the dichotomy of vision and reality and the borderline between the two in an intelligent and ingenious way. In one scene the artist Michael Ancker paints the portrait of a blind man. The man suddenly asks: 'Michael, am I ugly?' 'No,' Ancker replies and begins to describe the man's looks in words. Besides adjectives he also uses metaphors like 'you have the nose of a king'. The blind man touches the wet, half-finished painting, feels his fingers and smells them: 'Is it sky?' he muses thoughtfully. To the blind man, the texture and pungent smell of the oil paint connote the sky. In one single condensed scene the film thus describes many of the ways of expressing reality: image, words, metaphor, smell – and ultimately film as well.

Other areas of cinema that prospered under the management of the Swedish Film Institute in the 1980s were documentaries and animated films. This was not only possible through an allocation of quotas introduced in the agreement of 1982, but was dependent on the integrity and force of initiative of the producer responsible for these areas, Lisbet Gabrielsson. Thanks to her, films like *Inughuit* (Floreman, 1985), *Pica Pica* (Kristersson, 1987) and many others found their way to the cinemas. *Pica Pica* is a feature-long documentary about the magpies on the square in the Stockholm suburb of Vällingby. The film contains no dialogue and the viewer follows the daily life of the birds to the accompaniment of their incessant chatter. Naturally this film, like all good films, is also about something other than itself, namely man. This was a film that Lisbet Gabrielsson felt it was essential to make.

Animated films also had an upswing in Sweden in the 1970s and 1980s. One of the most noteworthy was Lennart Gustafsson's feature film *Rottis* (1990), a rock film about a teenage rat in love. *Linnea i Målarens trädgård* (Andersson and Björk, 1990) is based on a children's book in which a little girl, Linnea, visits the French painter Monet's garden and looks at his paintings.

There was relatively speaking plenty of money in the country as the Swedish Film Institute entered its second decade. In 1968 the film agreement between the representatives of the industry and the state had been revised. A new agreement was made in accordance with which the Film Institute was to be able to join as co-financier on various film productions. In 1972 the film agreement was altered once again. The state now for the first time gave direct economic support. Through this agreement the earlier quality grant was reduced by one-third. The general subsidy was dropped, as was the loss adjustment subsidy. Instead, a number of other foundations were instituted: the A-foundation gave a subsidy in proportion to ticket sales, as previously. The B-foundation, whose task it was to allocate the quality grant, remained as before; the others included the F-foundation which dealt with production loans and guarantees and the G-foundation which financed the Film Institute's own productions, and finally the H-foundation which granted what was called selective production loans and guarantees. At the start of the 1980s there were thus eight foundations and a revision was perhaps necessary.

A structural effect of the establishment of the Film Institute had been the decrease in importance of the major integrated companies as the work of the Institute became a regular feature in the industry. This trend became particularly noticeable when SFI began producing films in 1968. Many people questioned whether this development was a positive one, as the Institute was now in principle seen to be competing with others over the same production funds that it was appointed to administer and distribute. This situation was also altered in the agreement of 1992.

The faith in a strong society that was there to look after its people was still unshakeable. Both the state and the community welfare sectors offered extensive social services and several state and community agencies had the means to support cultural life in various ways. 'Increased equality' was the watchword of the social democrats in the 1960s and 1970s: the good folkhem was not to know of any 'privileged or slighted persons, nor any pets or step-children',[58] as Per Albin Hansson had once put it. In the 1970s there were yet more reforms: part-time pensions, an expansion of the health insurance scheme and parental leave of absence for the birth of children. In the 1970s a number of unpopular labour reforms were also introduced: the law concerning right of participation in decision-making

(MBL), employment security and the law concerning trade union repre-sentatives. The ominous fact was that these laws distinctly broke with the old principle which dictated that the labour market should be free of state intervention.

The year 1982 saw an increase in the problems of the Swedish model. The major devaluation of Swedish currency led to good times for the export industry and provided full employment for a while – but it also resulted in overspending and inflation. The public sector ended up in crisis because its expenses had increased dramatically and it was clear to everyone that taxes could no longer be increased. In order to avoid making unpopular cuts, the government borrowed in order to balance the budget deficit. The debt increased. It was also beginning to become clear that the force of Swedish economical expansion had been spent. The traditional products that the Swedes traded in – raw materials like ore, steel, lumber and the mechanized products of the engineering industry – were facing new competition from the Third World and elsewhere in the West. In order to take on the competition, demands for a severe restructuring and rationalization were voiced once again. But instead of an expansion in industrial areas, it was the real estate and financial markets which grew.

The weak spot of the Swedish model was its faith in never-ending growth, and now the unbelievable had happened: the growth began to decline, followed by a downturn in the nation's affluence. As the 1980s approached, the nation's dependence on the rest of the world became ever greater. Swedish companies established themselves in an increasing capacity abroad and the drain of foreign exchange escalated sharply, a situation that could only be checked by the country's decision to instigate negotiations regarding membership of the European Union. The exchange regulations were abandoned in 1989 and in one blow the possibility of pursuing an independent monetary policy vanished. After 1990 the country entered a profound recession, which continues to this day.

The period of saving that the state was forced to embark on at the beginning of the 1990s primarily meant reducing public expenditure which has principally affected low-paid women and families. Heavy industry has moved abroad, the industrial workers today have highly paid and skilled jobs and bear little resemblance to the proletarians of the 1930s: the parties that closed the agreement in the 1930s exist no more. Instead it is the low-paid women with little education and who work in the public sector who are the most vulnerable group in society. The boundary between the classes in Sweden today is no longer between certain professional categories, but between the sexes and certain age groups.

The economic development of the Swedish Film Institute follows the nation's financial situation in an interesting manner: during the economic upswing of the 1980s the Film Institute also experienced a particularly favourable development in its finances, but not through real estate or exchange deals. Rather, it had been decided as part of the film and video agreement of 1982 that, in addition to the 10 per cent of every film ticket sold that the Film Institute received, it was also to collect a fee from every video cassette sold or rented. None of the parties to this agreement could imagine the gold mine this was to be. For instance, when the Film Institute's revenue from the film theatre fees reached approximately 50 million SEK in the budget year 1985–86, the video fees brought in approximately another 30 million. In time, it was decided that the state would also contribute a direct subsidy. Thus, for example, the corresponding figures for the budget year 1991–92 were as follows: revenue from the cinemas supplied about 76 million SEK, video fees brought in 39 million and the state subsidy amounted to 29 million SEK. Sveriges Television had for a long time contributed a somewhat more modest sum to the Institute.

As of the agreement of 1982 the foundations were formed into committees: the quality jury disappeared but there was still a jury which appointed the recipients of the Swedish counterpart of the Oscar each year: Guldbaggen (the Golden Ram). The goal of the work of the committees was specified: the committees were to distribute the funds in the following way: (1) 20 per cent of the funds were meant for the foundations' commitment to produce Swedish film; (2) 35 per cent was set aside for production guarantees for artistic film; (3) 5 per cent was to be used for the production of short films; (4) another 5 per cent was set aside for the screening of culturally valuable film; (5) no more than 25 per cent was to be used for the maintenance of SFI and film cultural ends; (6) 3 per cent was for industry promotive purposes; (7) at least 2 per cent was to be used to subsidize the production and distribution of culturally valuable film; and (8) the remainder was to go to various projects.

Through the agreement of 1992, when dark clouds were already overshadowing the nation's economy, it was decided that the state would subsidize the film cultural departments of SFI, the library, the film club (Cinemateket) and the publishing business. Within the Film Institute it was generally believed that in such difficult times cinema attendance would decline further and that perhaps the industry should refuse to relinquish its diminishing revenues. One would suspect that the work that was not connected with film production would be subject to cuts first and that the state would protect the historical and cultural areas. This faith suffered a serious blow when the state subsidy to the Film Institute was diminished in the budget cuts in 1993.

Through the new agreement SFI's film production proper ceased. The film subsidy was once again distributed in proportion to ticket sales – in practice the most successful films were to be rewarded. As of the early 1990s an 'entertainment film' was eligible for a subsidy from the Film Institute: for instance, in the budget year 1991–92 Lasse Åberg's *Den ofrivillige golfaren* received a production grant. Instead of producing films itself, SFI employed a number of advisory officers for a limited period of time who were given a relatively free hand with the production funds at their disposal for various film projects. To a certain extent the advisory officers had their own areas to administer: one of them was to tend to the 'greenhouse' which grants funds to young film-makers to do brief short story-type films.

THE SOCIETAL MIRROR

It was in fact already in the 1970s that the Swedish model began to outgrow its creators. The country suffered from major financial difficulties even if no one (or few people) consciously understood the extent of these difficulties. The cause was partly due to the oil crisis (the rise in the price of crude oil), which not only affected the individual consumers, but to a greater extent, the heavy industries. The country found itself in a cost crisis, where high nominal withdrawals of salaries and high marginal taxes undermined the companies' market shares.

The basic premise of the Swedish model had always been the compromise between the parties of the labour market in the 1930s, which was founded on a voluntary agreement. This compromise was to be put severely to the test, however, when the issue of collective wage-earners' investment funds was addressed in the mid-1970s. The employers and the non-socialist parties were united against the proposition, which was passed in Parliament. The measure was felt to be a step towards too great a socialization and was dissolved immediately after the right-wing coalition came into government.

Against this background it is interesting to study the syndrome which had begun developing in the 1970s, namely the existence of the childhood films,[59] which feature children but are primarily addressed to adults. Childhood is a theme that has been worked into Swedish films for adults throughout the 1980s and 1990s. It is a theme whose frequency is fairly unique to Sweden and which can only be explained by the special historical phase that the country is experiencing. The childhood films are part of its ideological manifestation.

A fundamental feature of the planning and government of the social democrats has been that it has fairly singularly concentrated on future prospects without devoting itself to the past. Memories of the past, the country's history, have been traumatic. Sweden was for many centuries an imperialist state, which lost its largest dominion, Finland, in the early nineteenth century, and a little less than a century later the union with Norway was dissolved. The way the Swedes dealt with these losses was to transform its territorial imperialism into a moral imperialism, which among other things was to condemn the imperialist efforts of other countries in especially harsh terms. The country's own past was repressed, perhaps too eagerly since imperialism strikes a discordant note with the idea of solidarity which has prevailed in the country since the 1930s.

The teaching of history has been neglected and the study of history has focused on the living conditions of the workers and ordinary people, not on the kingdom that moved the borders. For many people, Sweden began with the founding of the labour movement a hundred years ago, and the time before that is shrouded in mystery. A country's people need a history, however, and a national memory on which to found its identity. People who are deprived of their national history often seek it in a more private, individual history. How else is one to explain the almost obsessive interest in children, children's culture and the importance of childhood that took place in the mid-1970s? As an interest, it goes hand-in-hand with the interest in psychology, psychotherapy and psychoanalysis that was the origin of a large amount of popular specialist literature written and translated *en masse*. There were also children's theatre groups, children's plays written, children's books published – and children's films produced.

The movement started with *Hugo and Josefin* (Grede, 1967). In the 1970s *Elvis Elvis!* (Pollack, 1977), *Mackan* (Svensson, 1978) and *Stortjuven* (Hellner, 1979) were produced. In the 1980s the theme was encapsulated in films like *Mitt liv som hund* (Hallström, 1986), *Åke och hans värld* (Edwall, 1984), *Fanny och Alexander* and in the nineties *Söndagsbarn* (1992) and *Kådisbellan* (Sandgren, 1993) – to name but a few. At the same time a systematic production of films based on Astrid Lindgren's books was initiated, with remakes of *Mästerdetektiven Blomkvist* and the *Bullerby* films, as well as stage productions of the *Mardie* books,[60] and filming of *Lotta på Bråkmakargatan* (Hald, 1993) and *Emil i Lönneberga* had begun earlier, as had films about *Pippi Longstocking*.

A trait common to both the childhood films and the Lindgren films – which, taken together, constitute a significant share of the film repertoire in Sweden over the past twenty-five years – is that they look back, they deal with the past. But they are about a utopian past, because in reality the middle classes were almost non-existent in Sweden and the country was one of the most poor and depressed in all of Europe. The later Lindgren films in particular portray a world that is if possible even more idyllic and designed to please than the first films made in the 1940s. The events take place in a small town or in the countryside in an idyllic community at the turn of the century, usually in a middle-class environment. People live in peaceful communities where illness, hunger and war have no place. The films are well made, lavish and consummately typical of the period, and the characters conventional. Even in the films where a child is deceived, he – because it is usually a boy – survives in the end.

A possible explanation for the frequent occurrence of childhood thematics – and especially the iconography of looking back at the past, through which this thematics is expressed – could be that it is a question of compensation for the loss of the idea of the folkhem. There is a thread connecting between the loss of a national history and its compensation in individual history: the image of the child in the past. In this image, an old trauma about the loss of national history is fused with the new trauma about the loss of the idea of the folkhem in the mid-1970s.

The idea of the folkhem (the Welfare State) has been the strongest metaphor that the social democratic rhetoric has presented to the Swedes. It was maintained that it was to be in the future, but it was not realized when that future would arrive. On the contrary the whole image collapsed. The extraordinary thing was that the metaphor of the folkhem could not be discarded, but was rather projected into the past. Both the childhood films and the Lindgren films create the concept of a utopian past and is a Swedish version of heritage cinema whose occurrence became a pan-European phenomenon in the 1980s. It is significant in this context that the childhood films are produced with such great care and financed through state funds. The images they display protect the Swedes from such repressed but real images that have now become frighteningly close. These phenomena are too contradictory to grasp, but they none the less belong together: for example, the rise of neo-Nazism in relation to the liberation of the Baltic states, questions about nationalism and the nation's identity. And racism.

As of the 1950s Sweden had been opened to immigrants from various countries – primarily from Finland, Italy and the former Yugoslavia who were attracted by the high wages earned by the Swedish industrial workers; and to political refugees from Greece, Spain and Latin America. A large number of economic and political refugees came from Turkey and the Arabic countries, and all these immigrants have contributed to the Sweden that exists today. The first feature film to portray the situation of the immigrants in a nationally heterogeneous Sweden opened in the early 1970s: *Jag heter Stelios* (Bergenstråhle, 1972) and was based on the novel by Greek author Theodor Kallifatides. Muammer Özer was one of the first immigrants to direct a feature film: *Splittring* (1984). His debut got a positive reception but was not a major success with the audience in spite of its suggestive play of symbols and topical subject.

Director Suzanne Osten has taken a militant attitude in the treatment of the immigrant issue by describing immigrants as a positive collective force in Sweden today. In *Bröderna Mozart* (1986), which is about a production of *Don Giovanni* at the Stockholm Opera house, the cleaning and repair staff are portrayed as the people who have the most authentic relationship with the music. In *Tala, det är så mörkt* (1992) Osten gives a frightening and intense portrait of a skinhead. Some of the more interesting productions are *Vägvisaren* (Simma, 1992) and *Freud flyttar hemifrån* (Bier, 1991). *Vägvisaren* takes as its subject matter the Sami legends and *Freud flyttar hemifrån* is about a girl called Freud who comes from a Jewish family and is the first feature film in Sweden to depict Swedish-Jewish culture.

The films *One Has to Live* (*Man måste ju leva . . .*) (Vinterheden, 1978) and *Johnny Roova* (Olsson, 1985) display Swedish immigrants in Sweden. These recount the problems that people face as they are forced to move south from Norrland in the north to find employment. Forty years after the nostalgic rural films, the countryside theme has again emerged and the upgrading of the national periphery has been reversed: the country-side is viewed as either comically backward or exotic. In Colin Nutley's *Änglagård* (1992), two delinquent children from the city – Fanny and her androgynous friend Zac – visit the Värmland village which Fanny's mother had left in her youth. The villagers view the couple with suspicion, distrust, hatred and delight. The Swedish audience loved seeing their prejudices portrayed by an Englishman and went as one man to see the film and its sequel, *Änglagård – andra sommaren* (Nutley, 1995). *Jägarna* (Sundvall, 1996) is a good example of a successful application of exoticism to northern Sweden where the film has a nebulous connection with reality. A conventional story about an investigation of a group of poachers is interwoven with a passionate family drama, a combination that explodes in fire and blood on the screen. In the first four months of its première *Jägarna* was seen by more than half a million people.

Sweden, which has always been conceived of as a heterogeneous country, has – and has had for many years – many cultures within it and today they emerge as images on the silver screen.

SELECT BIBLIOGRAPHY

Bono, Francesco and Koskinen, Maaret (eds), *Film in Sweden*, The Swedish Institute, Stockholm 1996.

Cowie, Peter, *Swedish Cinema, from Ingeborg Holm to Fanny and Alexander*, The Swedish Institute, Stockholm 1985.

Fullerton, John, 'AB Svenska Biografteatern: aspects of production A12–20', in *Current Research in Film: Audiences, Economics and Law, Volume 1*, Ablex, New Jersey 1985.

Kolaja, Jiri, 'Swedish feature films and Swedish society', in *Hollywood Quarterly*, 1950/51: 2, 189–94.

McIlroy, Brian, *World Cinema 2: Sweden*, Flicks Books, London 1986.

Oliver, Roger W. *Ingmar Bergman, An Artist's Journey on Stage, on Screen, in Print*, Little Brown, New York 1995.

Paulus, Alfred, Schwedische Spielfilmproduktion 1955–1963.

Steene, Birgitta, *Ingmar Bergman*, St Martins Press, New York 1968.

Sundgren, Nils-Petter, *The Swedish Cinema*, The Swedish Institute, Stockholm 1970.

Chapter 7

Conclusion

*Tytti Soila, Astrid Söderbergh Widding and
Gunnar Iversen*

By studying film production and culture as a whole in the five Nordic
countries separately, a pattern has become discernible which might not
be clear or unambiguous in all respects, but where common features as
well as mutual differences are evident. In summary, we would like to try
and draw a picture of a few such collective and separating features in
Nordic cinema. Is it moreover at all reasonable to talk about 'Nordic
cinema' as a homogeneous phenomenon? In spite of the similarities and
the collaboration between the countries, we are in fact discussing five
independent countries' film, where the general cultural traditions as well
as the production conditions specific to film differ to a far greater extent
than merely as regards details.

The perspective that has emerged during the course of our work
and which we have tried to argue in this book has been that the prevalent view of a uniform Nordic output in the area of film demands a
good deal of modulation. To attempt to construct Nordic cinema as
a monolith in the writing of history would be misleading. It would
be decidedly more reasonable to speak of Nordic cinema in the plural:
the field is that of Nordic films in five particular traditions. This is also
in accord with the general revision of film history as a whole, where
today one prefers to speak of recording film histories rather than one
history.

Finally, we wanted to examine three different areas more closely.
First and foremost there is state control and support of film production
which is accredited to the joint account on our balance sheet on Nordic
film. After that we discuss the film cultural characteristics, both those
which seem to point in the direction of a unity in Nordic contexts
and those peculiarities which define each country respectively. Finally,
we discuss actual film production from the perspective of content as
well as form, and try to indicate a direction. Where is Nordic cinema
headed?

THE RELATION OF THE STATE TO
FILM PRODUCTION

The connection between the government authorities and the film industry in a number of aspects is something which unites the cinema in all the Nordic countries, and which separates them from film production in the rest of the world. In the Nordic context it has been natural for the state to intervene both negatively and positively in film production as well as distribution. The censorship has been directed towards a limiting function with regard to production as well as import, while the production subsidy on the contrary has been aimed at performing a stimulating function. This production subsidy has included contributions to film culture in general. The state has thereby come to exercise a unique control over the film medium in the Nordic countries as a whole.

An exception to this rule is the Norwegian law of 1913 which delegated state control of film screening to the municipal level, as a consequence of which the counties took over the running of cinemas. That this model has been kept as far as video is concerned in the 1987 revision of the law is interesting, and is also unique to Norway. However, one has never questioned control as such – the difference in relation to other Nordic countries is that the control has been decentralized. An exception in the opposite direction from state control is Denmark's abolishment of adult censorship – the first real step towards another relationship between state and film industry in the Nordic countries.

Even if the censorship has for a long time been a project common to all the Nordic countries, the degree of control has still varied from country to country, as have the elements against which one has taken action. In Finland, censorship has often been clearly political. Finland's relationship with Russia has caused major fluctuations in the political climate, even as regards the censor's attitude towards individual films. Apart from the films' political content, censorship intervention in Finland has concerned sex, and above all alcohol. The state subsidies have also functioned as a form of censorship by allowing for films to be exempt from tax, depending on whether the film was deemed art or entertainment. It is striking that it is the censor which has made these decisions in Finland. Finland also censors all films on video before distribution as opposed to the other Nordic countries. In Norway, the censor has in particular looked unfavourably on sex, regardless of the films' otherwise cultural status. Bergman's *The Silence*, for example, was severely cut. In Sweden however, where there is assumed to be a more liberal approach to erotic elements in film, violence is cut. One of the more debated examples in recent years was Scorsese's *Cape Fear* which was finally released uncut after a court decision.

The forms of support and control exercised by the state have also been transferred to television in the Nordic countries, even if deregulation is on the agenda in the 1990s. Television has at the same time become imperative to film production. In current practice, if television is not involved there is no film. The situation has become the reverse of the one which arose when the new visual medium was born and caused a crisis for the feature film.

FILM CULTURAL DISTINCTIONS

The Nordic countries form a small film culture, even when considered as a whole. It is therefore hardly surprising that this culture is also governed to a large extent by the American import which dominates the market and as a rule also scores the highest audience ratings today. Nordic film production is therefore, as we have seen, most often in opposition to American film, regardless of whether one has chosen the strategy of trying to incorporate and 'Scandinavianize' American hit concepts or on the other hand to distinguish oneself through individual, distinctive productions. One could maintain that the Nordic countries' film culture has in this respect been consistently determined by a love-hate relationship with Hollywood.

The Nordic countries' numerous filmings of literature throughout its film history is an example of the strategy of making one's mark, a way of differentiating between the domestic productions, and American films. The choice of using the individual countries' literature in this context has had a dual purpose. A basic intent has been partly to raise the quality of the films in general. If the Nordic countries have been aware of their marginal status as regards film, the situation in the field of literature has been wholly different; there they have been able to assert the qualitative status as well as the production quantity. Partly and primarily, however, the purpose has been to give a national standing to film. This is particularly striking, as the choice of literary originals to be filmed have been almost exclusively limited to domestic or Fenno-Scandinavian works of high literary prestige.

Something which amply illustrates the existence of a Nordic affinity as well as the awareness of national distinctions within the confines of this affinity is the exchange which has taken place between the Nordic countries throughout film history. One could speak of a historical circle of sorts, which can be illustrated by the fact that the dominating figure in Norwegian film during the 1910s, Peter Lykke-Seest, had previously worked at the Danish Nordisk Films Kompagni among other things. His scripts were also filmed in Sweden, for example, by Victor Sjöström. When this circle is completed today it is inconceivable to imagine a Norwegian film without Swedish actors. This Nordic exchange has thus included staff, but to an equal extent also various kinds of material; for example, books that have been filmed. It has also found a direct outlet in a long line of

Nordic co-productions, not least in latter years. Paradoxically, these co-productions have often been received rather badly and have been rejected by the audience. One example is *Hip Hip Hurra!*, Kjell Grede's film about the Skagen painters. There are many problems with these films, but a deciding factor as regards the audience is without doubt the different languages, at least in those cases where one mixes actors of several Nordic nationalities.

The confusion of tongues has undoubtedly also had an impact on the distribution of domestic films between the Nordic countries. Few Finnish films have been shown in the other Nordic countries, for instance. In Norway, however, many Danish as well as Swedish films have been shown, while only a small number of Norwegian films have travelled in the opposite direction. In other words, the circulation of films between the Nordic countries is generally poor, even if there are exceptions. This strengthens our hypothesis that there is no monolithic Nordic film, but instead several distinct film cultures, which are sufficiently different for it to be impossible to transfer film arbitrarily from one country to the other. Ideas, novels and the like can be brought from a neighbouring country, but they must be subject to national decoding and be given specific national characteristics. There is thus no obvious interchangeability between the Nordic film cultures. A statistical survey may illuminate the problem (see Tables 1 and 2).

Table 1 Audience ratings per country for Nordic film (1991)

	Domestic film	Other Nordic films	Total
Denmark	264,706	1,631	266,337
Finland	28,621	1,535	30,156
Iceland	19,092	1,734	20,826
Norway	52,500	51,150	103,650
Sweden	41,000	7,925	48,925

Table 2 Nordic film export to the Nordic countries 1985–92

	Denmark	Finland	Iceland	Norway	Sweden
Denmark	–	19	15	28	28
Finland	11	–	0	15	16
Iceland	1	3	–	4	1
Norway	9	5	1	–	14
Sweden	33	34	5	77	–
Total	54	61	21	124	59

Source: Scandinavian Films

Yet another factor that on the contrary tends to unite the Nordic countries is the different countries' mutually similar positions on the range which locates film somewhere between art and entertainment. In the Nordic countries, film has been viewed decidedly as an art form to a far greater extent than in any kind of hypothetical average of film in the world as a whole. As a rule, film has been able to lay claim to a higher status than mere amusement. This has been a consequence of its relationship with the state. The subsidy for quality film on the one hand and the censorship on the other, which have functioned for a long time as surety for some sort of cultural hallmark, have given film an established position in society and placed it under the aegis of culture and art. What is more, it is not a question of any narrow 'l'art pour l'art', but of an art which has at the same time had close ties to the public good. This view becomes apparent not least by the connection between the quality subsidy and the societal public good aspect of film which we recognize from several Nordic countries. Film has thus been considered generally as a potent social agent in the Nordic countries. Ibsen's old dictum 'to put the problems under debate' is a motto which could be extended to all Nordic film. But film does not only have a social influence, it has also been regarded as an important national bearer of culture since the silent era. The social critique has been closely linked with a national identification process. As opposed to American film, it is implied that Nordic film often gives an adequate reflection of domestic problems, and thereby has also contributed to the society's understanding of itself. An especially clear example of this is films made during and after the Second World War, when, for instance, Denmark and Norway relived their experiences from the years of Occupation in various ways which all had to do with the nation's identity. As we have seen, this could take the form of comedy, by lionizing theories of the Resistance or by addressing the problems that followed in the wake of the war: lack of housing, increased poverty, criminality, etc. We will return to this point in our concluding discussion of the content of the films.

In this context, however, something should be said of acting style and heroic ideals where the Nordic countries differ substantially from American cinema. This is in fact largely to do with the anti-American distinctions that have been cultivated within Nordic film. Characteristic of these Nordic heroes is their sobriety or matter-of-factness. There are seldom heroes who are larger than life. It is both a question of stylistic choices and of an emotional tone in the films, and, in taking a stand between constraint and spectacle, Nordic film is decidedly modest in its aspirations. We find a similar view of the hero and a similar acting style in all the Nordic countries with the exception of Finland, which has had a weakness for grand and lavish costume dramas. However, an exception in this context is the Finnish costume film of the war years, which is to a large extent an expression of the wish to display a grasp of technical know-how.

In production on the other hand, the structure differs vastly between the countries. The film companies are an excellent example of this. The difference is most clearly defined when comparing Sweden and Norway. In Sweden, Svensk Filmindustri (or SF – Swedish Film Industry Co) was established as early as 1919, and it is still the most stable of the film companies today. In addition to SF however, there are today a number of stable and competitive film producers in Sweden, most notably Sandrews and the Swedish Film Institute. This puts SF in the position of competitor, but also of collaboration partner. Norway is in a wholly different way dominated by one sole producer – Norsk Film A/S (Norwegian Film Co), which was originally owned by a local municipality, but which is today owned by the state. This is the indisputable flagship of Norwegian production which has existed since 1932. In addition to this there are a number of transient companies – small companies which, once started, produce one, or at the most two films, and then go bankrupt.

Common to all the Nordic countries is that the cinema ratings once again, after several years of decline, began to rise in the early years of the 1990s. A statistic comparison reveals an interesting picture of the different countries' mutual relationships as regards the increasing trend of cinema visits. The comparison is based on figures from 1992–93. Denmark presents the most drastic increase: 18 per cent. In 1992 Denmark's cinema attendance was 8,648,000, which in 1993 had increased to 10,222,000. On average, the country had 1.98 cinema visits per inhabitant in 1993. In second place we find Norway with 9,590,000 cinema visits in 1992, which in 1993 rose to 10,933,000, an increase of 14 per cent. Norway rates higher than Denmark as regards the number of cinema visits per inhabitant, which in 1993 was 2.56. Finland finishes a good third in the increasing statistics with a 6.63 per cent increase: from 5,398,000 cinema visits in 1992 to 5,756,000 in 1993. On the other hand, the number of cinema visits per inhabitant is only 1.14 and thereby rates lower than Sweden which shows 1.8 visits for 1993. Here the increase from 1992 to 1993 is only 1 per cent however, from 15,686,335 to 15,977,064. As regards Iceland the statistic information is incomplete, and the relation between 1992 and 1993 cannot be accounted for. In 1992 there was a small decline (2.4 per cent) in relation to the year before, but the number of cinema visits per inhabitant in 1992 is still well above the other Nordic countries: 11.85 per cent! (*Source*: Nordisk Medie Nyt 1/94.)

What kinds of films attract the audience? American film dominates heavily of course, but domestic film has also defended its position, as can be seen if we take Denmark as an example. During 1993, American film cornered 74.1 per cent of the market in Denmark, while Danish film had 17.2 per cent of the market despite the fact that only eleven Danish films premièred during that year. Among the ten most seen films we find a total of four Danish films. Rather similar results are found in the other Nordic countries. This brings us to the last point of our discussion, namely the question of the films themselves. In the chapters on each respective country we have seen how film production has developed as regards the content and form of the films. It is time now to offer a comprehensive comparison between the countries.

FILM PRODUCTION: CONTENT/FORM

The image of Nordic cinema in other countries has to a large extent been determined by the Anglo-American view of what is typically Nordic. These clichés have also at times been adopted into the films for the purpose of marketing them as Nordic. Let us briefly try to pinpoint some features in this portrait of what is Nordic.

1 Perhaps the most important aspect, and one which is constantly fore-grounded as characteristic of the films of all the Nordic countries, is the portrayal of nature. Film historical surveys speak of the proximity to nature as a Nordic feature which has been given expression on the screen, whether during the golden age of Swedish silent film or, in later years, Finnish peasant melodramas. Nature often displays an exotic trait in this popular understanding of it. It is closely connected to the ethnic, as, for instance, in the depiction of the life of the Lapps.

2 Beside nature and exotism, melancholy is a basic Nordic quality, if regarded objectively. Here, as in the view of the central role of the description of nature, film historical writing goes hand-in-hand with the history of literature: in both art forms nature and melancholy are abundantly represented. Prominent names in Nordic literature (Ibsen, Lagerlöf, Strindberg, Salminen, Undset) have readily been heralded as representatives of an interpretation of human melancholy coupled with gloom which would appear to be inherent in the very Nordic natural scenery, with its deep pine forests. This has yielded yet more weight to the arguments in the area of film: it has here been possible to view film as part of a long and well-documented tradition.

3 Closely related to the melancholic quality is the religious streak, which in Nordic film is usually portrayed as an introverted, aescetic and life-denying Lutherianism. It is a private religion, focused on the individual's relationship to God, not on community life. On the other hand, it is also connected to strong social demands and taboos, for example, the rejection of gambling, alcohol or the pleasures of the table in general. Its most famous filmic expressions are portrayed in films like Bergman's *Winter Light* or Axel's *Babette's Feast*.

4 In paradoxical opposition to this religious trait we have the infamous Swedish sin, which often goes hand-in-hand with references to Nordic

heathenism. It was primarily in later years, after the breaching of the sex barrier, that these types of films were made. Here we also find one of the most obvious examples of how film production has attached itself to and used a cliché for export purposes. The numerous erotic films of the 1970s, several of which were Nordic co-productions, live off this myth. *Fäbodjäntan* (*The Shack Girl*) is an example of such a film which combines a sex theme with hazy reminiscences of the heathen traditions of the ancestors. Furthermore we find here a postcard-like Swedish scenery and melancholy missionaries.

A film like *Fäbodjäntan* displays in an almost overly explicit fashion the stereotyping of this prevalent image of Nordic quality. The problem is not, however, the stereotypes of the image, but the fact that they have been snatched from its context: societies as a whole and the social changes they have undergone during the last century. A further problem is that in practice this image originates almost totally in Swedish film. Nordic film abroad has been almost exclusively identified with Swedish film, and moreover with the most restricted part of the Swedish film: Bergman and Mattsson among others.

Most problematic, however, are the claims to want to establish some kind of unity in the image of the Nordic film, whether it concerns an internal unity in each country right through film history, or between the countries. It is not possible to find a homogeneous list of a uniform Nordic cinema. Nor is it possible to make snap judgements about similarities between the different societies as far as film is concerned. An excellent example of the latter is the log-drivers which have been equally important societal phenomena in Norway, Sweden and Finland. In spite of this it is only in Finnish film that they have become cliché and a national mythical figure of sorts.

Another example of the difficulty in describing Nordic film in homogeneous terms is the portrayal of the relation between countryside and city in connection with the modernization process following the Second World War. This has been handled in different ways within separate film cultures – as is the case in the Nordic countries. The theme of the countryside in relation to the city is particularly instructive if one wishes to examine the very national differences in the Nordic states. The Swedish films cause one to look back nostalgically to the good old days. The countryside is made to represent a closeness between people and an affinity with one's origins, with nature. There were at this time a large number of films which were set in the countryside, both with regard to the number of films produced and the attendance. In Finland there was a more marked contrast between countryside and city than in Sweden. The films of the countryside were about the peasant community and its lasting values, and was generally a more heavy genre than in Sweden. The difference could be summed up by giving the Finnish films the title 'peasant melodramas' and the Swedish, 'rural film', where the farmer's wife keeps the house in order and safeguards tradition while the farmer is out drinking in town. It is a wider rift between the values which each category respectively represents than in any other Nordic country. Norway, in sharp contrast to the Finnish as well as the Swedish film, is distinguished by a near complete absence of rural and scenic depictions during this period. One solitary feature film made in the 1950s takes place in the countryside: *Thrush in the Ceiling Lamp*. Interestingly, the countryside in this film is also portrayed as hypocritical, in singularly negative terms – anyone who sticks his or her neck out gets mercilessly struck down. Denmark assumes a sort of middle position: the urban films were plentiful in the latter half of the 1940s, but in 1950 the 'hyggefilm' or the 'genial film' became popular. With its breakthrough there was a significant increase in films with a rural theme, but here the corruption and decadence of the city have more clearly than in Finland or Sweden also reached the countryside.

It is also interesting to note how a specifically Nordic type of film, the military farce, has circulated between the countries. In the 1930s it enjoyed enormous popularity in Sweden. During the war Finland assumed an interest in such films and produced a wave of them, which was followed by yet another wave at the beginning of the 1950s. In Denmark a series of military farces were produced during the 1950s which continued well into the 1960s.

There are thus clear similarities between the different countries, but there are also constant displacements in time as well as focus between them. It is here that we may seek the origins of the myth of the homogeneous Nordic film: the recurrent phenomena that can be discerned in different decades have been separated from their historical contexts in each respective country and bundled together in ahistoric universality. Yet another contributing reason has been the aforementioned factors which have played a part in film export, where film production has at times been adapted to meet apparent foreign expectations.

A feature common to all the Nordic countries – it too is historically determined, however, and valid in a larger historical context than the Nordic one – is the influence of the French new wave. The 1960s meant a shift in generations for all the Nordic countries. In this new generation the female directors began to make themselves known to a larger extent than previously. It was furthermore in the 1960s that the starting of film schools was begun to a hitherto unseen extent. Film institutes were also founded in several Nordic countries. The decade also brought about a breakthrough for the new modernistic film style on a wide front in the North. This went hand-in-hand with a political radicalization and an incipient internationalization of film culture. This in turn laid the foundation for a greater mutual similarity between the Nordic countries and between the North and the film world at large.

On discussing Nordic film it is important to keep in mind something which should have already become apparent, namely that there exists in no Nordic country a genre system in the American sense. In its place, one can speak of recurring themes which constitute groups of films. Only in individual cases can these quantitatively and structurally be said to make up genres. One can also discern specifically Nordic variations on established genres, for example, the comedy. Here, the exceptionally most popular variant has been light comedy in Denmark, Finland and Norway as well as Sweden. This has furthermore been the most popular genre throughout film history in the Nordic countries. Apart from this there are smaller sub-genres such as the aforementioned military farce. However, these have to a strikingly small degree been attempts to make pure genre films in accordance with American patterns, even if this has occurred only once in a while in the course of film history. It was only in the 1980s that genre film began to be made, but then only as a form of pastiche, as, for instance, with the brothers Kaurismäki or in modern Icelandic versions of film noir.

The 1980s in the Nordic countries on the whole mark both the return of fiction and the triumph of internationalization. The national subsidy to domestic productions and to various film cultural phenomena simultaneously increased steadily during the decade, with the purpose of safeguarding the home nations' film production and culture, while the films on their part clearly developed in the direction of becoming less and less national. It is this paradoxical situation that determines Nordic cinema at the beginning of the 1990s.

Notes

3 FINLAND

1 The Finnish soldiers who belonged to the army of the Swedish King Gustav II Adolf during the Thirty Years' War were legendary for their bravery and were called Hackapelitas because of their battle cry 'Hakkaa päälle!' – 'Beat them!'
2 OY is the Finnish abbreviation for Ltd.
3 The company got its name from the initials of the young owners of the company: Lennart and Alvar Hamberg and Yrjö Nyberg – (later Norta).
4 The Finnish national anthem.
5 i.e. a length of at least 200 m.
6 Among these there were a dozen or so companies which managed to produce one or two films: one short-lived company, Eloseppo, produced five films between 1939 and 1940.
7 Domestic Work – a patriotic federation, the purpose of which was to promote Finnish products and industry.
8 Even today the war of 1917 to 1918 is sometimes referred to as the 'Independence War', 'Class War', or 'Rebellion', depending on the political correctness of the period and the background of the person speaking.
9 A 'yager' is a specially-trained soldier.

6 SWEDEN

1 'Sverige dröjde tjugo år för länge med /att bygga uta/ järnvägarna och trettio år för länge med den allmänna rösträtten.'
2 'otroliga passions- och kriminalförvecklingar till atmosfärladdade dynamiska och märkvärdigt rörande bildoperor.'
3 'Våra tändstickor, kullager och telefoner och separatorer bära det svenska namnet på ryktets vingar.'
4 'utländsk filmsmak.'
5 'En halvmullig och okryddad köttbulle, som varken kittlar eller mättar.'
6 'Jag begriper inte hur hon fotograferades i första avdelningen – eller var det jag som inte var disponerad att se vackert?'
7 'Antingen har /filmerna/ betraktats som /den litterära/ textens förrädare eller dess ödmjuka tjänare.'
8 'ett urlakat extrakt.'
9 'ett plastiskt mimisk framställning av den inre handlingen (hos karaktärerna och deras inbördes relationer). Men', menade författaren: 'det krävs att /manus/ författaren helt vänder sig bort från varje tanke på verbala uttrycksmedel.'

10 'Hjalmar Bergman är vår ende filmförfattare av litterär betydenhet [sic] –
   litterär även in den meningen att han helst rör sig i en något dekadent soci-
   etet, som likt marionetter virvlar omkring i en lindrigt naturlig handling.
   Elegant, spirituell och bizarrt originellt men föga av kött och blod och levande
   gripbart liv.'
11 'talar dess eget språk.'
12 'Kronvrak', literally 'Crown Wreck' – a person who was a 'wreck' and hence
   not suitable to serve the Crown: men who had a chronic or congenital disease
   (anything from flat feet to a heart condition) or some sort of injury could not
   do military service.
13 'Jag finner inte ord för min sorg. Gode Gud, skänk honom frid och hjälp oss
   arma som måste leva utan honom.'
14 'att sätta igång arbeten, vanliga nyttiga arbeten med vanliga löner i öppna
   marknaden.'
15 'I det goda hemmet råder likhet, omtanke, samarbete, hjälpsamhet.'
16 Literally: crisis in the population issue.
17 'befria filmkonsten från den tvångströja av kommersialism som den hade
   hamnat i mot slutet av tjugotalet.'
18 'skamfläck för vår kultur.'
19 Literally: Swedish cinema – culture or culturally dangerous.
20 'förhindra osvensk opinionsbildning och befrämja nationellt tänkande.'
21 Swedish name: Internationella Filmkammaren.
22 'samhällsanda, vaksamhet, tystnad.'
23 'En stram, saklig svensk och manlig film utan alla falska brösttoner och försök
   till uppskruvad heroism.'
24 'Vår beredskap är god.'
25 'Förlåt att jag inte skrivit till dig på länge men jag har inte haft pengar till
   frimärke.'
26 'Där fanns ett ursinne och en politisk tydlighet som bröt sig tvärs igenom hela
   det tyngande utanverket och konstlat teatraliska tonfall.'
27 The film's title.
28 'En förutsättning för en konstnärlig film som befinner sig på en hög kulturell
   nivå är en kvalificerad publik, som är tillräckligt stor för att den här sortens
   filmproduktion skulle vara sund i ekonomiskt avseende: m a o borde publiken
   vara mogen och ha lämnat bakom sig de enklare underhållningsformerna och
   vara bered för att uppskatta konstnärlig film. Den allt överskuggande frågan
   är således frågan om publikens andliga mognad och dess aktva efterfrågan på
   kultur.'
29 'Det förefaller som om de svenska landsbygds filmerna bidragit med någon
   sorts fiktionsterapi till den psykologiska bearbetningen av detta kollektiva
   trauma/som folkflyttningen från landsorten till städerna innebar.'
30 'Varför inte unna dessa efterblivna element ett oskyldigt nöje också på bio?'
31 'samtidsdramatiserande.'
32 'Hjälp mor, byt skor!' literally: Help your mother, change your shoes.
33 'Tvärtom kan man med små medel skapa en vacker ram till måltiden!'
34 'en av [i] dessa filmer förekommande män i den vita rocken som kan allt och
   vet allt.'
35 'Hyland's Corner.'
36 'en ovanligt charmfull gosse, behaglig, vänlig, på ett älskvärt sätt förälskad i
   sin egen artist värld.'
37 'Det är en utmärkt reklamfilm för bananbolag och bananätning, och som all
   utmärkt film är den underhållande.'

38 'ungdom på glid.'
39 'Visst är det en betydande bildartist som regisserat *Ljuvlig är sommarnatten* och där finns förledande grepp i själva berättar tekniken med glidningar i tid och rum, i dröm och verklighet. Det fatala är bara det – och här kommer vi till Arne Mattsons skötesynd som filmregissör – att denna raffinerade form inte inspirerats av det föreliggande ämnet. Han sätter upp en liten enkel deckare som om det gällde att skapa ett vidunder av skönhet och märkvärdighet.'
40 *The Vision in Swedish Film.*
41 'Man dricker vatten från en pöl tills man får tillfälle att smaka från en källa, och efter man gjort det går man hellre törstig än återvänder till pölen.'
42 'ta sitt ansvar.'
43 'en mera expressiv stil som bättre skulle kunna beskriva de levnadsförhållanden som /filmernas karaktärer/ levde i.'
44 'spörsmål gällande människors värdighet och ansvar såsom de förekommer och ventileras i deras egen omgivning.'
45 'våga ta risker i nya och nyskapande projekt.'
46 'Det som Bergman exporterar till utlandet består av ljusmystik och ohöljd exotism – inte förslag till alternativa handlingssätt eller moraliska möjligheter. Bergman förstärker de mest banala myterna om Sverige och svenskarna,' skriver Widerberg och fortsätter: 'Den fråga som Bergman film efter film framhåller – mest sannolikt ställd av Max von Sydow mot en bakgrund av mörk barrskog – är huruvida det finns någon Gud, huruvida det finns någon högre rättvisa. Han riktar nästan alltid sina frågor uppåt, eller – skämtsamt – nedåt men mera sällan i sidled, mot människor. Han gör vertikala filmer i en situation där vi mer än någonsin behöver en horisontell film, en konst i sidled.'
47 'privat nostalgi.'
48 *Can We Afford Culture.*
49 'förnyelse av filmens uttrycksmedel och formspråk, angelägenhetsgraden i filmens ärende, intensiteten eller fräschören i dess verklighetsuppfattning eller samhällskritik, graden av psykologisk insikt och andlig nivå, lekfull fantasi eller visionär styrka, episka, dramatiska eller lyriska värden, den tekniska skickligheten i manus, regi och spel samt övriga artistiska komponenter hos en film.'
50 'förråande och skadligt upphetsande.'
51 'tukt- och sedlighetssårande framställning.'
52 'bitsk och rivande vital', 'en aktiv politisk handling just här och nu', 'fränt och hårt språk.'
53 'kulturmyglare.'
54 'Fortfarande utgör /*Myglaren*s publiksiffror/ det totala, och förhoppningsvis oslagbara bottenrekordet för svensk film.'
55 '/På sextiotalet framträdde/ en filmsyn som kort kan karakteriseras på så vis att man önskade en film som gjorde den verklighet människor levde i tydlig och gripbar, som trängde under skeendets yta och tog ställning genom att låta verkligheten komma till tals realistisk och osminkad. Filmarna började se sig själva som en liten men aldrig så oviktig del i sammanhang som gick långt utanför filmens och konstens snäva verklighet. Som filmare med speciella yrkeskunskaper hade man ett uttalat mål att ställa sig i tjänst hos människor och grupper som hade svårt att hävda sin rätt.'
56 *Tjorven, Båtsman och Moses* (1964), *Tjorven och Skrållan* (1965), *Tjorven och Mysak* (1966), *Skrållan, Ruskprick och Knorrhane* (1967) and *Vi på Saltkråkan* (1968). Saltkråkan was the fictive name of the island where the events take place – in reality Norröra in the northern archipelago outside Stockholm.

57 'Ledarparet /visade sig/ vara en skäligen misslyckad konstellation. Donner offentliggjorde så småningom sin kommentar till samarbetsfiaskot. Den var präglad av perfid vältalighet. Ahlmarks är ännu inte publicerad.'

58 'några priviligierade eller tillbakasatta, inga kelgrisar eller styvbarn.'

59 Birgitta Steene holds that the thematical childhood films constitute a genre and calls it child-adult films.

60 *Du är inte klok, Madicken* (Graffman, 1979), *Madicken i Junibacken* (Graffman, 1979).

Subject index

Name index

Film index

DATE DUE